MARY AND JOHN GRAY LIBRARY
LAMAR UNIVERSITY

Purchased

with the

Student Library Use Fee

S0-FAE-220

Ethnoreligious Conflict in the
Late Twentieth Century

Ethnoreligious Conflict in the Late Twentieth Century

A General Theory

Jonathan Fox

LAMAR UNIVERSITY LIBRARY

LEXINGTON BOOKS
Lanham • Boulder • New York • Oxford

BL
65
W2
F69
2002

LEXINGTON BOOKS

Published in the United States of America
by Lexington Books
A Member of the Rowman & Littlefield Publishing Group
4720 Boston Way, Lanham, Maryland 20706

12 Hid's Copse Road
Cumnor Hill, Oxford OX2 9JJ, England

Copyright © 2002 by Lexington Books

All rights reserved. No part of this publication may be reproduced,
stored in a retrieval system, or transmitted in any form or by any
means, electronic, mechanical, photocopying, recording, or otherwise,
without the prior permission of the publisher.

British Library Cataloguing in Publication Information Available

Library of Congress Cataloging-in-Publication Data Available

ISBN: 0-7391-0418-7

Printed in the United States of America

♾™ The paper used in this publication meets the minimum requirements of American
National Standard for Information Sciences—Permanence of Paper for Printed Library
Materials, ANSI/NISO Z39.48–1992.

In memory of Irving Nathan. You were always there for me and will always be with me.

Contents

Acknowledgments

I would like to thank Ted R. Gurr, without whom this book would not have been possible, both for his insightful advice and criticism and for making the Minorities at Risk data so accessible. I would also like to thank the staff of the Minorities at Risk project, especially Michael Dravis, Deepa Kholsa, Anne Pitsch, and Pamela Burke, who helped out with the backup codings, as well as Michael Haxton, Shinwa Lee, and Steve Kurth, who helped out at other stages of the project. I would also like to thank R. Scott Appleby, Charles E. Butterworth, Eliezer Don-Yehiya, Hillel Frisch, Ollie A. Johnson, Shmuel Sandler, Shlomo Shpiro, William T. Stuart, Bernard Susser, and Jonathan Wilkenfeld, all of whom provided useful advice at various stages of this project. Any errors of fact or interpretation that remain are mine alone.

Chapter 1

Introduction

Throughout history, scholars have pondered the role religion plays in conflict. Many ancient scholars, like St. Augustine in *The City of God*, pondered the role religion ought to play in war. The more recent scholarship, including luminaries such as Durkheim and Weber, has begun to ponder the role it does, and sometimes does not, play in society and conflict. Given this large volume of scholarship on the subject, it is difficult to say anything new about the role religion plays in conflict. Most of what there is to say about religion and conflict has already been said. Yet, it is argued here that the existing explanations are lacking. That is, there is no adequate theory of religion and conflict. However, the building blocks for such a theory exist. In other words, while the existing literature on religion and conflict does not provide an adequate theory to explain the phenomenon, the concepts and ideas within the various parts of that literature can be reassembled into a more organized framework to create a better theory.

Twentieth century scholarship on religion and conflict provides an example of some of the inadequacies of the body of theory on religion and conflict. For the first three quarters of the twentieth century, little attention was paid, at least in Western circles, to the issue of religion and conflict. This is true of academic and policy-making circles as well as the media. However, since the late 1970s all three of these circles have begun to pay considerable attention to what many call a resurgence of religious conflict across the globe. Whether this is a resurgence of a phenomenon that has lain dormant for decades or simply renewed attention to a phenomenon that has never gone away is an open question.

In any case, the watershed event that seems to have caused this renewed attention by Westerners to religion and conflict was the Iranian revolution of 1979. Since then, it seems that academics, policy-makers, and the media have been constantly occupied by conflicts that have religious dimensions. These include, but are by no means limited to, Afghanistan's Islamic rebellion against the country's

Communist government throughout the 1980s, which resulted in a civil war followed by a fundamentalist Islamic state, and the current Islamic resistance movements in many Middle Eastern, North African, and Asian countries. In the case of Algeria, this Islamic resistance has reached the level of open and bloody rebellion. There has also been what appears to be a revitalization of the religious right as a political phenomenon in the United States.

Many of the conflicts with religious dimensions that have received attention by academics, policy-makers, and the media have been ethnic conflicts. The more well known of these conflicts include the civil war in Lebanon between Sunni Muslims, Shi'i Muslims, Maronite Christians, and several other ethnic groups; the rebellion of Shi'i Muslims against Saddam Hussein's Sunni Muslim dominated government in the aftermath of the Gulf War; the conflict between the Christian Armenians and Muslim Azerbaijanis in the former USSR; the independence movements in East Timor and Tibet, and the several conflicts in the former Yugoslavia.

Despite the considerable attention paid to the issue since the late 1970s, academic literature is ill prepared to deal with these questions on a general level. That is, while many contextual explanations of specific conflicts are insightful, the more general explanations of the role of religion in conflict are weak. This inadequacy of the existing literature's explanations for the role of religion in conflict exists on many levels: the small number of theoretical works and theoretically driven studies; the even smaller number of attempts to integrate the existing body of theory on religion and conflict with general conflict theory; and the absence of cross-sectional, large-n (studies including many cases), empirical studies.

Consequently, the object of this book is to fill these gaps in the academic literature. This is done in three steps. The first is to assess the state of the existing scholarship on the role of religion in society, politics, and conflict. This includes an assessment of this scholarship's inadequacies and why these inadequacies exist. The second is to use elements of this scholarship to build an improved general theory of religion and conflict. This involves taking the building blocks that exist in the literature and drawing from them a comprehensive list of the ways religion can become involved in conflict. While it is argued here that the principles contained in this list apply to all types of religious conflict, the primary focus of this book is ethnic conflict. Accordingly, the third step is to test this theory using data on ethnic conflict. This is done by incorporating the list of ways that religion can become involved in conflict into the Minorities at Risk model of ethnic conflict, thus creating a dynamic model of ethnoreligious conflict. This model is then tested in a large-n cross-sectional format.

Criteria and Research Design for a Theory of Religion and Conflict

In order to build a better theory of religion and conflict, the criteria for what constitutes a good theory must be specified. It is argued here that an adequate theory of religion and conflict should be both dynamic and comprehensive. A dynamic theory is one that goes beyond simply listing the ways in which religion influences conflict. In addition, a dynamic theory would account for the interrelationships between each of these factors. For instance, one can list many factors that are believed to influence whether states go to war with each other. These factors include, but are not limited to, whether the states are both democracies, military power, economic power, and alliances. However simply providing such a list is not enough. Whether a state is a democracy affects its economic system, military spending, and which states it will choose for allies. Economic power is one of the bases for military might. Also, alliances can bring increased trade, thereby increasing economic power. A dynamic theory must take interrelationships like these into account.

A comprehensive theory must account for all of the ways religion can become involved in conflict. Providing an explanation for one way religion can become involved in conflict but not placing it in the context of the other ways religion can become involved is like completing only part of a jigsaw puzzle. It may provide part of the picture, but it is only part of the picture. Furthermore, even that part of the picture cannot be fully appreciated until it can be placed in the context of the entire picture. For instance, if one were to complete a part of a jigsaw puzzle depicting a soldier, some aspects of the context in which that soldier exists can be understood or inferred from the fragment of the puzzle; the full context can be better understood only by completing the entire puzzle. Is the soldier going to battle, taking part in a battle, or returning from a battle? Or, perhaps is he part of a parade or simply enjoying himself about town? From what army is the soldier? In what historical context is he situated? While the answer to some of these questions can possibly be inferred from the fragment of the jigsaw puzzle, completing the jigsaw puzzle will clearly provide a better set of answers. So, too, with explanations and theories. A complete, or comprehensive, theory of religion and conflict should provide a better explanation for that phenomenon than the sum of its parts considered separately.

For a theory of religion and conflict to be truly comprehensive, simply explaining all of the ways religion can become involved in conflict is not enough. The theory must also incorporate the general body of theory on conflict. This is because religious conflicts are rarely one hundred percent religious. They are usually influenced by other economic, political, and social factors. For instance, the origins and dynamics of the conflict in Afghanistan cannot be understood without an understanding of the East-West conflict during the Cold War. Similarly, the conflicts in the former Yugoslavia cannot be understood without taking the international repercussions of the end of the Cold War and the fall of the USSR into account.

In addition to being dynamic and comprehensive, a useful theory should also be falsifiable. This means that the theory should be made up of propositions that are specific enough that they can be disproved. Falsifiability is essential to any empirical study. This is because the purpose of an empirical study is to test whether a theory or set of propositions is true or false. If there is no way to prove a theory is false, there is no point in this exercise.

When building a predictive theory, it is also important to define the object of prediction. In this case what is being predicted, or at least explained, is religious conflict. However, religious conflict can mean many things, ranging from a theological debate to civil war. When the term "conflict" or "religious conflict" is used here, it is referring to political conflict. This means that there are two groups who have different political goals and agendas and are pursuing them in the political arena. The means used to pursue these goals can be peaceful, including but not limited to peaceful protest, supporting or running political candidates, and/or lobbying activities. The means used to pursue these goals can also be violent, including rioting and various forms of rebellion. This connection between politics and violence is a long recognized principle that has probably been best put by Karl Von Clausewitz when he stated that "war is nothing more than the continuation of politics by other means."

Overview

The first part of this book looks at the connection between religion and conflict on a general level. The definition of conflict is intentionally kept at its most general and inclusive level because the object of the first few chapters, up to and including chapter 5, is to establish the nature of religion and how it causes conflict, rather than the nature of that conflict once it has been caused. Chapter 2 addresses the issues of defining religion and its role in society. The emphasis is on a social science perspective of religion's role in society rather than a theological definition. This is because, while the nature of God is an important issue, a more practical look at the function of religion in society is more essential to understanding its role in conflict.

The question of whether religion is even relevant to conflict is addressed in chapters 3 and 4. The literature on this topic is divided into two major schools of thought. The first, which is addressed in chapter 3, is the modernization/secularization school, which argues that the process of modernity has made religion irrelevant in today's world. The second school, the functionalists, which is addressed in chapter 4, argues that even when religion seems to be relevant to politics or conflict, it is merely acting as an agent for more basic and important social, political, and economic forces.

These schools of thought pose important questions because if either of them is correct, there is no point in studying the role of religion in conflict. It is argued here that these schools of thought are flawed. Not only has modernity not reduced the relevance of religion to politics and conflict, it may have actually contributed to many of today's religious conflicts. If nothing else, the unfortunate abundance of conflicts with religious elements makes it clear that modernity has not eliminated religion as a cause for conflict. Also, while religion may often act as an agent or catalyst for other forces, it can and does contribute directly to conflicts.

In any case, it is clear that these schools of thought, which have their roots in the writings of eighteenth and nineteenth century social thinkers, were dominant in academic circles until at least the late 1970s, when events began to cause many to reconsider their arguments. Until around 1980, and even to some extent after then, a considerable amount of resources was spent on the debate over whether or not religion is relevant to conflict and less was spent on developing and testing theories explaining how it is relevant. The prominence of these schools of thought in academic thinking can, perhaps, explain the failure of the literature to provide an adequate body of theory on the role of religion and conflict. It is likely that they discouraged many from addressing the topic and forced those that did to spend more time defending the legitimacy of their work than actually developing a theory of religion and conflict. Thus, examining the debates over these schools of thought also helps provide insight into the evolution of the study of religion's role in society, politics, and conflicts.

The existing academic literature on religion and conflict is described in chapter 5. Most of the literature on religion and conflict, even now, over two decades after the Iranian revolution, is limited to case studies with little if any theoretical content. In fact, one could literally bury oneself in the case study literature on any one of many religious conflicts (the Iranian revolution probably being the best example of this). There are comparatively few works devoted to developing a body of theory on religion and conflict. Those few that do are lacking in the sense that few, if any of them, develop theories that are both comprehensive and dynamic. That is, few theories of religion and conflict take into account all of the ways that religion can become involved in conflict as well as take into account the interrelationships between the ways religion becomes involved in conflict. Few of these theories are integrated into the general body of theory on conflict. In addition, no theory of religion and conflict has been tested in a large-n cross-sectional format.

As already noted, the purpose of this study is to address both the lack of an adequate theory of religion and conflict and the lack of empirical testing in the field of religion and conflict. The basic building blocks for a theory of religion and ethnic conflict used here are developed in chapter 6. This is done in two stages. First, it is argued that the role of religion in society, politics, and conflict can be described by four social functions of religion. Second, these four social functions are used to develop a set of propositions that form the basis for a general theory of religion and conflict.

In chapter 7, the comprehensive list of ways religion can become involved in conflict constructed in the previous chapters is combined with the Minorities at Risk model of ethnic conflict in order to create a comprehensive, dynamic, and falisfiable model of ethnoreligious conflict that is tested empirically in a large-n cross-sectional format. In this chapter, the definition of conflict is more precise. The type of conflict explained in the model is ethnic protest and ethnic rebellion. The exact nature of these types of conflict, as well as their predicted causes, are specified by variables that are specific enough to allow statistical techniques to be applied to them. Chapter 8 explores the general implications of this study as well as the applicability of the findings on ethnoreligious conflict to other types of religious conflict.

The Minorities at Risk Project

Most of the data on ethnic conflict used in this study are taken from the Minorities at Risk Phase 3 dataset. These data are supplemented by data collected specifically for this study. However, while the use of the Minorities at Risk dataset makes this study possible, it also complicates and places some restrictions on this study.

The Minorities at Risk dataset contains data on 268 politically significant ethnic minorities worldwide.[1] The unit of analysis is the ethnopolitical minority within a specific state. The groups included in the dataset meet one or more of the following criteria: they are subject to discrimination at present; they are disadvantaged because of the results of past discrimination; and/or the group (in whole or in part) supports one or more political organizations that advocate greater group rights, privileges, or autonomy. They also must constitute at least 1 percent of the population of the state in which they reside or number at least 100,000 in that state (Gurr, 2000).

Of these 268 groups, 105 are religiously distinct and, therefore, included in this study. These groups are ethnic minorities whose religion differs from that of the dominant group. While, as shown in chapters 3 and 4, religion is not an important issue in all of these conflicts, it is assumed here that because the religions of the groups involved in these conflicts differ, the potential exists for religion to become involved in the conflict. Also, when asking the question of when, why, and how religion becomes involved in a conflict, one is also implicitly asking when and why it does not become involved. For more details on case selection and a full list of the cases included in this study, as well as all of the cases included in the Minorities at Risk study, see appendix A.

This dataset focuses on the relationship between the minority group and the state. For this reason, many ethnic groups are coded as a separate group in each state in which they meet the above criteria. For instance, ethnic Russians are included in the dataset several times because they meet the above criteria in Azerbaijan, Kazakhstan, Kyrgyzstan, Tajikistan, Turkmenistan, and Uzbekistan, as well as in several other of the former Soviet republics.[2]

The nature of the dataset has several implications for this study. First, this study is limited to the same unit of analysis as the Minorities at Risk dataset: the ethnic minority within a state controlled by a coherent government. This eliminates from the study all cases of religious conflict within the same ethnic group, especially conflicts between secular and religious elements within a state. For example, while this study does look at the Christian Coptic minority in Egypt, it does not include any evaluation of the Islamic militant challenge to Egypt's government. This is because the Copts are a religiously distinct ethnic minority in Egypt, but the Islamic militants are members of Egypt's ethnic majority. That is, these militants constitute a contemporary political movement in Egypt, but are not a distinct social entity that persists over time. While it is clear that cases such as the Islamic militants in Egypt are worthy of study, the nature of the available data places such cases beyond the scope of this study.

Second, because the data focus on the relationship between a dominant ethnic group that, more or less, controls a state's government and an ethnic minority, there must be a working state government for a group to be included in this study. That is, if a country is in a state of anarchy where there is effectively no state government and the country's ethnic groups are in a state of total war, there is no relationship between a state government and an ethnic minority to be measured. Thus, even though they are worthy of study, minority groups in states like Bosnia and Afghanistan, where there were effectively no governments during the 1990 to 1995 period, are not considered here.

Third, in order for the information on religion to be as compatible with the Minorities at Risk dataset as possible, it is best collected in a similar manner. That is, the religion variables were modeled after the ethnicity variables used by the Minorities at Risk project. While this can potentially complicate the data collection process, in this case it did not. However, it does influence the structure of the religion variables.

Fourth, that the unit of analysis is the ethnic minority greatly complicates the analysis. That is not to say that the issue of religion and conflict is not complicated in and of itself. The model developed here is not particularly simple, and many real-world factors can complicate the dynamics predicted in this model. These include, but are by no means limited to, the type of government involved and economic conditions within the state. However, ethnic conflicts can be complicated by all of these factors as well as many others. These include, but are by no means limited to, discrimination directed against the ethnic minority, a desire for autonomy by the ethnic minority, linguistic and cultural differences between the ethnic minority and the dominant group, and the level of ethnic conflict among similar groups elsewhere, otherwise known as contagion or diffusion. This means many more independent factors can complicate the predicted relationships and, accordingly, must be taken into account.

Some Limitations of This Study

The limitations on this study caused by the nature of the Minorities at Risk data are overshadowed by a more basic structural limitation: that the empirical portion of this study is limited to ethnoreligious conflict. This means that while the theoretical portion of this study is meant to apply to all forms of religious conflict, the empirical section looks only at one particular type of religious conflict. As a result, major religious phenomena such as fundamentalism are left out of the empirical portion of this study.

Ethnoreligious conflict is a specific type of religious conflict. As discussed in the chapter 2, ethnicity overlaps with religion and religious fundamentalism, but not all ethnic conflicts are religious and not all religious conflicts are ethnic. Ideally, an empirical study, such as this one, would deal with all types of religious conflict. However, as is discussed more fully in chapters 7 and 8, the scarcity of data on religion and conflict forces reliance on the data which is currently available. This is especially true given that collecting this kind of data is a time consuming and expensive process.

Thus, the empirical findings of this study are limited to ethnoreligious conflict. However, this study attempts to transcend this limitation in the following manner: first, every attempt is made to constrain the impact of this limitation to only the empirical portion of this study. This includes the specific model for ethnoreligious conflict and the discussion of the empirical testing of this study, which is contained in chapter 7 and small portions of chapters 4 and 5. In this portion of the study, it is not appropriate to broaden the discussion to other types of religious conflict because it is important to avoid confusion over which conclusions are directly related to the data analysis and which are not. Second, the overlapping concepts of ethnicity, religion, and fundamentalism are discussed in chapter 2. Third, the general discussion of the state of the study of religion and conflict, in chapters 3 through 5, as well as the discussion of the impact religion has on conflict, in chapter 6, discusses the study of religion in general and is not limited to ethnicity and religion. Finally, chapter 8 contains a discussion of how the results of the empirical study impact on other forms of religious conflict.

Conclusion

While it is not claimed that the theory that is developed here is the last word on religion and conflict or on ethnoreligious conflict, it is claimed that it is an improvement over previous theories. It provides a more comprehensive explanation of religion and conflict than most previous theories. With regard to the more specific case of ethnoreligious conflict, the theory is also dynamic, falsifiable, and testable in a large-n cross-sectional format. In addition, the building blocks from which the model of ethnoreligious conflict is built can be used to develop dynamic and falsifiable models of other types of religious conflict.

Notes

1.The Minorities at Risk dataset has increased to 275 groups since the study, upon which this book is based, was performed. The additional groups are not included in this study.

2. They are also coded in the Minorities at Risk Phase 3 dataset in Belarus, Estonia, Georgia, Latvia, Moldova, and Ukraine. However, in these states ethnic Russians are not religiously distinct minorities and are, accordingly, not considered in this study.

Chapter 2

Defining Religion's Role in Society

In order to understand the relationship between religion and violence, we must first ask the question what is religion? And more importantly, what role does it play in society? This is because it is religion's active role in society that most affects conflict. That is, while the exact nature of God is of great interest to theologians, it is how these beliefs affect actions by people and institutions that is of interest to anyone examining the role of religion in conflict. Accordingly, the focus here is not on what religion is, but what religion does. This approach is problematic in that it avoids a direct definition of religion, but defining religion has always been a problematic undertaking.[1] Focusing on the role religion plays in society has the double advantage of focusing on how religion actually influences real world events while avoiding complex philosophical issues.

Several definitions of religion and ideology are examined here in order to derive from them the social functions of religion. Each of these functions is then examined in detail. Finally, modern fundamentalism, one of the newest manifestations of religion, is examined in the context of these social functions.

Definitions and Social Functions of Religion

Most would agree that religion is, among other things, a form of ideology. Accordingly, an examination of various definitions of ideology, as well as those of religion, should prove useful in defining the term "religion" and its social functions. The goal of this exercise is to draw from these definitions the essential properties ascribed to religion, with an emphasis on the roles religion plays in society. It should be noted that there are many different definitions of religion and ideology. Some, like Max Weber, avoid defining religion at all. Accordingly, the definitions presented here are a sampling of the many such definitions that are available and should be sufficient to provide a better understanding of the term "religion."

Rokeach (in Taylor, 1991: 85) defines an ideology as an "organization of beliefs and attitudes–religious, political, or philosophical in nature–that is more or less institutionalized or shared with others, deriving from external authority." This definition defines ideology as constituting a framework of belief, or belief system, which is referred to as an "organization of beliefs and attitudes" that is associated with formal institutions.

David Apter (1964: 16) asserts that ideology "links particular actions and mundane practices with a wider set of meanings and by doing so lends a more honorable and dignified complexion to social conduct." Like Rokeach's definition, this definition includes a belief system, which he refers to as "a wider set of meanings," as one of the properties of an ideology. It adds that this belief system also influences the actions of believers, including their "mundane practices" and "social conduct," but does not refer to formal institutions.

Similarly, Taylor (1991: 87) defines ideology as "[a] common public and broadly agreed set of externally derived rules which influence an individual and which help to regulate and determine behavior, giving it consistency with past action and helping to generate appropriate behavior in novel environments." This definition, like the others, defines ideology as having a belief system, which is referred to as "externally derived rules." It also explicitly connects the actions, or "behavior" of believers to this belief system.

From these definitions of ideology, three properties emerge. First, ideologies include some sort of belief system. Second, ideologies affect the behavior of those who adhere to them. Third, ideologies are often associated with institutions. Similarly, three properties of religion emerge from most definitions of religion: that religions constitute belief systems; that these belief systems usually include rules and standards of behavior; and that they are divine in origin. However, few of these definitions contain all three of these properties, nor do most of them contain references to institutions. Rather, they tend to focus on the nature of religious belief systems.

David Martin (in Kowalewski & Greil, 1990: 523) defines religion as "an acceptance of a level of reality beyond the observable world known to science, to which are ascribed meanings and purposes completing and transcending those of the purely human realm." This definition defines religion as a belief system, or "meanings and purposes," that is supernatural in origin in that they transcend "the purely human realm." Richard Wentz's (1987) definition of religion also contains these two properties. However, he uses a very broad definition of belief system. For him, any ritual activity (including watching a football game) that allows one to transcend biological existence and has a broader meaning to the self is considered engaging in "religiousness."

Durkheim (1975: 93) argues that "phenomena held to be religious consist in obligatory beliefs, connected with clearly defined practices which are related to given objects of those beliefs." This definition defines religion as a belief system, referred to as "obligatory beliefs," that contains rules and standards of behavior, which he calls "clearly defined practices." But Durkheim (1968: 30-34) specifically argues that religions are not necessarily divine in origin.[2]

Geertz's anthropological definition of religion describes in detail the nature of religious belief systems, infers that they are related to rules and standards of behavior and, like Durkheim, does not define them as divine in origin.[3] He defines religion as "(1) a system of symbols which acts to (2) establish powerful, pervasive and long-lasting moods and motivations in men by (3) formulation conceptions of existence and (4) clothing the conceptions with such an aura of factuality that (5) the moods and motivations seem uniquely realistic" (Geertz, 1973: 90).

Lewy's definition of religion includes all three properties of religion noted above. He defines religion as "a cultural institution, a complex of symbols, articles of faith and practices adhered to by a group of believers that are related to and commonly invoke the aid of supernatural powers and provide answers to questions of ultimate meaning" (Lewy, 1974: 4).

Perhaps the most complete definition for both ideology and religion is provided by Juergensmeyer. He describes several properties that religion and ideology have in common: both conceive of the world in coherent and manageable ways; both provide levels of meaning behind the day-to-day world that give coherence to things unseen; both provide the authority that gives social and political order its reason for being; both define for the individual the correct way of being in the world and relate individuals to a social whole (Juergensmeyer, 1993: 30-31). This definition includes all of the properties of religion discussed above, as well as that religions are often associated with formal institutions and can confer legitimacy upon actions and institutions. Perhaps the reason Juergensmeyer's definition is the most comprehensive is that he is more concerned with the social impact of religion than the nature of religion itself.

Using these definitions, a general list of the properties that religion and ideology have in common can now be constructed:

- Both provide a meaningful framework for understanding the world.

- Both provide rules and standards of behavior that link individual actions and goals to this meaningful framework.

- Both are usually derived from an external framework.

- Both link individuals to a greater whole and sometimes provide formal institutions which help to define and organize that whole.

- Both have the ability to legitimize actions and institutions.

These properties of religion merit a further and more detailed discussion.

A Meaningful Framework for Understanding the World

Religions provide meaningful frameworks for understanding the world. In doing so they fill a basic human need to make sense out of a complex reality. These religious frameworks, otherwise known as belief systems or world views, become a tool to place the seemingly chaotic information provided by one's senses into an understandable and meaningful context. Although it is true that religions are not the only source for such frameworks, it is indisputable that they are one of the major tools used by humankind in order to understand the world around them.

Stark and Bainbridge (1985: 366) note that sociologists of religion accept this assertion: "There is a powerful tradition among sociologists of religion to regard human beings as theologians or philosophers. It is assumed that people almost universally possess a coherent, overarching, and articulated 'Weltanschauung,' 'world view,' 'perspective,' 'frame of reference,' 'value orientation,' or 'meaning system.'" However, Stark and Bainbridge (1985: 367-393) themselves argue that not everyone has a coherent religious framework. While this is undoubtably true, they do accept that religious frameworks exist and serve the function of interpreting the world for many, if not all.

Spiro feels that such a framework is essential to the definition of religion. He argues that "belief in superhuman beings and in their power to assist or to harm man approaches universal distribution and this belief . . . is the real variable which ought to be designated by any definition of religion" (Spiro, 1996: 94). He continues to say that "every religious system consists . . . of a cognitive system; i.e. it consists of a set of experiences and implicit propositions concerning the superhuman world and man's relationship to it, which it contends to be true" (Spiro, 1996: 101). Thus, Spiro argues that the essential characteristic of a religion is whether it has a set of beliefs that define man's understanding of the world. Similarly, Williams (1994: 790-791), in his discussion of fundamentalist social movements, describes their belief systems as "frames" which are the "schemata of interpretation" that people use to "give meaning to events, organize experiences, and provide guides for actions."

It is implicit in Max Muller's (in Durkheim, 1975: 76) definition of religion that he would agree with this assessment:

> Religion is a mental faculty or disposition which . . . enables man to apprehend the Infinite under different names and under varying disguises. Without the faculty, no religion, not even the lowest worship of idols and fetishes, would be possible; and if we will but listen attentively, we can hear in all religions a groaning of the spirit, a struggle to conceive the inconceivable, to utter the unutterable, a longing after the Infinite.

Clifford Geertz not only argues that religions contain interpretive frameworks, he describes how they work. He posits that people use sacred symbols to form their religious frameworks. "Sacred symbols function to synthesize a people's ethos–the tone, character, and quality of their life, its moral and aesthetic style and mood–and their world-view–the picture they have of the way things actually are, their most comprehensive ideas of order" (Geertz, 1966: 3). This view of religious frameworks as consisting of symbols is also evident in Geertz's definition of religion, which was discussed earlier in this chapter.

Geertz also believes that most people need their religious framework to be able to interpret and explain anomalous events, human suffering, and evil. Not surprisingly, he argues that it is sacred symbols which allow us to recognize "the inescapability of ignorance, pain and injustice and the human plane while simultaneously denying that these irrationalities are characteristic of the world as a whole . . . in terms of a symbolism relating man's sphere of existence to a wider sphere in which it conceives to rest" (Geertz, 1973: 108). For this reason, he concludes that, according to anthropologists, religion's social importance "lies in its capacity to serve, for an individual or for a group, as a source of general, yet distinctive, conceptions of the world, the self and the relations between them" (Geertz, 1973: 123). Furthermore,

> religious concepts spread beyond their specifically metaphysical contexts to provide a framework of general ideas in terms of which a whole range of experience–intellectual, emotional and mental–can be given meaningful form . . . . A set of religious beliefs is also a gloss upon the mundane world of social relationships and psychological events. It renders them graspable. But more than a gloss, such beliefs are also a template. They do not merely interpret social and psychological processes–in which case they would be philosophical, not religious– but they shape them. . . . The tracing of the social and psychological role of religion . . . is a matter of understanding how men's hopes . . . of the "really real" and the dispositions these notions induce in them, colors their sense of the reasonable, the practical, the humane, and the moral (Geertz, 1973: 124-125).

Thus, Geertz is arguing that, in addition to shaping our understanding of the world, religious frameworks shape the world itself.

Geertz (1966: 12-13) also argues that "if sacred symbols did not at one and the same time induce dispositions to human beings and formulate, however obliquely, inarticulately, or unsystematically, general ideas of order, then the empirical differentia of religious activity or religious experience would not exist." Thus, not only does Geertz argue that a religion needs to include a framework for understanding the world, he also argues that a religion would not be a religion unless it provided such a framework. That all of the definitions of religion and ideology discussed earlier in this chapter contain some reference to a belief system provides strong confirmation for Geertz's assertion.

Greely, like Geertz, argues that religious symbols, images, and stories are important elements of religious frameworks. For Greely, a religious symbol "is a picture or image which resonates and articulates and re-presents the experience of grace. It also may be used to share this experience with others by re-presenting to the others parallel experiences of their own" (Greely, 1982: 53). This experience of grace validates the human experience by affirming that human existence has meaning and is part of a greater whole. The experience of grace is reinforced by "creation and renewal images." These images are so important that if a religious group is unable to provide them, its members often look elsewhere to fulfill their need for such images (Greely, 1982: 53-56).

For this reason, according to Greely, "religious heritages" consist of systems of symbols and stories designed to transmit and replicate the experiences that created them in the first place (84-90). Once these images have been transmitted to the individual, that individual reflects upon them and develops a "world view" based upon them. This world view becomes something more elaborate than the story and images that have been transmitted and is able to provide a response to critical questions with which it must deal, including the problems of human suffering and death (pp. 97-98).

Thus, Greely pictures religious frameworks as being very flexible. While the symbols, stories, and images which influence them remain constant, each generation facing a new set of historical, social, political, and/or economic circumstances is free to evolve a new interpretation of the basic framework to fit their particular circumstances. This understanding of the concept of frameworks also accounts for how different individuals who adhere to the same religion can often develop very different frameworks.

Durkheim (1964: 36-37) also argues that religions provides frameworks for understanding the world. He argues that religion is divided into two parts, rites and beliefs. While rites are relevant to providing the rules and standards of behavior which link individual goals and actions to the framework that religion provides, and will, accordingly, be discussed later, beliefs are Durkheim's concept of a religious framework for understanding the world. Durkheim defines beliefs as "states of opinion" which "consist in representations" that divide all things into profane and sacred. For Durkheim "beliefs, myths, dogmas and legends are either representations or systems of representations which express the nature of sacred things, the virtues and powers which are attributed to them or their relations with each other or profane things."

Durkheim also has some interesting comments on the natures of some religious frameworks. For instance, he argues that belief in a deity and/or the supernatural are not necessary elements in religious frameworks. He argues that religions like Buddhism, Janism, and Brahmanism do not have conceptions of deities within their frameworks and that "even within deistic religions there are many rites which are completely independent of all ideas of Gods or spiritual things"[4] (Durkheim, 1964: 30-34). Durkheim also argues that in primitive societies there is no conception of the supernatural within their religious framework. This is because Durkheim (1964: 24) defines the supernatural as "all sorts of things which surpass the limits of our knowledge." Yet, according to Durkheim (1975: 77-78), for primitive man there is no distinction between natural and supernatural. "Far from seeing the supernatural everywhere, primitive man sees it nowhere."

In other words, according to Durkheim, anything that is at variance with the natural laws as we understand them is supernatural. Thus, we must have a conception of the natural to have the supernatural. Both what modern man would consider natural and supernatural is understood by primitive man within one framework, with no distinctions between the two. To primitive man, the natural and the supernatural are the same thing. Because of this, mystery, or our lack of understanding of what cannot be explained by natural laws, does not exist for primitive man and is invented by modern man. This is because mystery can only come with knowledge that differentiates between the natural and the supernatural. Mystery, according to Durkheim, therefore plays an important part in some advanced religions.

While religions are a major source for frameworks that help man understand the world and his identity and place in it, they are not the only such source. For example, Horowitz argues that ethnicity can play a similar role. He argues that "ethnic affiliations typically fulfill needs that might otherwise go unmet ... blood solidarity, and personalistic help in an increasingly impersonal environment–in short, ascription in an ostensibly nonascriptive world" (Horowitz, 1985: 74). Ethnicity is an extension of kinship which meets "the need for familiarity and community, for family-like ties, for emotional support and reciprocal help, and for mediation and dispute resolution–for all the needs served by kinship, but now on a larger canvas" (Horowitz, 1985: 81). This extension in scale of family bonding also fills other human needs, including increasing the predictability of daily existence and providing more familiar relations with other groups and the government.

In all, it is clear that there is a considerable body of literature which argues that religion provides a framework within which one can understand the world. A major function of religion is to pass this understanding from one generation to the next through the use of sacred symbols, images, and stories. This function of religion fills a basic need to explain the unexplainable and bear the unbearable. In fact, human beings need such a framework in order to comprehend the world around them and without it they would be lost. While religions are not the only source of such interpretive frameworks, that they provide them is one of their essential functions in society.

Rules and Standards of Behavior and Formal Institutions

Religious frameworks usually include a set of rules and standards of behavior which influence the actions of the adherents of those frameworks. That is, religions usually contain some form of rules to which their believers are expected to adhere. In addition, religious frameworks often cause their adherents to form institutions to assist in the task of reinforcing those frameworks and transmitting the religion's belief system and guidelines for behavior to the next generation as well as to converts. This inclusion of rules and standards of behavior and the formation of institutions in religious frameworks are the logical result of the existence of such frameworks. It is logical that anything which affects how people see the world will also influence how they react to it.

Spiro (1966: 96-97) implicitly makes this connection between religious frameworks and action. He argues that religion consists of, in part, "an institution consisting of culturally patterned interaction with culturally postulated superhuman beings." This interaction consists of "activities which are believed to carry out, embody or be consistent with culturally postulated superhuman beings" as well as activities "believed to influence superhuman beings to satisfy the needs of the actors." Thus for Spiro, the belief in superhuman beings, which is a core concept of his version of a religious framework, has a strong influence on the behavior of those who have such beliefs.

Weber also links religious frameworks to behavior. He argues that the existence of a world view is necessary, but not sufficient, for that world view to influence action. His version of the link between belief and action is a concept called psychological premiums. He argues that salvation religions put psychological premiums on actions which create constraints and opportunities that influence actions. In other words, these religions create a system of psychological rewards for some actions and psychological punishments for others. Thus, psychological premiums serve as filters for world views and translate them into action orientations. However, he limits the use of this concept to some extent by arguing that only salvation religions, due to their capacity to bestow psychological premiums, have the potential to translate on a continuous basis the comprehensive ideal thrusts of world views into daily action (Kalberg, 1990: p. 63-66).

Durkheim also connects religious frameworks to actions taken by the adherents of those frameworks. As noted earlier, he divides religion into two parts. While belief, as discussed earlier, is Durkheim's version of an interpretive framework, rites are "determined modes of action" which can only be "defined as distinctive from other human practices . . . by the special nature of their objects" (Durkheim, 1964: 36). For Durkheim, rites and beliefs are closely related. "Religious beliefs are the representations which express the nature of sacred things and the relations which they sustain, either with each other or with profane things. . . . Rites are the rules of conduct which prescribe how a man should comport himself in the presence of these sacred objects" (Durkheim, 1964: 41).` The collective consciousness of religion is only possible and can only realize itself through action. In fact, in order to "reaffirm" its collective sentiments, a society, according to Durkheim, engages in reunions, meetings, and assemblies. These activities can only be described as rites, and the reunions, meetings, and assemblies in which they take place can be described as religious institutions. Thus, not only does Durkheim argue that religious frameworks can only be sustained if they require actions by their adherents, he also infers that these actions take place within the context of institutions. The reunions, meetings, and assemblies which Durkheim describes constitute, at the very least, a simple form of religious institution and can often take place within the context of more formal institutions, including formal houses of worship.

While it can be inferred that Durkheim considers religious institutions an important tool for transmitting religious frameworks, Greely puts it more bluntly. He argues that "in a complex society all major religious heritages seem to develop institutions which one way or another strive to guarantee fidelity to the original religious heritage" (Greely, 1982: 93). However, Greely notes that there are several limitations on the ability of religious institutions to accomplish this task, including the difficulty of transmitting a clear message from the top of a religion's bureaucratic structure (if it has such a structure) to the rank and file members of that religion (Greely, 1982: 94); the ability of religious institutions to control their followers, which is limited by the consent of those followers, especially in the "modern world" where churches are voluntary organizations (Greely, 1982: 95, 128); and the fact that the family is often more important than religious institutions in transmitting religious frameworks (Greely, 1982: 125).

Greely (1982: 107-117), like Durkheim, also argues that rituals, including prayer, are an important means for transmitting religious frameworks. He argues that although "ritual does not teach religious truths, it passes on religious symbols and stories and the experience of hopefulness contained in these stories, as well as symbol systems or arrangements" (Greely, 1982: 113). However, he also argues that rituals can become less effective in this task when they become "ritualized, formal, routine, unchangeable, and rigidly constrained by regulation." When this happens, as often seems inevitable, rituals can become a chore rather than a vital and meaningful experience. While it should be the task of religious institutions to revitalize such routinized rituals, it is often the case that they oppose any attempts to change the rituals.

Thus, there is strong support for the assertion that belief in a religious framework is fundamentally linked with behavior. That is, those who believe in a religious framework also accept upon themselves a set of rules and standards of behavior which they are obligated to follow. Conversely, the actions or rituals required by a religious framework's rules and standards of behavior play a role in transmitting and reinforcing that framework. There is also strong support for the assertion that religious institutions play an important role in transmitting religious frameworks, as well as in organizing and guiding the actions and rituals advocated by such frameworks. Thus, religions affect society through their influence on behavior and this influence is often perpetuated through institutions.

The Ability to Legitimize Actions and Institutions

Despite the fact that the issue of legitimacy is not included in most definitions of religion, there seems to be considerable agreement among scholars that, as is argued here, religion can act as a legitimizing force in society for both governments and those who oppose them. Kokosalakis (1985: 371) argues that even though, currently, the justification of state power usually rests on ideologies like nationalism, pursuit of democracy, humanitarian values, etc., a "strong residual element of religion, which clearly exists even in western societies, can still perform basic legitimizing or oppositional functions within such ideologies."

Geertz (1977: 267-278) similarly argues that "thrones may be out of fashion and pageantry too; but political authority still requires a cultural framework in which to define itself and advance its claims, and so does opposition to it."

Little (1991: xx) also considers religion important to political legitimacy. He argues that "religion or similar beliefs often play an active and prominent part in defining group identity and in picking out and legitimating particular ethnic and national objectives." This is because of the human need to "elevate given political and economic arrangements in reference to sacred or cosmic standards."

Turner (1991: 178-198) engages in a detailed discussion of religion and legitimacy. He discusses the history of legitimating political power through religion in Christian Societies. This legitimacy comes from a descending theory of legitimacy in which power descends from God to the rulers (divine right) and, accordingly, people have no right of resistance and no power over their ruler. However, over time, the Western world has switched to an ascending theory of legitimacy, in which power comes from people, thus giving them a right of resistance. He attributes the current "crisis of capitalism," in part, to "the inability of legal formalism to provide a system of normative legitimation" (Turner, 1991: 197).

While this brief discussion of religion and legitimacy is by no means complete, it is sufficient to make the point that religion is a powerful source of legitimacy. This legitimacy can be used to justify actions that might otherwise have been unthinkable. It has been used to justify mass suicide, mass murder, and suicide attacks on unarmed civilians. The potential effects on society of this social function of religion should not be underestimated.

Derived from an External Framework

The major difference between religion and ideology is the source of the external authority and the type of meaning that it provides. The type of external authority found in most religions was best described in Martin's definition, which, as is recalled, referred to a "level of reality beyond the observable world known to science," or, in other words, a supernatural and/or divine external authority. The meaning that religion supplies can also be a spiritual meaning that is not realized on this earth, such as the concepts of Heaven and Hell. However, it will usually relate these otherworldly phenomena to actions that must be taken on this earth. That is, while Heaven and Hell are not part of the physical world which we normally experience, our actions in this world can affect the experience of our souls in the afterlife. Also, religion can, like ideology, provide a set of meanings that are directly related to this world.

However, as noted earlier, there are those who argue that religion does not necessarily need to come from a supernatural source. Durkheim and Geertz, as discussed earlier, make this argument, as do others.[5] Be that as it may, the major emphasis of this work is an examination of the role religion plays in society and conflict. Whether a religion must be of supernatural origin or not is less important for our purposes than how religions, whatever their origin, affect social and conflict behavior. Thus, while the origin of religion is an interesting issue, it is not dealt with extensively here except where it affects social and conflict behavior.

Fundamentalism and Fundamentalists

Recently, a substantial amount of attention has been given to fundamentalist movements by scholars, the media, and policy makers alike. Despite the perception that fundamentalism is a wholly new phenomenon, fundamentalist interpretations of religious frameworks are not fundamentally different from other religious frameworks. They are, rather, a specific type of framework. The defining character-istic of the various manifestations of fundamentalism is a particular type of interpretation of their respective religious frameworks. These fundamentalist frameworks place an emphasis on what is perceived by the fundamentalists to be a return to the true, authentic origins of their religion. Thus, while fundamentalism represents a new and unique form of religious framework, the fundamentalist view of the world is still a form of religious framework.

The source of the term fundamentalism comes from a series of ten paperbacks published between 1910 and 1915 called *The Fundamentals,* which consisted of edited essays written by leading American conservative theologians who defended biblical inerrancy and attacked what they perceived as the evils of secular, theistic modernism (Misztal and Shupe, 1992: 7). As will be seen, these conservative theo-logians were, to a great extent, cut from the same mold as the people we today call fundamentalists.

Marty and Appleby (1991: 3), in their groundbreaking study of fundamental-ism, define it as:

> a tendency, a habit of mind, found within religious communities and paradigmatically embodied in certain representative individuals and movements, which manifests itself as a strategy, or a set of strategies, by which beleaguered believers attempt to preserve their distinctive identity as a people or group. Feeling this identity to be at risk in the contemporary era, they fortify it by a selective retrieval of doctrines, beliefs, and practices from a sacred past. These retrieved "fundamentals" are refined, modified, and sanctioned in a spirit of shrewd pragmatism: they are to serve as a bulwark against the encroachment of outsiders who threaten to draw the believers into a syncretistic, areligious, or irreligious cultural milieu. Moreover, these fundamentals are accompanied in the new religious portfolio by unprecedented claims and doctrinal innovations. By the strength of these innovations and the new supporting doctrines, the retrieved and updated fundamentals are meant to regain the same charismatic intensity today by which they originally forged the communal identity from the revelatory religious

experiences long ago.

Therefore, fundamentalism is both derivative and original. In the effort to reclaim the efficacy of religious life, fundamentalists have much in common with other religious revivalists of past centuries. A renewed religious identity becomes the basis for a recreated political and social order oriented on the future. Inspired by this order, fundamentalists pay special attention to values, motivations, incentives, and ideals which serve to order the intimate zones of life including marriage, sex, family life, child rearing, education, morality, and spirituality. Boundaries are set, enemies identified, converts sought, and institutions are created and sustained to accomplish these goals (Marty and Appleby, 1991: 3).

Furthermore, fundamentalism is particularly modern. Fundamentalists feel that their tradition is at risk in the modern secular world and take measures to protect their tradition from these threats. The structuring of the private lives of fundamentalists and the boundaries built between them and others are manifestations of this desire (Appleby, 2000: 101).

While frameworks of belief and the distinction between "us" and "them" can be found in most religions, the nature of the fundamentalist frameworks and ingroup-outgroup distinctions make fundamentalists unique. Fundamentalists believe "that they have a clear and detailed picture of the beginning and typological pictures of the end, along with a clear blueprint of the rules for right living in the present." Individuals and societies who stray from this path are doomed. For fundamentalists, there is a clear and distinct contrast between salvation and damnation. The world is best understood through the fundamentalist framework, which becomes the standard for evaluating all aspects of life. "All other knowledge, all other rules for living are placed in submission to the images of the world found in sacred texts and traditions. All other authorities and credentials are de-legitimized, or at least put in their place" (Ammerman, 1994b: 149-150).

The conviction that their frameworks of belief constitute an absolute truth results in fundamentalists applying their imperatives both inwardly and outwardly. Applying their framework inward results in an "intense preoccupation with individual conduct and interpersonal relations" (Marty and Appleby, 1993: 5). This preoccupation is so intense that fundamentalists reject the public/private distinction. God's will is absolute and applies in all instances, public or private. They believe that God is active in the world, see His purpose in mundane events, and believe that He guides history (for example AIDS is seen by many fundamentalists as a punishment for homosexuality). Accordingly, they use traditional religious ideology as a guide for how to deal with modern problems and place an emphasis on "traditional values." In fact, the very idea of deriving law from sacred texts is a repudiation of public/private distinction. (Garvey, 1991)

Furthermore, fundamentalists' greatest successes have been in the private realm. That is, fundamentalists are most able to affect interpersonal relationships, especially within the family. This is because the family is the primary unit for most religions. Fundamentalists consider the family a microcosm of the universal moral order. It is also essential to both religious observance, education, and transmission of religious knowledge from one generation to the next. For this reason, fundamentalists tend to pursue social programs to shape the family in accordance with their values. On a more practical level, the fundamentalist framework is most developed with regard to domestic relations, and these rules are probably the easiest to enforce (Hardacre, 1993; Marty and Appleby, 1993: 5-7).

Fundamentalists also often attempt to apply their frameworks of belief outward, to society as a whole, as well as the government. This is because "the fundamentalist message is not only about being an individual believer, but also about being a believing nation." Therefore, fundamentalists often become activists trying to bring the nation onto the true path. In fact, they often claim that they are the keepers of the nation's true traditions. They argue that the nation's founders followed the fundamentalist framework and established the nation based upon it. In this way, fundamentalists try to define the past in order to make claims on the present. They become cultural critics, defining society's problems and demanding that society readjust itself back to the original intents of its founders under the guidance of fundamentalist principles and leadership (Ammerman, 1994b: 152-155).

For example, most fundamentalists agree that the "decoupling" of religion and science by secular modernists disrupts the relationship between knowledge and wisdom. This has resulted in the "destruction or loosening of normative restraints that would otherwise harness the dehumanizing forces of modern technology." Fundamentalists therefore believe that these restraints should be reintroduced (Marty and Appleby, 1993: 6).

However, Appleby (1994: 42-43) points out that "fundamentalists have seldom proven themselves capable of governing effectively." They can usually find society's problems, but not their solutions. For this reason, fundamentalist movements must often resort to the services of professional politicians and non-fundamentalist allies. Also, it is often the case that secular politicians often support fundamentalists when their goals coincide. Similarly, the use of violence by fundamentalists has generally failed in that it has most often resulted in resentment and divisiveness rather than the unification of believers and the punishment of those deemed responsible for the ills of society. The use of violence has also sapped the moral standing of those who use it (Appleby, 2000: 121).

Thus, it is the belief in a divine and absolute truth that must, at almost all costs, be applied to both individual and societal behavior that both distinguishes fundamentalists from non-fundamentalists and defines what all fundamentalists have in common. Marty and Appleby (1993: 5) make this argument when they note that "fundamentalists seem to have more in common with one another across traditions than they do with their nonfundamentalist coreligionists, at least with regard to seminal questions such as the role of revealed truth in guiding human inquiry."

Similarly, Appleby (1994: 16-18, 40) argues that such movements have "family resemblances." Fundamentalist movements thrive when the masses are dislocated by rapid and uneven modernization, haphazard change in economic and cultural patterns occur, and education and social welfare systems fail. They all see religion as an encompassing way of life that meets their needs. They all tend to establish codes of behavior which apply to political and international arenas as well as family life and serve to unite their movements. Accordingly, the term "fundamentalist" connotes a certain kind of believer who wishes to form or defend a state based in some explicit way upon sacred history, laws, customs, traditions, and/or moral obligations" (Appleby, 1994: 15). In general, religious ideologies and sacred texts provide the blueprint for a course of action used to attain this goal in society. While some moderates work to achieve this within the law, others use extralegal and violent means.

However, the cultural context in which fundamentalists exist places some limits on the scope of their frameworks. Fundamentalist "movements must demonstrate that they are different and better–rejecting the existing wider culture as corrupt–without falling so far beyond the pale that their beliefs and practices appear to be madness." For example, extreme indiscriminate violence tends to go beyond the limits of what is acceptable in most cultural contexts. However, when fundamentalist frameworks are in line with local culture and tradition, they can have considerable appeal (Williams, 1994: 804-805).

Another limitation on fundamentalist frameworks seems to be self imposed. Fundamentalist frameworks tend to be selective. That is, they emphasize some aspects of the religion and ignore others. Appleby (2000: 87-91) argues that this tendency of fundamentalists to emphasize and reinterpret some aspects of their tradition at the expense of others is a hallmark of fundamentalism. This selectivity and innovation is justified by the perceived need to find a way within the tradition to maintain the community within the context of the modern world.

To some extent, what aspects of religious doctrine are selected for emphasis is probably influenced by the cultural context in which fundamentalists exist. An editorial makes this point in response to the U.S. Southern Baptist declaration based on the Epistle to the Ephesians, which may or may not have been written by the apostle Paul, that a wife should submit to her husband as a servant:

> But does this mean that Southern Baptists condone slavery (as Paul does in his Epistle to Philemon)? Do the Southern Baptists pool all of their property and hold everything in common as the first Christians did? Do they condemn usury as do all biblical texts that refer to the subject–and if so, how do they manage to invest in the stock market, put savings into pensions or even have a bank account? Christ taught that we should not lay up treasure at all. What about the teaching of Jesus in the Sermon on the mount, that we should bless our enemies and not resist evil? Does the Southern Baptist Convention embrace pacifism?
>
> Even the most fervent fundamentalists have to be highly selective in their fundamentals. They want to believe that every word of Scripture is God's word, and therefore infallible. But paradoxically, their hero is St. Paul, who entirely overturned the Jewish reverence for the letter of the law and regarded the Torah as a dirty word.[6]

It is important to emphasize that fundamentalism is not synonymous with violence. For instance, Appleby (2000: 103-104) demonstrates that many movements considered fundamentalist are not violent and many religious movements which use violence are not fundamentalist. Rather, fundamentalists are differentiated from other religious movements by the nature of their religious beliefs and practices. Fundamentalist practices are designed to protect religious traditions from the perceived threats of modern secular culture. In order to protect the religious community, the distinctions between insiders and outsiders are strengthened. The lives of those within the movement are regulated, and sometimes efforts are made to export these regulations and perhaps impose them on others. These practices are justified by the selective interpretation of religious tradition, which emphasizes some aspects of that tradition at the expense of others.

In sum, it is clear that fundamentalism represents a particular brand of religious framework. This framework is in many ways a reaction to modernity that is intended to preserve or defend religious traditions in a modern secular world. Accordingly the rules and standards of behavior contained in fundamentalist frameworks involve a selective interpretation of those religious doctrines that are intended to meet this goal. Nevertheless these interpretations are considered to be an authentic and, in many cases, literal interpretation of original religious scriptures and doctrines that describe an absolute truth. These rules and standards emphasize the proper modes of behavior that must be adopted in private life and are intended to also build a distinction between insiders and outsiders. They also sometimes include the imperative to use the political system to enforce these standards on others.

The Overlapping Concepts of Religion and Ethnicity

Religion and ethnicity are often overlapping and even intertwined. Religion is included in most definitions of ethnicity as one among many potential traits that can define an ethnic group. For example, Gurr (1993a: 3) argues that

> in essence, communal [ethnic] groups are psychological communities: groups whose core members share a distinctive and enduring collective identity based on cultural traits and lifeways that matter to them and to others with whom they interact.
>
> People have many possible bases for communal identity: shared historical experiences or myths, *religious beliefs*, language, ethnicity, region of residence, and, in castelike systems, customary occupations. Communal groups–which are also referred to as ethnic groups, minorities and peoples–usually are distinguished by several reenforcing traits. The key to identifying communal groups is not the presence of a particular trait or combination of traits, but rather in the shared perception that the defining traits, whatever they are, set the group apart.

Thus, Gurr defines religion as being salient to ethnicity when it is a defining trait that sets a group apart in that group's own eyes and/or in the eyes of others. Because the importance of religion to ethnic identity is based on perceptions, the relevance of religion can vary over time.

Horowitz (1985: 64-74) also argues that the boundaries of group identities change over time. This happens through the processes of "differentiation" and "assimilation." He defines assimilation as the "simplification of identities in a more heterogeneous environment" and differentiation as the "drawing of fine distinctions among people in a less heterogeneous environment" (Horowitz, 1985: 68). Thus, like Gurr, Horowitz believes that the manner in which individuals perceive themselves is the most important factor in how these processes create new identities. He also argues that the process of ethnic conflict itself affects these boundaries. Conflict with other groups can cause an ethnic group to reexamine its boundaries, for example emphasizing traits that differentiate it from its enemy and deemphasizing internal differences. It can also increase the importance of the ethnic identification itself. Carment and James (1997a: 207, 216-217, 1997: 2, 255), Deutsch (1981: 55), Greenfeld (1992, 12-13), Kasfir (1979: 373), and Kriesberg (1997: 232-233) make similar arguments.

Thus, religion is potentially a very important element of ethnicity. It is even arguable that many of today's ethnic groups have their origin in religion.[7] This is probably true of most of the Christian minorities in the Middle East who are generally indistinguishable from the region's Muslim population other than through religious affiliation. In a few cases, the two coincide almost fully, as is arguably the case with the Jewish religion.

Religion and ethnicity, as social and political concepts, have many similarities. While ethnicity is not always congruent with a framework of belief, it is often associated with nationalism, which does provide a such a framework. This framework can include rules and standards of behavior such as the requirement or at least the desirability of forming or maintaining a state for one's ethnic group. Even for ethnic groups which do not express such national sentiments, ethnicity is a basis for identity that can influence beliefs and behavior. Ethnicity, both in its nationalist and other manifestations, can provide legitimacy for a wide variety of activities and policies and ethnic symbols can be as potent a political and social mobilizing force as religious symbols. Ethnicity is also often associated with institutions.

In practice, the distinctions between religion and ethnicity as bases for nationalism are rarely clear. They are often "intertwined and mutually reenforcing." Religion can justify ethnic aspirations and ethnicity can be the birthplace of religions (Appleby, 2000: 61-62). Yet, clearly, not all ethnic groups are religiously homogeneous and not all religions coincide fully with a particular ethnicity. For instance, many fundamentalist movements are not coincident with ethnicity. The religious right in the United Sates and most of the Islamic fundamentalist opposition movements throughout the Islamic world are opposing members of their own faiths and ethnic groups in the political arena in order to pursue their aims of protecting their religious traditions in the modern era.

However, even in this, fundamentalist movements are not completely dissimilar from ethnic groups. Both have political goals that they pursue using a similar repertoire of strategies and tactics that range from peaceful protest and other legal political activities to violent rebellion. Also, the goals that both types of groups pursue are linked to the preservation of important concepts. For fundamentalists, this concept is their religious tradition. For ethnic groups, this concept is the group's physical and economic well-being, the desire to have some form of input in political decisions concerning them, and the preservation of the group's identity as expressed through culture, language, religion, and often self-determination.

However, these goals differ in the nature of the political demands made by ethnic minorities and fundamentalists. Ethnic minorities have two major ways to attain their political goals; voice and exit. Voice means gaining more say in governmental decisions, at least with respect to decisions that affect the group. Exit is the more radical solution of pursuing group interests through exiting the state, either partially in the form of autonomy or fully through establishing a new state or joining a bordering state that is ethnically similar to the group.

While the desire of some fundamentalists to withdraw into their own communities and have little to do with outsiders can be considered a form of exit, it is qualitatively different from the exit sought by ethnic groups. This is because most states do not feel threatened by a religious community that keeps to itself and wishes to be left alone but does not seek political separation from the state. Whereas, few states are willing to grant an ethnic group political autonomy, and fewer states are willing to cede territory to another political entity, whether that entity be a new state or an existing bordering state. Also, the nature of the voice sought by fundamentalist groups is fundamentally different from that sought by ethnic groups. Ethnic groups seek only to defend their own interests, whereas fundamentalist groups often want to enact policies that will affect every citizen in the state, regardless of their religious beliefs. Clearly, if one views political power as a zero-sum game, the pursuit of power by an ethnic minority impinges on that of other groups in a state. However, this is not the same as an attempt to remold the state in a more fundamentalist image or perhaps replace a secular government with a religious one.

For example, Israel's granting of regional autonomy to the Palestinians was clearly a difficult decision that has had security implications that affect the lives of most Israelis. Yet, despite tensions, inconveniences due to increased security measures, and occasional tragedies caused by the low-level conflict between Israel and the Palestinians, Israel's political structures remain unchanged. However, should Israel's Haredi (Jewish Fundamentalist) parties take over the government and enact many of the religious laws that are on their agenda, life in Israel would change radically, especially for secular Israelis. Given that the birthrate of Haredi Jews in Israel is considerably higher than that of secular Jews and that Israel's government is democratically elected, demographics makes this scenario a distinct possibility at some point in the future.

That is not to say that fundamentalism and ethnic nationalism never coincide. Many ethnic resistance movements are also fundamentalist movements. For example, Hamas and Islamic Jihad are Palestinian fundamentalist movements that participate in the Palestinian conflict with Israel. However, these movements are only two among many Palestinian groups, and Hamas is part of the international Islamic Brotherhood movement. Thus, while fundamentalist movements may sometimes coincide with ethnicity, such movements often have connections outside their ethnic group and rarely represent the entire ethnic group. In the case of Hamas, the movement behaves both as a fundamentalist movement and as an ethnic movement. They pursue their interpretation of the ethnic-based exit strategy against the Israelis while at the same time pursuing the fundamentalist goal of transforming Palestinian society into a more religious one.

Another major difference between religion and ethnicity is the nature of membership. It is much harder to change one's ethnicity than it is to change one's religious affiliation. In many cases, ethnicity is based on unchanging traits such as the color of one's skin, but one's religious affiliation is a matter of choice. While there may be social consequences or even barriers to changing one's religion, it is often a more viable option than changing one's ethnicity.

This is especially true when this change involves a change in the level or nature of one's religiosity within the same religion. Thus, fundamentalists can recruit new members among nonfundamentalists who adhere to their tradition, while the membership of an ethnic group is relatively fixed. In fact, fundamentalist movements are often successful in gaining new recruits (Marty and Appleby, 1991: 630; Don-Yehyia, 1994: 268), and one of the major goals of these movements is to increase their numbers in order to increase their political clout (Williams, 1994: 788-790).

To return to our example of Israel, it is clear that changing ethnicity from Palestinian to Israeli Jew is nearly impossible. Even intermarriage between Palestinians and Israeli Jews is extremely rare. Yet among both Palestinians and Jewish Israelis, there has been considerable recruitment by fundamentalist movements. Hamas has been very successful at recruiting new members among Palestinians, and Shas, a Jewish fundamentalist political party, has been equally successful at recruiting new members among Israel's Sphardi Jewish population (Jews of Middle Eastern and North African origin). Both movements use the similar tactic of providing educational opportunities and charity work among populations where authorities have failed at meeting these needs.

This difference in the nature of membership has two additional implications. First, the importance of ethnic identities varies over time, place, and individuals. That is, ethnicity is more important in some times and places than others and to some individuals than it is to others in the same time and place. While this is also true of religion, it is considerably less true of fundamentalism. An important element of fundamentalism is the belief that the religious tradition is important to the extent that active steps must be taken in order to preserve it. While this can be true of ethnic identity, it is not always the case. In all probability, most ethnic groups have members who would rather not be members but have been unable to successfully extricate themselves from being identified by others as members of the group.

Second, while fundamentalist movements are more often than not politically active, ethnic groups are generally not politically active in pursuit of group interests. Gurr (2000) notes that while there may be as many as 5,000 ethnic minorities worldwide, he only includes 275 in his study because these are the minorities that were politically active or potentially politically active during the 1990s. In contrast, a basic element of fundamentalism is to take active steps to preserve the tradition; this often includes steps to export fundamentalist values to other elements of society and almost always includes enforcing these values within the movement.

In sum, while religion and ethnicity have many similarities and overlaps to the extent that they are sometimes indistinguishable, they are not the same. The nature of membership and the type of demands they tend to make on the state are very different. However, as shown in later chapters, the combination of religion and ethnicity in the political arena is potentially very explosive.

Conclusion

In all, religion serves four social functions. First, it provides an interpretive framework, or belief system, for understanding the world. Second, it contains rules and standards of behavior which guide the actions of believers. Third, religions are generally associated with institutions that transmit religious frameworks from one generation to the next. Finally, religion can legitimize all forms of actions. While ideologies also serve these functions, they are different from religions because religions are usually believed to have divine origins while ideologies are accepted as the creation of man.

As will be discussed in later chapters, these social functions of religion are essential to understanding the role of religion in conflict. This is because they define the context in which religion interacts with society. It is through these interactions that religion can also inspire or influence violence, conflict, and rebellion.

Notes

1. For a discussion of some of the problems inherent in defining religion, see Stark and Bainbridge (1985: 3-5).
2. Durkheim also infers that religions are also associated with institutions. This is discussed more fully later in this chapter.
3. Geertz's views on the nature of religious belief systems are discussed more fully later in this chapter.
4. It should be noted that this argument of Durkheim's is not undisputed. For example, Spiro (1966: 91-94) argues that Buddhism does actually contain something analogous to a belief in superhuman beings.
5. See, for example, Luckman (1967), Bellah (1970), and Yinger (1970).

6. A. N. Wilson, "The Problem with Fundamentalists," *International Herald Tribune* 6/17/98.
7. Anthony Smith (1999 and 2000) makes this argument with regard to the origins of nationalism, a concept closely related to ethnicity.

Chapter 3

Religion in a Modern and Secular World

Although a basic argument of this book is that religion considerably influences society, politics, and conflict, it is important to emphasize that this argument is not universally accepted. In fact, there are many scholars who believe that religion has no affect on conflict or, for that matter, on modern politics and society in general. While this argument was more common several decades ago, there are many who still posit that religion is not important or even relevant in modern times. The prominence of these arguments in social science theory provides a possible explanation for the lack of an adequate theory of religion and conflict. This is because first, many scholars think no such theory is necessary. Second, many who do think religion affects conflict have been forced to divert a large portion of their resources in order to defend the validity of studying the topic at all rather than on developing a theory of religion and conflict. The centrality of this ongoing debate requires a detailed discussion of the arguments presented by both sides.

There are two major schools of thought which contend that religion has become an "epiphenomenal" factor, having no effect in politics and society. That is, these schools of thought consider religion to be irrelevant and to have no important effect on worldly events. The first school of thought, known as the modernization or secularization thesis, posits that, due to various processes, the modern world has become secularized and religion is no longer a relevant political or social force. The second school of thought, which is described in more detail in the following chapter, is known as the functionalist or instrumentalist argument. This argument posits that religion is actually the tool of other more basic social forces and has no independent influence. If either of these schools of thought is correct, there would be no point in studying the effects of religion on any type of conflict because there would either be no such effects or those effects would actually be manifestations of other forces. However, as the following discussion illustrates, these arguments are seriously flawed.

It is clear that many would question the value of devoting entire chapters of a book to an evaluation of the argument that religion is not an important factor in society. This is especially so considering that there exists a large body of scholarship which considers the fact that religion influences society, politics, and especially conflict a "no brainer." Anyone who studies Islam and the Middle East, for example, is very unlikely to conclude that religion is of little import. Despite this, a full evaluation of the debate over religion's relevance is essential for several reasons. The most obvious and perhaps the least important is that many continue to argue that religion is not relevant in modern times and, as will be shown, these arguments were for a time the dominant paradigms within large portions of the behavioral branches of sociology and political science. Furthermore, many who make this argument do so in unambiguous terms. If these prophets of religion's demise are correct, a study of religion and conflict, such as this, would be a waste of time. Therefore a response to such arguments is necessary. Yet, this alone would merit a brief description of the arguments against religion's relevance and a brief retort. However, the other reasons for a more in-depth discussion are more convincing.

Perhaps the most convincing reason to evaluate this debate is that the past prominence and continuing presence of these nay-sayers has significantly influenced the evolution of thought on religion and conflict. As noted above, this includes the fact that many have devoted resources to defending the study of religion, society, politics, and conflict rather than building theories on the exact nature of this influence. Also, it is probable that the presence and sometimes dominance of these paradigms deterred many from addressing the topic of religion at all. It is hard to understand why it is possible to make the argument, as it is made here, that the study of religion lacks an adequate theory of religion and conflict without taking this into account.

Another important reason for examining the arguments against religion's relevance and the responses to them is that doing so helps to shed light on both the nature of religion's influence in modern times as well as religion's reaction to modernity. This is because the debate is precisely over this issue, with one side arguing that modernity has made religion irrelevant and the other saying that modernity has, in fact, caused a resurgence of religion while at the same time altering the nature of religion's interaction with society. Also, this examination reveals something about the differing perspectives of those who engage on both sides of the debate. That is, those who argue that religion is becoming less relevant tend to be those who focus only on Western society or use paradigms influenced by Marxism. Those who argue for religion's continuing, or even increasing, influence in modern times more often, but by no means exclusively, have focuses that include the non-West.

It is important to reiterate that the purpose of this chapter is not to disprove the argument that religion is an epiphenomenal force in modern times, although the review presented here of the debate on this topic can be said to have this result. Rather, the goal here is twofold: first, to understand the context in which the existing body of theory on religion and conflict has evolved; and second, to provide a deeper understanding of how religion itself and religion's role in society, politics, and conflict has been influenced by modernity.

The Expected Demise of Religion in Modern Times

The argument that, in modern times, primordial factors like ethnicity and religion are becoming irrelevant was at one time dominant in the disciplines of political science and sociology and today continues to have many supporters. While this school of thought is by no means monolithic, and spans a wide range of social science disciplines, the general argument that modernity has made religion "epi-phenomenal," having no relevance, remains a consistent theme. If this is the case, any study of the role of religion in politics and society would also be irrelevant.

The arguments presented in this section are intended to be representative of the arguments as those who support them have presented them in the past and should in no way be taken as an endorsement.

The Modernization and Secularization Theses

During the 1950s and 1960s, many social scientists, especially political scientists, argued that modernization would reduce the political significance of ethnicity. They argued that factors inherent in modernization, including economic development, urbanization, growing rates of literacy and education, as well as advancements in science and technology, would inevitably lead to the demise of the role of primordial factors like ethnicity in politics. While the modernization literature usually dealt with ethnicity in general, its predictions were also intended to apply specifically to religion.[1] In fact, modernization theory predicted that the same factors which were believed to be causing the demise of ethnicity would lead to the process of the secularization of society.[2]

In a good summary of the attitudes of modernization theorists toward religion, Sahliyeh (1990: 3) notes that

> students of social development hypothesized that exposure to education, urbaniza-tion, the presence of modern opportunities for employment, technology, scientific advancement, as well as new and more complex social organizations, would inevitably lead to the spread of secularization, pluralism and political differentia-tion throughout the world. These changes were also expected to lead to the adoption of new values and modern life styles that would sharply clash with religious traditions. It was thought that with the spread of modernization, traditional religious institutions would decline or disappear and religion's grip over various cultures and societies would be loosened. Rather than being a force for collective action, social control and political mobilization, religion would

simply become a private affair for the individual.

Furthermore, nationalism and other secular ideologies are expected by modernization theorists to replace religion in the role of granting legitimacy (Sahliyeh, 1990:
4). This argument is known as the *secularization thesis.*

While the modernization argument has its roots in political science, the
arguments for this trend toward secularization are not limited to that discipline and
are more prominent in the discipline of sociology. In fact, while political science's
modernization theorists focused on the demise of ethnicity and only included the
demise of religion as an afterthought, sociologists focused directly on the demise
of religion through the process of secularization. From World War II until recently,
most sociologists have subscribed to the secularization argument. For example
Westhus (1976: 314) notes that

> when interest in the sociology of religion revived after World War II, it took three
> primary forms. Some sociologists of religion focused on the declining functional
> capacity of religion to solve people's problems of meaning and identity. Others
> took to measuring religion in extreme empirical detail. A third group concentrated
> on the deviant and exotic fringe of phenomena whose relevance to what most
> sociologists considered to be the major developments of the time was severely
> limited. In each case, religion was usually assumed to be epiphenomenal, a
> declining force in a fully secularized world.

In a similar vein, Wilson (1982: 53), another sociologist, argues that "the
general culture of day-to-day life in advanced nations, whether of the east or west,
is not, in modern times, markedly religious. . . . Advanced societies–in their very
nature of being advanced–are essentially secular in their orientation." This process
of secularization is facilitated by the growth in the effectiveness of the modern state
and its increased role in economic and social life. The modernization theorists are
correct in that the modern state no longer needs religion for legitimacy and state
power is self-justified or legitimated as the will of the people. Moreover, because
the modern state is the center of large-scale coercion and communication, "transcending legitimation" is not necessary. Thus, the modern state is based on the
assumption that it can manufacture conditions for social order. In addition, religion's traditional role of "interpreting both the natural universe and social order"
has been replaced by science and other secular philosophies (Wilson, 1982: 53-54).

Thus, as part of the processes of modernization and secularization, secular
political and social forces take over many functions formerly filled by religion. This
process of secularization includes several related processes. First, the property and
facilities of religious agencies are "sequestered" by society's political powers and
the various functions and activities of religions shift to secular control. Second,
there is a decline in time and resources devoted to religion and a decay of religious
institutions. Third, religious definitions of social behavioral norms and proper
modes of thought are replaced by technical, rational, and empirical criteria. This

entails an "abandonment of mythical, poetic and artistic interpretations of nature and society for matter-of-fact description" (Wilson, 1982: 149).

Fourth, the basic focus of social organization shifts from the community to the society. This is because society has replaced the community as the primary locus of the individual's life. Accordingly, religion, which helps to maintain order within community, is no longer needed to maintain social order in a society that is no longer communally based. Thus, "social organization itself is the result of processes of secularization." Once this process of secularization gains sufficient momentum, anything that impedes the process of shifting from a religious-based to a rational and secular-based society tends to be eliminated by "the imperatives of the system itself" (Wilson, 1982: 153-157). This means that not only is secularization inevitable, any social force that impedes it will be destroyed in the process.

Similarly, Turner (1991: 118) argues that the process of "secularization can be regarded as the transfer of religious disciplinary practices to the secular domains of the polis." He further elaborates that

> in the process of secularization, various forms of moral restraint, internal disciplines of asceticism, external rituals of public control and public codes of representation are transformed and transferred into secular practices of dietary control, narcissism and intimacy. With these changes in interpersonal intimacy, there was a corresponding elaboration of the apparatus of social control. Regulative panopticism emerged as a new principle organization of mass society. The intimacy of the private world is conjoined with detailed regulation of public space (Turner, 1991: 133).

Thus, it is clear that modernization theory goes hand in hand with secularization theory. The processes believed to be associated with modernization are also expected to erode the hold of religion on society and replace it with secular social and political structures.[3]

These two bodies of theory also have one other thing in common. They are both the product of almost exclusively Western academics who, in one way or another, generally focus on the West. Sociologists who support the secularization argument focus mostly on the West, and often only on the United States, rarely dealing with non-Western cultures. In political science, however, modernization theorists did deal with the non-West but tended to assume that economic, social, and political development in the non-West would follow paths similar to those followed by Western states. In other words, they believed that ethnicity and religion were becoming things of the past in the West and that this would also occur in the non-West.

Globalization and Dependancy Theory

Other major Western theories, including the closely related globalization and dependency schools of thought, also predict the secularization of society. These schools of thought, which are heavily influenced by Marxist and neo-Marxist deterministic assumptions, represent one of the major bodies of theory that competed with the modernization literature in predicting the future of global politics. These schools of thought predict the globalization of nations into a single integrated, interdependent world system of economic and political relations. However, the exact nature of this global system varies among the proponents of these theories (Haynes, 1994: 23-25; Shupe 1990: 21).

Like modernization theory, most proponents of these schools of thought also "marginalize the effect of religion and other cultural factors on politics." Scholars of this school of thought focused on the formation of modern state institutions and the impact of these institutions on traditional society. They assumed part of this impact would be to marginalize the role of tradition in society (Haynes, 1994: 25). Thus, it is clear that the globalization and dependency schools of thought are consistent with the secularization thesis that religion is a spent "epiphenomenal" force in the global arena and that they are based on Western political thought.[4]

Modernization and Secularization Theory in the Eighteenth and Nineteenth Centuries

While modernization/secularization theory seems to have had its heyday in the post-World War II era, it has its roots in eighteenth and nineteenth century thought. For instance, in the eighteenth century Voltaire argued that an "age of enlightenment" would replace superstition and authoritarian religious order (Appleby, 1994: 7-8). Also, "nineteenth century theorists such as Auguste Comte, Emile Durkheim, Ferdinand Toennies, Max Weber, and Karl Marx all prepared Western intellectuals for this expectation" (Shupe, 1990: 19). Neither time nor space permits a full analysis of this literature. Accordingly, this discussion relies on a comprehensive evaluation of the literature by Turner (1991).

There was a debate over progress in nineteenth century philosophy and sociology over the nature of industrialization. The majority view held that the collapse of the old military/theological system created a crisis in social organization and human consciousness. However, it was believed that a better state of social welfare could be created by a modern industrial/secular society that increases the productive base of society and encourages greater social freedom. The minority view was that the benefits of industrialization are costly and precarious. Industrialization was believed to have destroyed a society in which everybody had a place. Furthermore, this view held that industry caused individuals to be dislocated and "did not necessarily result in greater existential certainty and happiness." Therefore, "secularization . . . divides sociology into two camps: one that treats secularization as a loss of faith and authenticity; and another that regards secularization as a gain in personal freedom and autonomy." What both of these nineteenth century schools of thought have in common is the argument that the process of secularization was already under way (Turner, 1991: 134-135).

The origins of the secularization thesis can be seen in the writings of many individual nineteenth century Western thinkers. For instance, Nietzsche's "God is dead" thesis refers to the loss of credibility of Christian belief and the loss of commitment to absolute values (Turner, 1991: 40-42, 192). According to Nietzsche:

> The loss of certainty and conviction of religious assumptions and natural law . . . resulted in cultural relativism with widespread, momentous effects: the loss of political legitimacy, the collapse of social consensus, the insanity of the solitary individual, and the absence of purpose in natural phenomena. The consequence was that modern people inhabit a world where "everything is false, everything is permitted."
>
> Nietzsche thought that the crisis of European culture provided conditions for the generation of new forms of moral authenticity, of which his own philosophical standards constituted a starting-point. Nietzsche did not, however, get beyond an announcement of the need for moral revaluation. In the absence of this "revaluation of values," modern society is the product of contingent conflicts under the dominance of the nation-state. It was for these reasons that Nietzsche treated the collapse of the credibility of religious belief as the most significant event of modern history. In this respect, Nietzsche's Godless theology outlined the major themes of the sociology of religion which came to fruition in Weber's condemnation of modern society as an "iron cage" in *The Protestant Ethic and the Spirit of Capitalism* (Turner, 1991: 42).

Thus, Weber's views on the bankruptcy of contemporary politics originated in Nietzsche's "death of God" thesis. Weber argued that "legal-rational domination and rational compliance had gradually replaced tradition and charisma as the principle basis of control in capitalism" (Turner, 1991: 190). However, this legal-rational domination is fragile, leading to a crisis of legitimacy in nineteenth century politics. Thus, like Nietzsche, Weber argued that secular ideologies were replacing religion as the basis of legitimacy in nineteenth century society. That Weber's speeches on politics and science as vocations are riddled with "Old Testament metaphors about the loss of innocence and the effects of the tree of knowledge (rational science)" illustrates this point (Turner, 1991: 193).

According to Durkheim:

> there is, in short, a concrete, real and persistent reference to religious symbols which explains the continuity of religious practice and the resilience of religious belief. The real referent of religious symbols, which is external to individuals and survives the death of individual practitioners, is not the totem or god, but society itself. It is society which possesses the supra-individualist authority, continuity and externality to impress awe and obedience on the solitary individual (Turner, 1991: 47).

That is, it is society and not God which stands behind religion. A social consequence of this is that it is actually collective involvement in practices rather than consensus of belief which leads to the social integration that religion provides. However, such social cohesion on the basis of religious practices, according to Durkheim, is impossible in the differentiated society created by industrialization. Accordingly, "in the absence of traditional religious ceremonies and beliefs, Durkheim identified nationalist sentiments and national ceremonial as the main roots of social cohesion" (Turner, 1991: 52). Thus, society had shifted from religion to secular ideologies as the basis for its social cohesion.

Marx and Engles also subscribed to the secularization thesis. Their "dominant ideology thesis" argues that the dominant class controls "the means of mental production" and thus, is able to control the ideology through which the subordinate classes express themselves. In feudal times, the dominant ideology was religion, and peasant rebellions during this time expressed themselves through the "linguistic cloak" of religious ideologies. However, the transition to capitalism was resulting in the collapse of the "religious props of bourgeois political control" and secular ideologies were emerging to replace them. While Marx and Engles are not wholly consistent in their adherence to this argument, their alternative theories are generally consistent with the secularization thesis (Turner, 1991: 40-42, 192).

While it is clear that there are some major disagreements between these and other nineteenth-century Western thinkers, it is also clear that there was considerable agreement on several points. First, religion is based on its social context; thus the truth of religion is relative rather than universal. Second, society was experiencing a crisis of religious belief. Third, industrialization was breaking the hold of religion on society. Thus, it is fair to say that there was a considerable body of nineteenth century thought which subscribed to the modernization/secularization thesis. It is also fair to say that these arguments were made by Western thinkers regarding the West, with little attention paid to the rest of the world.

Religion's Resurgence in the Late Twentieth Century

The modernization/secularization argument constitutes a serious challenge to the validity of the study of religious influences on conflict and society. In sum, the various forms of the modernization/secularization argument, more or less, agree on several basic points. They agree that a new modern, secular, and scientific society is replacing or has replaced the old traditional religious society of the past. In this new society, modern institutions based on the new secular, scientific arrangement are taking or have taken the place of the primordial traditionally and religiously based social institutions. These new institutions provide a new secular basis for legitimacy, morality, social norms, and understanding of the world. In the wake of this modernization or secularization, traditional society, including religion, has been or will be left behind and is no longer or will no longer be an important determining factor in any important aspect of society, including politics and conflict.

It is likely that this school of thought, which was very influential among Western and especially U.S. social scientists through the 1970s, contributed to the scarcity of theoretical and empirical work on the subject of religion. However, since the late 1970s, and especially in the 1990s, there has been what many call a resurgence or revitalization of religion, and perhaps more importantly, a resurgence and revitalization of the study of religion's role in society, politics, and conflict. This has resulted in, among other things, the development of arguments to counter those who posit that religion has no place in the modern world. These counter arguments provide one of the major justifications for the study of religion and conflict. They also provide a better understanding of the influences of modernity on religion.

Perhaps the strongest counter-argument against the voluminous body of literature predicting religion's demise is factual rather than philosophical. That is, events in the 1970s, 1980s, and 1990s have shown that religion continues to influence politics in the late twentieth century. The most well known of these events include the Iranian revolution in 1978 and the war between the Communists and Islamic fundamentalists in Afghanistan, which then reverted into an ethnic conflict that still had some religious aspects. It then transformed into a conflict between multiple factions and the Taleban, a militant Islamic fundamentalist movement which then took over the country and established a theocratic state which, in turn, was overthrown in the wake of the events of September 11 2001. Other well-known instances of religious conflict include the Islamic opposition and revolutionary movements throughout the Islamic world, the role of liberation theology in oppositional politics in Latin America, and the ethnoreligious wars in Bosnia, Chechnia, Tibet, East Timor, Sudan, and Sri Lanka. While these events may have received the lion's share of media attention and have disproportionately affected the views of policy makers, they take place in the context of what many call a revitalization or resurgence of religion across the globe.

It is also interesting to note that most of these events took place outside of the West. Thus, Western social scientists who, arguably, had become ethnocentric and had formed the modernization/secularization argument based on that insular perspective, most likely began to be convinced that religion was, in fact, an important factor judging by events that took place outside of the West. It is possible, even likely, that if the Iranian revolution, in particular, did not intrude into the Western consciousness through the highly publicized and dramatized hostage crisis, this realization may have occurred much later, if at all.

Be that as it may, there are three major philosophical arguments explaining religion's resurgence in the late twentieth century: first, that religion never left politics; second, that the imperatives of modernization itself and other systemic factors have led to a revitalization or resurgence of religion; and third, that the end of the Cold War has created an ideological vacuum, which religion is able to fill, while at the same time removing systemic restrictions on religious conflicts. These schools of thought are not incompatible and, in fact, reinforce each other's arguments.

Religion's Persisting Influence

The first argument posits that there has been no resurgence of religion in the late twentieth century because religion and ethnicity have always been inseparable from politics and that modernization has not changed this. Gurr (1993a; 1993b; 2000) provides strong empirical support for this argument. He documents the more or less continuous rise of ethnic conflict in general and ethnoreligious conflict specifically from World War II through the early nineties, followed by a slight drop. If the modernization/secularization school of thought was correct, one would have expected to see a continuous drop in the levels of ethnic and religious conflict during this period. That Gurr finds the opposite is true is strong evidence that ethnicity and religion continue to be factors that are very relevant to conflict and, by implication, politics and society in general.

The arguments stating that religion has always been an important factor are varied and deal with many aspects of religion from many perspectives. For instance, religion is said to be one of the pillars upon which civilization has been built, thus making it inseparable from the politics and society of modern civilization. Furthermore, it is recognized that religion played important roles in political processes and social change in those premodern civilizations which are the basis for today's civilization. Historically, "religions provided some components of the broader civilizational premises and frameworks, and this partly determined the ways which religious activities and organizations became related to the political process" (Arjomand, 1993: 13). This occurred to the point where it was difficult to distinguish between culture/civilization and religion. This intertwining of religion and civilization has occurred to the extent that the importance of the impact of religion on political processes "can be best understood not in terms of the direct impact of religious beliefs or patterns of worship on politics, but rather through the mediation of civilizational premises of which religious beliefs constitute an important component" (Arjomand, 1993: 37). For example, Judaism and Christianity helped to shape the West's "preference for legal and political, that is, nonviolent conflict resolution" (Weigel, 1992: 174). Also, religion is posited by some as one of the bases for nationalism (Smith, 1999 & 2000) and the Westphalian state system. (Philpott, 2000)

Not only has religion always played a role in society and politics, but efforts to change that situation have been unsuccessful.

> Since about 700 B.C.E., in urban and civilized societies, whose inequitable social relations were always present to offend tender consciences, energetic groups or reformers have persistently and perpetually sought to remake the world along juster, religiously sanctioned lines. . . . The appeal of secular, rationalistic doctrines is limited mainly to the privileged and mainly comfortable persons . . . [but] even in affluent communities, most persons do face hardship and disappointment of one sort or another and need the comfort and support that cold reason and individualistic pursuit of happiness cannot provide (McNeil, 1993: 561-565).

Furthermore, efforts to convince the populace of the advantages of modernization have failed because "popular tolerance of market relationships, and of inequalities between rich and poor that were generated by market exchanges, took centuries to establish in Great Britain–centuries during which merchants and bankers . . . had operated in defiance of public opinion but protected by the monarchy" (McNeil, 1993: 561-566). Thus, especially in the Third World, as well as many Western countries which have not had as much time for the populace to develop a "popular tolerance of market relationships," religious ideologies should remain a major source for ideologies of social reform.

Religion is also influential on the individual level, at least in liberal democracies. This is because "religious convictions of the sort familiar in this society bear pervasively on people's ethical choices, including choices about laws and government policies" (Greenwalt, 1988: 30). In fact, it is possible to determine when an individual is relying on religious convictions to support his beliefs and opinions using several criteria. First, the clearest instance of a reliance on religious convictions is "when the person is certain he would make a different choice if he disregarded those convictions" (Greenwalt, 1998: 36). Second, an individual is relying on religious convictions when that person is questioned about the "whys" of his beliefs and "if such questions, answered without any change in belief, revealed the centrality of premises that are religious" (Greenwalt, 1988: 37). A third way to determine such reliance is if the abandonment of religious convictions would cause one to seriously reconsider his position.

Using these criteria, it is easy to show that most citizens in liberal democracies do make use of religious convictions to resolve many political issues and "theories that exclude many nonreligious premises as well as religious convictions do not leave ample grounds for citizens to resolve many political issues . . . [and,] no adequate reason exists for preferring all nonreligious premises to religious convictions as bases for political judgements" (Greenwalt, 1988: 49). Furthermore, despite efforts to encourage citizens to use nonreligious criteria for their decisions, practical decisions tend to be affected by value judgements because "when people must decide about claims that gravely affect their lives and are not subject to easy external confirmation, they understandably give weight to their own personal convictions" (Greenwalt, 1988: 75).

Many studies based on survey data have also shown that religious affiliation affects political attitudes and behavior. Hayes (1995) found that both the denomination and the strength of religious affiliation affect political attitudes.[5] She finds that apostates and independents (those who do not identify with any specific religious sect but believe in God) are more liberal on all issues[6] than Protestants or Catholics, except on the issue of capital punishment. Campbell and Curtis (1994: 225), based on similar data,[7] conclude that there is a high level of belief in God in all nations and that "beliefs in heaven, life after death, a soul, and sin" are moderately high. Leak and Randall (1995) found that religiosity is correlated with authoritarianism. Bolce and De Maio (1999) found that in the United States, those with antifundamentalist sentiments are likely to feel antipathy toward Republicans.

Scheepers and Van Der Silk (1998) find that religious denomination is a good predictor of moral attitudes. Also, Miller (1996) found differences in how Jews and Christians form their political attitudes.

Another version of the argument that religion has never ceased to be an influence in society is that what appeared to be a general revival of religion in the 1980s was actually "a shift of influence among the various strains of religion" in which "the fundamentalist wing of Protestantism, Islam and Judaism in the 1980s gained greater influence largely at the expense of the more moderate wing" (Barnhart, 1990: 28). That is, there was never a decline in religion, rather there was a shift to more fundamentalist interpretations of religion which made the eternal presence of religion more conspicuous.

This shift can be explained as a result of basic forces in the religious economy. While dominant religions tend to become more worldly, there is always a demand for less worldly religions. This is because there are always those who desire the "compensators" religion provides to those who feel they are not receiving rewards in this world. That is, while elites often desire more worldly religions to legitimate their desires, those on the bottom often seek less worldly religions to provide them solace for their lack of ability to fulfill their worldly desires. This results in both movements to renew the faith of the dominant religion and the creation of new religions. Thus, secularization is a self-limiting process. The secularization of one element of the religious economy does not mean the end of religion because at the same time, another element is moving toward religion (Stark and Bainbridge, 1985).

The current religious resurgence can also be explained as a part of a cyclical phenomenon that has been going on for at least sixty years; the only thing that has changed is "the growing awareness of these events by the Western world, and the perception that they might be related to our interests" (Smith, 1990: 34). This resurgence may be limited by factors inherent to the resurgence itself. "Oppositional politics is the forte of religion, and the arena in which it has achieved its greatest successes. [Accordingly,] the most basic limit of religious resurgence is in moving beyond the oppositional role to institutionalize some version of a modern religious state" (Smith, 1990: 44). Similar arguments are made by Williams (1994: 805) and Tarrow (1988).

Stark and Bainbridge (1985: 1-2) combine the previous two arguments, positing that the process is cyclical and that different types of religion vary in their influence over time. They

> acknowledge that secularization is a major trend in modern times, but argue that it is not a modern development and does not presage the demise of religion. Rather . . . secularization is a process found in all religious economies; it is something that is always going on in all societies. While secularization progresses in some parts of a society, a countervailing intensification of religion goes on in other parts. Sometimes the pace of secularization speeds or slows, but the dominant religious organizations in any society are always becoming progressively more worldly, which is to say, more secularized. The result of this trend has never

been the end of religion, but merely a shift in fortunes of religious faiths that have become too worldly and are supplanted by more vigorous and less worldly religions.

In sum, the basic argument of this school of thought, that religion has never ceased to be a factor in society and politics, has considerable support. One major drawback, however, is that it does not explain how Western theorists could have failed to see the presence of religion in society for such a considerable amount of time. Marshall (1998: 13) makes a similar argument when he notes that "I do not know if religious influence is increasing. This is not because I think current analysts exaggerate it but because earlier analysts ignored, downplayed or redefined it." Smith's argument for the cyclical resurgence of religion and Barnhart's arguments that the current resurgence is merely a shift in power between factions are partial but not adequate answers.

One possible answer to this problem is that the perceptions of Western theorists were affected by their theories. That is, Western theorists may have fallen into the trap of seeing only what their theories told them they would see. Any counter-examples were either ignored or explained away. It was not until the counter-examples were too blatant to be ignored that the current widespread reassessment of the modernization/secularization thesis occurred.

Several who ask this question come to the same conclusion and take the argument a step further. The culture of enlightenment and the assumption of humankind's reasonableness is believed to have caused scholars to ignore religion, often redefining it as an ethnic, psychological, or quasi-Marxist phenomenon (Lawrence, 1989: 62-63; Luttwak, 1994: 8-10). Some sociologists are even accused of entangling their own values and group interests with their study of secularization. Their focus on societies, groups, and social structures caused them to ignore religion as a factor in society (Marshall, 1998). Similarly, governments, bureaucrats, diplomats, and political elites are accused of being afraid to address religion at all because their power is based on secular ideologies (Gopin, 2000: 37-40).

Rubin (1994: 20-21) argues that U.S. foreign policy often misreads the importance of religion in politics for several reasons, including the assumption that modernization would cause the decline of religion, that religion was seen as a theological and not a political issue, and the assumption that Marx was right and religion is the opiate of the masses. It is easy to see how this occurred, given that liberalism, which is the dominant paradigm of most Western scholars, assumes that modernization "will result in the proliferation of the rational and universal values of capitalism, which are antithetical to the premodern basis of ethnicity" (Smith, 1981:2). Stack (1997: 11-12) suggests that this refusal to acknowledge ethnicity and religion is also due to wishful thinking. Many consider primordial factors like religion and ethnicity "a deadly political virus" that must be isolated and eliminated. The belief that this virus will go away on its own would be a comforting thought. However, as described above, the evidence shows that this is not happening.

Another contributing factor to Western social scientists missing the importance of religion is based on where they were looking. Western social scientists tended and, to a lesser extent, still tend to focus on the West where, especially until the 1980s, the influence of religion is less obvious than it is elsewhere. For example, it is unlikely a scholar focusing on the Islamic world would conclude that Islam has no influence on politics and society.

Modernity as a Cause of Religion's Resurgence

The second counter-argument to modernization/secularization theory posits that rather than causing the decline of religion, modernization and other systemic factors have led to its revitalization. This argument is not inconsistent with the first counter-argument, which argues that religion never left politics. Most proponents of the second school of thought agree that religion has never ceased to be a factor in politics but they believe that its involvement has increased during the past twenty years due to the imperatives of modernity, which have also altered many aspects of religion's interaction with society.

It is clear that the advocates of this school of thought agree that religion has never ceased to be a factor in society. For instance, Sahliyeh (1990) argues that the modernization literature incorrectly posited that a single global community would gradually replace the diverse cultures and religions of the world and that religion would become an insignificant factor in world politics. Similarly, Haynes (1994: 7) argues that the mistake of Western theory "was to see ethnicity, caste, clientism and (when it was mentioned at all) religion simply as manifestations of tradition. . . . It is insufficient to view modernization as merely reactivating and reinstating such 'traditional' concepts as religion or ethnicity into the political framework without taking into account their dynamic nature." Because of this, it became clear by the 1980s that "mono-casual, deterministic and universal explanations of development" that did not take other factors like religion into account were not enough to explain its complex nature. In other words, modernization and other Western theories failed to predict the resurgence of religion because they ignored the fact that it had never ceased to be a factor in politics.

As already noted, what differentiates this school of thought from the first is the argument that not only did modernization not cause the demise of religion, it actually contributed to its revitalization. There are several processes associated with modernization that are believed to have contributed to this revitalization. First, unsuccessful attempts at modernization and the failure of much of the non-Western world to end its dependence on the West have added to the grievances of religious movements. These failures have also created an ideological vacuum which religion is able to fill. Second, there have been many unsettling social and intellectual consequences of modernization. Modernization has contributed to a "widespread feeling of dislocation, alienation and disorientation resulting from the process of modernization and from the rapid disappearance of habitual lifestyles and traditions" (Sahliyeh, 1990: 9) as well as the breakdown of community values. Put more simply, many people have simply become disillusioned "with a 'modernity' which reduces the world to what can be perceived and controlled through reason, science, technology, and bureaucratic rationality and leaves out considerations of the religious, spiritual, or the sacred" (Thomas, 2000: 816). Haynes (1994: 34) makes this argument noting that

> the arrival and consolidation of contemporary religious militancy is rooted in the failed promise of modernity. Our era is one where God was in danger of being superseded by a gospel of technical progress and economic growth, a process identified . . . as "modernization." Yet all of this is very confusing and (especially over the past 50 years) has been very swift, with traditional habits, beliefs and cultures under constant pressure to adapt. In an increasingly materialist world, one's individual worth is increasingly measured according to standards of wealth and status, and hence, power. . . . The result of [this] cultural and economic confusion was to provide fertile ground for the growth of religious militancy and conservatism.

Thus, Haynes argues that the failure of many to attain the materialist goals of modernity has played a role in causing the recent revitalization of religion.

Third, both the state and religious bodies have expanded their spheres of operation; this has often, but not always, resulted in a confrontation between the two. As modernization and globalization enable and sometimes cause governments to expand their roles in society, they inevitably expand their influence into the realm which was formerly the exclusive domain of religion. As a result,

> any secularization trajectory that accompanies globalization, because it involves culture conflict and challenges to the truth-claims of various traditional religions, is ultimately self-limiting. There is, to put it simply, a ceiling-effect that comes into play. At some (as yet imprecisely specified) point, globalization sets in motion the dynamic for a search for ultimate meaning, values, and resacralization (Shupe, 1990: 23).

As a result of this, "New religions . . . thrive where secularization has mostly eroded traditional religious practice and allegiances, and do worst where secularization has not achieved some general but unspecified level" (Shupe, 1990: 24). This has resulted in a situation where "there are few nations or cultures where the sacred and secular realms are not intimately intertwined" (Shupe, 1990: 26). This can also be said to be true of ethnicity because the indifference of increasingly powerful national bureaucracies caused the alienation of ethnic minorities and, thus, the surge in the importance of ethnicity (Stack, 1997: 21).

Fourth, inherent in the process of modernization is the "admission of the masses into politics." It is true that these changes incorporate into the polity "a broadened elite of professionals, business people, military officers, government bureaucrats, and teachers [who] are hallmarks of the modernization process."

However, these changes also incorporate those religious sectors of the population who wish to impose their views on the rest of society. Thus, modernization can give the religious segments of the population the political power to make sure that religious ideologies and issues remain an important influence in politics and society (Rubin, 1994: 22-23).

Fifth, modernization has made the world smaller. Modern communications technology and ease of travel have resulted in the globalization of many issues, including religion. Because of this, religious groups around the world are becoming more and more aware of each other's activities as well as the possibilities of religious opposition. Also, the modern media has contributed to the rise of religious intensity because it is easier for the media to deal with caricatures than complicated events and issues, thus portraying them as "black and white as well as archetypical scenarios of villains and heros. . . . In such a medium those groups adept at reductionist, absolutist and simplified frameworks of reference will excite and mobilize news consumers" (Shupe, 1990: 22).

Televangelism in the United States is but one example of this use of communications technology. Also, that the Iranian revolution took place in a world where all knew about it instantly arguably influenced Islamic movements everywhere. It proved that powerful Western-supported states could be successfully challenged by religious movements. The demonstration effect of this event and others like it, which can be viewed instantly by the entire world, should not be underestimated.

Sixth, a new trend in the sociology of religion, known as the rational choice or economic theory of religion, posits that the freedom of choice in many modern societies to select one's own religion has led to an increase in religiosity. This approach basically applies economic market behavior theory to religious behavior in a manner similar to the way Mancur Olson (1971) applied it to collective action theory.[8] Iannaccone (1995a and 1995b), one of the major proponents of this theory, lists its three basic assumptions. First, the approach assumes that people, or religious "consumers," engage in maximizing behavior. That is, they use a cost-benefit analysis when selecting a religion. The benefits can include expected rewards in a future life, feelings of spiritual well being and moral justification, and the social benefits that tend to go along with membership in a group. The costs of religious participation can include monetary costs, such as church dues and the expectation to give to charity, the time costs of church attendance, and the fact that most religions place restrictions on people's behavior.

The second assumption of this theory is that the church and clergy, or religious "producers," attempt to maximize their membership, net resources, support from the government, or any other good which they believe will enhance the institutional success of their religion. Accordingly, these religious "producers" market and sometimes even alter their religions based on "the constraints and opportunities found in the religious marketplace." The final assumption is that the combined actions of religious "consumers" and "producers" in a free religious marketplace tend toward equilibrium. That is, as in the economic marketplace, the "consumers" and "producers" of the religious marketplace are constantly altering their behavior in response to each other and the general environment.

The result of all this is a number of dynamic religions, at least one of which should be more appealing to the average religious "consumer" than the monolithic religions found in states where religious diversity is discouraged. Consequently, people, on average, should be more religious in societies with such religious diversity. Warner (1993) notes that it is not the diversity of alternatives that is most important to this theory, rather it is the incentives of religious "producers" to meet the "consumers" needs. Thus the rise of religiosity in the United States, for example, "was neither a residue of Puritan hegemony nor a transplantation of a European sacred canopy but an accomplishment of 19th-century activists" (Warner, 1993: 1057). It should be noted that despite the calculating behavior attributed to religious "producers," there is no assumption that their efforts are insincere.

The rational choice approach to religion explains behavior at several levels of analysis. At the ecological level, it explains the variation in religious rates across states. At the institutional level, it explains denominational growth, especially of conservative groups in the United States. At the individual level, it explains the variations in individual religious behavior including affiliation, mobility or switching between denominations, and commitment (attendance and contributions) (Ellison, 1995).

However, there are also several criticisms of this theory. First, many scholars consider this formal theory approach to religion too rigid in its oversimplification of a complex and dynamic process. That is, religion cannot be explained by so simple a theory (Ellison, 1995). Second, this theory falls into the trap of seeing the world as one would like it to be rather than as it is, or as Demerath (1995: 105) puts it "whereas most sociologists try to shape explanations to fit the world, most economists try to shape the world to fit their explanations." Third, religion is not rational, the and rational choice theorist's assumption of rational religious behavior does not reflect reality. Fourth, religious choices tend to be stable, inhibiting the dynamism of the religious marketplace (Ellison, 1995). Fifth, people often join or remain in religions because of the social benefits of a religion and not due to the religious goods being offered; however, there tend to be social sanctions when one leaves a religion including the loss of social benefits and the negative reaction of others (Ellison, 1995). Sixth, religion is often correlated with ethnicity, thus increasing the social pressure to stay in a religion (Ellison, 1995). Seventh, rational choice theorists ignore the fact that religious behavior is usually based on "social-ization, institutionalized custom, and ingrained habit," all of which are factors that resist change (Demerath, 1995). Eighth, rational choice theorists are criticized for assuming it is lone individuals making calculated choices that form the bulk of those who switch religions. In fact, lone individuals are less likely targets of recruitment than people hooked into social networks (Williams, 1994: 788-789). Stark and Bainbridge (1985: 353-354) make a similar point in their discussion of limits on the expansion of cults.

A final criticism of the rational choice approach to religion is that the empirical evidence does not reflect its predictions. Most of those who leave a religion move away from all religions rather than switching to another (Demarath, 1995). Also, Verweij, Ester, and Nauta (1997) show that religious participation is higher in monolithically Catholic countries than in countries with more religious diversity. Be that as it may, rational choice theorists have their own empirical evidence to support their conclusions, and their theory has the benefits of simplicity and explanatory power. While these criticisms should be taken into account, the argument that modern market-like religious practices have contributed to a rise in religiosity cannot be dismissed. It is also important to note that the arguments regarding this theory tend to focus on Western society.

A seventh way in which modernization has contributed to a resurgence of religion is the processes of colonialism and the creation of the nation state, both modern processes which have strengthened ethnic identities. Colonial governments differentiated ethnic groups, often choosing one as its official or unofficial representative. Nation states, led by a particular ethnic group or in which political parties are defined by ethnicity, also increase the extent of ethnic awareness (Fenton, 1999: 44-47, 216 and Horowitz, 1985). In addition, nationalism often institutionalizes group boundaries. (Heisler, 2000)

Finally, modernization has caused a crisis of legitimacy for secular ideas, ideologies, and institutions. This crisis includes the inability of elites to replace traditional institutions and norms with modern ones; the illegitimacy of imported Western beliefs; in some cases, military weakness; and external threats to ethnic identity.

Mark Juergensmeyer, in his book *The New Cold War* (1993), presents a detailed explanation of the current resurgence of religion that hinges upon the argument that the secular values of modernization are suffering from what he calls a crisis of legitimacy. Juergensmeyer believes that secular nationalism attempts to be a super-religion or anti-religion beyond any single religious allegiance and tries to replace religion with an all-embracing ideology unaffected by any other affiliation. Secular nationalism is based on the Euro/American notion of the nation state, in which loyalty to the state is "forged entirely from a secular sense of citizenship." It is an ideology that goes hand in hand with the Western theories which predict the secularization of politics. Juergensmeyer's notion of secular nationalism includes most Western ideologies, including liberalism (democracy), socialism, and communism.

To Juergensmeyer, secular nationalism, like religion, is what he calls an "ideology of order." This concept has many of the characteristics and societal roles which ideologies and religion have in common. It has a framework for understanding the world, that of liberal democracy. This framework provides rules for behavior and defines the place of the individual in society. It is a potential source of legitimacy for the state, as well as those who challenge the state, and it has myths and rituals which constitute an external authority as the source of this ideology. Juergensmeyer also notes that both religion and secular nationalism can legitimize violence.

Since both religion and secular nationalism are ideologies of order, serving the same functions in society, they are potential rivals. In fact, their worldviews are different and incompatible. Accordingly, they compete with each other for control over society's collective mind, its government, and its institutions. According to Juergensmeyer, it is secular nationalism that currently serves these societal functions in the modern world, but religion waits as potential challenger. Although it is possible for there to be a limited synthesis between religious and secular ideologies, and they can form a coexistence between them based on mutual respect, there can be no true convergence of the two types of ideology. Thus the potential for conflict between the two also exists.

Accordingly, religion will not always stay bridled by secular nationalism. Those who adhere to religious ideologies see their religion as superior to secular nationalism and often feel it is better to start a new society based on religion. Also, attempts by secular nationalist governments to accommodate religion through compromises often lead to the double frustration of being seen as traitors to both sides.

It is implicit in these arguments that the worldviews of religion and secular nationalism are, to an extent, incompatible and because of this religion is always waiting in the wings to replace secular nationalism in a time of weakness. Although the level of this incompatibility varies according to the particular brands of secular nationalism and religion that are involved, the theory holds wherever religion competes with a dominant secular nationalist ideology. However, it takes more than this incompatibility of religion and secular nationalism to prompt a religious revolution. A religion must wait for the dominant secular nationalist ideology with which it competes to weaken before that religion can successfully become the dominant ideology.

Juergensmeyer believes that the loss of faith in secular nationalism in the non-Western world has resulted in such a weakness and that this weakness has resulted in a crisis of legitimacy for secular nationalism. He cites several reasons for this loss of faith. First, secular nationalism promised political freedom, economic prosperity, and social justice but many governments which have subscribed to this ideology have failed to fulfill these promises. This failure has been highlighted by the world's mass media, which shows the world all the troubles in Western society which are perceived to be failures of secular nationalism.

Second, secular nationalism is perceived by many in the non-Western world as a foreign ideology imposed from outside. It does not have any local authenticity or legitimacy. The people of the non-Western world no longer see secular nationalism as an expression of their own identities or as being related to their economic or social situation. In addition, it has failed to provide a vision of what they would like themselves to become. Although Juergensmeyer does not discuss it, it is fair to say that there are many in the Western world who also feel that secular nationalism is unauthentic.

Third, and along a similar vein, secular nationalism has become identified with the issue of colonialism. The imposition of secular nationalism by governments in former colonies has led to the accusation that the leaders of these former colonies are perpetuating colonialism through their espousal of secular nationalism.

Fourth, secular nationalism has been associated with cultural colonialism, which is said to erode the traditional aspects of society along with the influence of religion in society. Advocates of secular nationalism are seen as being in league with the West (the enemy) in a global conspiracy against religion. In fact, secular nationalism is seen as a "sinister religious entity" that is responsible for society's moral decline. This has, in some cases, been taken to the point where anything the West does is part of this plot and anything secular is considered, by definition, illegitimate.

Thus, according to Juergensmeyer's version of the second school of thought, the secular nationalist ideologies which go hand in hand with modernization and other Western theories that predict the secularization of world politics have failed to fulfill their promises and are perceived as unauthentic by many in the non-Western world. This failure has resulted in a resurgence of religious ideologies. Although Juergensmeyer does not give much attention to the subject, it is implicit in his arguments that religion never ceased to be a factor in politics; rather its advocates waited in the wings while being overshadowed by the advocates of secular nationalism. Although his arguments deal mostly with the non-western world, many of them also apply in the Western context.

In a later work, Juergensmeyer (1997:20) puts this argument more succinctly:

> What is significant about the Enlightenment three centuries ago was its proclamation of the death of religion; what is significant about the present period is the perception of the death of secularism. By that I mean the widespread impression that secular culture and its forms of nationalism are unable to provide the moral fiber that unites national communities, or offer the ideological strength to sustain states that have been buffeted by economic and military failures. In other words, there is the widespread perception that politics is immoral and public life desperately needs the sacred cleansing religion can offer it.

The scholarship on Islamic militancy reflects Juergensmeyer's arguments. For example, Deeb's (1992: 53-54) list of factors under which militant Islam is likely to emerge is similar to Juergensmeyer's criteria. These factors include political stagnation, a weakening of central authority, economic stagnation, income gaps, deteriorating social conditions, a perceived "invasion" of Western culture and values, and the government is perceived as encouraging this cultural change and as being secular. Piscatori (1994: 361-363) provides a similar list of causes but adds that it is the failure of the secular leadership to effectively deal with these factors, combined with the association of traditional Islamic leaders with this failed leadership, which is the true cause of Islamic fundamentalism. Layachi and Haireche (1992: 70) also seem to agree when they argue that "the development and expression of the Islamist opposition in the Maghrib reflects much less a simple desire for the institution of Islamic states than a clash between popular movements desiring change and regimes that lack legitimacy resisting change." Finally, Nasr

(1998) argues that there is a correlation between the decline of the secular state and religious activism and that this is especially true for Islam.

While, most of those discussed so far have focused their arguments on the non-Western world, there are some who make similar arguments regarding the West. Shupe (1990), for instance, argues that statistics on popular religion, like church attendance and religious book buying, show that religion is on the ascent in the industrialized West. He notes that the emergence of new religious groups includes a revitalization of old ones and that religion has been "a visible, significant factor in political mass movements" (Shupe, 1990: 20).

The literature on religious fundamentalism posits that fundamentalism is, at least in part, a consequence of modernity. For instance, Williams (1994: 798-803) argues that modernization has created an "institutional differentiation" between various aspects of public and private life, including the polity, the economy, the family, and religion. This has led to a "disarticulation of statuses" where someone's position in one of these areas is not automatically transferable to another. As a result, life has been "compartmentalized" into categories wherein different norms apply. These distinctions created by modernity, especially between public and private life, have created the social space in which fundamentalism has been able to flourish. In addition, like Juergensmeyer, he argues that the political instability caused by the economic transition to modernity has created a credibility problem for modern governments and has created a "fertile soil for fundamentalism."

Marty and Appleby (1991: 602, 620) in their landmark study on the nature of religious fundamentalism also link the current resurgence of religious fundamentalism to modernization. They argue that rapid modernization in formerly traditional societies has caused a considerable amount of social and personal dislocation. This problem has been exacerbated by the absence of mediating institutions capable of meeting the human needs caused by this dislocation. Accordingly, religious fundamentalism is concerned with defining, restoring, and reinforcing the basis of personal and communal identity that is being shaken or destroyed by modern dislocations and crises. Similarly, Esposito (1998) argues that fundamentalists claim to ameliorate problems of modern society.

This has led to the criticism of many aspects of modernity by fundamentalists. For instance, fundamentalists believe that the "decoupling" of religion and modern science has removed the normative restraints from modern technology. Accordingly, "the ultimate subordination to sacred authority similarly marks fundamentalists' approaches to modern science and technology" (Mendelsohn: 1993). Tehranian (1993: 314) similarly argues that fundamentalists criticize "the failure of secular ideologies of progress to address (let alone resolve) the human conditions of finitude, fragility and evil." This rejection of secularism is considered by Tehranian to be a necessary but not sufficient condition for fundamentalism. He also describes seven models for understanding fundamentalism: antielitist; antiimperialist; anti-communist; antimodernist; antifeminist; and antidecadence. Each of these models describes a manner in which fundamentalism reacts to an aspect of modernity.

Fundamentalist movements also display many modern characteristics. They use modern communications, propaganda, mobilization, and organizational techniques as well as modern institutions. Their ideologies are influenced by modernity both in that they use modern ideas to construct their ideologies and that their ideologies are a rejection of modern phenomena like the Enlightenment (Eisenstadt, 2000: 601-603).

Rabbi Haym Soloveitchik,[9] in a discussion on why he thinks orthodox Judaism has taken a "swing to the right" during his lifetime describes how modernization contributed to the rise of Jewish fundamentalism. According to him the basic change that has occurred is the "new and controlling role that texts now play in [Jewish] religious life." Originally *Halakhah* (Jewish law) was transferred between the generations to a great extent through the example of parents and tradition, as practices in the community as well as through scholarly institutions. According to Soloveitchik, this dual tradition of law as taught and as practiced began to break down at the end of the nineteenth century. This breakdown in traditional society resulted in increased emphasis on religious law as written in religious texts as the source for determining the correct interpretation of Jewish law (Soloveitchik, 1994: 65-68).

Soloveitchik (1994: 71) attributes this breakdown of traditional society to the fact that

> alternatives [to being a practicing orthodox Jew] now exist and adherence is voluntary. A traditional society has been transformed into an orthodox one, and religious conduct is less the product of social custom than of conscious reflexive behavior. . . . Behavior once governed by habit is now governed by rule. If accuracy is now sought, indeed deemed critical, it can be found only in texts.

Furthermore, this has resulted in "a tireless quest for absolute accuracy, for 'perfect fit'–faultless congruence between conception and performance–is the hallmark of contemporary religiosity. The search is dedicated and unremitting; yet it invariably falls short of success" (Soloveitchik. 1994: 73).

This rise of a text culture in orthodox Judaism came only after sustained exposure to modernity by the Jewish community. Modernity eroded at the "otherness" of Jews and brought them out of their insulated communities into the modern world and general culture. Simple ethnicity was no longer enough to maintain this "otherness." The new climate of inclusiveness, especially in the United States, reduced the costs of distinctiveness. What Soloveitchik calls the "embourgeoisment" of religious community ended the traditional ascetic ideal that had been an integral part of Judaism for over a thousand years. As a result of this, the traditional community, as it had existed for over a thousand years, ceased to exist. This weakened, if not destroyed, the role that tradition, which was based in the community, played in transmitting Jewish law from one generation to the next. This left the scholarly interpretation of Jewish texts as the primary source of Jewish law (Soloveitchik, 1994: 74-80).

There are three effects of this shift to texts as the primary source of Jewish law.

First, it caused the school to replace the home as the primary place for transmission of values. Yeshivas (Jewish theological schools) became mass, rather than elite, institutions emphasizing religious, rather than academic, education. This occurred because the Jewishness which was once taken for granted now has to be instilled. Second, the shift to institutions to transmit Judaism from one generation to the next increased the influence of the educators. As a result, political and social issues which had once been outside of the rabbinical sphere of influence are now determined, at least in part, by Torah scholars. This was able to occur because tradition and community are no longer a source of religious legitimacy and identity, thus causing Jewish lay leaders to lose their base of religious legitimacy. Finally, orthodox Jews no longer have a primal belief in God as an explanation for the way the universe works or in God's direct involvement in daily life (Soloveitchik, 1994: 87-102). That is, as Soloveitchik (1994: 102) puts it, "individual Divine Providence, though passionately believed as a theological principle . . . is no longer experienced as a simple reality."

While Soloveitchik's observations are limited to the orthodox Jewish faith, his basic argument that the breakdown of the traditional community by modernization has resulted in a shift to texts as the major source for religious education and practice is applicable to other religions. This is particularly true of Islam. A shift from tradition to texts as the source for determining the proper behavior for Muslims goes a long way toward explaining the rise of Islamic fundamentalism across the globe.

The literature on ethnic conflict also contains arguments consistent with this school of thought. Connor (1972) argues that, especially for the new multiethnic states in the Third World, loyalty often does not extend beyond one's ethnic group, and this is a major threat to stability. Efforts at modernization, state building, and assimilation have exacerbated ethnic conflict rather than making ethnicity epiphenomenal. Horowitz (1985: 105) also documents various theories in the ethnic conflict literature which argue that ethnic conflict is caused by processes associated with modernization. These arguments include that the social mobilization caused by modernization, as well as the uneven distribution of the benefits of modernization, contribute to ethnic conflict.

These arguments with regard to fundamentalism are important for another reason. They show that even if secularization is occurring, religion is still an important political factor. This is because fundamentalism is precisely a reaction in defense against modern secular culture. Fundamentalists clearly take part in politics and are influential in many parts of the world. They are also responsible for a number of violent acts. Thus, even if secularization is occurring, it could be seen as a contributing factor to the creation of a new type of religious movement that is clearly influential in society, politics, and conflict. This creates an interesting paradox where the very phenomenon that is believed by some to be the cause of religion's demise actually has the opposite effect.

In sum, the advocates of the second school of thought make several points in their explanations for the recent resurgence or revitalization of religion. First, the first school of thought is correct and religion has never ceased to be a factor in politics and society. Second, governments espousing secular Western ideologies have failed to live up to the promises made by those ideologies. This has led to a disillusionment with those ideologies and the governments which espouse them. Third, that these ideologies are Western in origin has contributed to this disillusionment in non-Western states. Fourth, the tools provided by modernization have facilitated the spread of religiously based opposition movements. This is especially true of the improvements in communications technology which have made the world a smaller place and have made fundamentalists aware of the activities of their counterparts across the world. The Iranian revolution of 1979 was one such activity which had a profound effect in the global arena. It proved that Western-supported secular authoritarian regimes could be successfully challenged and that Islamic fundamentalist movements are capable of posing such a challenge. Also, more recently, the fall of the Soviet Union and other eastern European authoritarian regimes provided more proof that authoritarian regimes are not invulnerable.

Fifth, the religious resurgence is, in part, a reaction to the challenges posed to and breakdown of religious values by the new secular values. This breakdown has often caused a feeling of dislocation, alienation, and disorientation in individuals, making them more receptive to the appeal of religions which minister to the needs caused by this feeling. Sixth, the freedom of choice of religions in many societies has increased the ability of people to find and join religions more appealing to them. Finally, the increasing government involvement in the realm that was formerly the exclusive domain of religion has provoked a reaction.

While, as noted earlier, many of these points are made mostly in the context of the non-Western world, most of them are also applicable to Western industrialized states. Despite the formal separation of church and state in many Western democracies, issues with religious overtones have continually been part of their political agendas and many of these issues deal with how far the government may intrude into the realm of religion. Although the failures of modernization are not felt as strongly in such countries, there is no reason to assume that those effects that are felt do not play a role in the recent religious revitalization that is also taking place in the West. It is clear that, in the United States for example, communications technology is being used by religious fundamentalists. It is also clear that religious fundamentalist in Western industrialized countries are fighting against secular values. The current push for "family values" in the United States by the Christian right is an example of this. The only point made by the proponents of the second school of thought which may not apply to Western industrialized states is that of resentment against Western ideologies because they are not indigenous. However, one could argue that the clash between the secular Western ideologies and religious ideologies creates a similar situation.

Religion in the Post-Cold War Era

The third counter-argument posits that the end of the Cold War has contributed to the rise in religious conflict. That is, the imperatives of the Cold War forced many conflicts motivated by religion and ethnicity under the surface. The end of the Cold War removed these constraints. An analogy often used in the media during the early 1990s was that the end of the Cold War blew the lid off of the pressure cooker of ethnic and religious conflict.

This argument is popular with many policy makers who believe religious fundamentalism will be the new ideology to threaten the West.[10] It is also compatible with the first two schools of thought. There is no assumption that religion disappeared, only that many types of conflict, including religiously inspired conflicts, were repressed by the Cold War. Also, that modernization has contributed to the resurgence of religion is an element of the arguments made by this school of thought.

Huntington is, perhaps, the most prominent advocate of this school of thought. Earlier in his career, he was one of the major advocates of the modernization school of thought. This is a strong indication that this school of thought is being seriously reconsidered. In fact, he now argues that modernization, rather than inhibiting religion, tends to produce renewed commitment to indigenous cultures, which often take the form of religion (Huntington, 1996b: 37). The decline in Western (American) power since the end of the Cold War has accelerated this process. This is because "as Western power recedes, so too does the appeal of Western values and culture, and the West faces the need to accommodate itself to its declining ability to impose its values on non-Western societies. In many fundamental ways, much of the world is becoming more modern and less Western" (Huntington, 1996b: 38).

Huntington (1993) also argues that the end of the Cold War resulted in a change in the nature of world conflict and that the new conflicts are more religiously based than those that occurred during the Cold War. He argues that, during the Cold War, most of the world's conflicts were between Western ideologies (the conflict between democracy and communism), but now that the Cold War is over, most of the world's conflicts will be between civilizations, specifically between the West and the non-West. This will be due to clashes between civilizational ideologies.

Huntington (1993: 24) defines a civilization as "the highest cultural grouping of people and the broadest level of cultural identity people have short of what distinguishes humans from other species. It is defined by both common language, history, *religion*, customs, institutions and by the subjective self identification of people."[11] Also, his method for dividing the word into civilizations seems to be largely based on religion. Huntington divides the world into eight major civilizations: Western, Sinic/Confucian, Japanese, Islamic, Hindu, Slavic-Orthodox, Latin American, and "possibly" African. That four of these categories are religious is telling. Also, the others, except the African civilization, are largely religiously homogeneous and differentiated from the others by religion (Huntington, 1993; 1996a). Thus, Huntington is, in part, arguing that the end of the Cold War will result in a rise in religious conflict. This rise in religious conflict is made possible by the lifting of the Cold War restraints on such conflict. This infers that religion has never been divorced from politics and society, rather it has merely been restrained by other forces.[12]

Many disagree with many of Huntington's arguments; however, they generally do not oppose his argument that identity is an important influence on politics. They, rather, argue that post-Cold War identities will not be civilizational. Some argue that the relevant level of identity will be national or even subnational (Kirkpatrick et. al.,1993; Halliday, 2000; Hunter, 1998; Kader, 1998; Rosecrance, 1998). Others argue that the world is unifying into a single identity (Anwar,1998; Ikenberry, 1997; Tipson, 1997). Others oppose Huntington on other grounds. Some argue that Huntington ignored important factors that significantly influence the nature of conflict. These include improved conflict management techniques, the importance of population and environmental issues (Viorst, 1997), the strength of secularism and the desire for economic prosperity (Ajami, 1993), information technology (Barber, 1998), the continuing importance of military and economic power (Rosecrance, 1998), and the desire of the non-West to emulate the West (Kirkpatrick et al., 1993). Some contend that Huntington's theory does not fit the facts (Anwar, 1998; Hassner, 1997a; Heilbrunn, 1998; Kader, 1998; Neckermann, 1998; and Walt, 1997), and some even accuse him of ignoring or bending the facts (Pfaff, 1998; Hassner, 1997b). Most quantitative studies of Huntington's theory contradict his claims.[13] Finally, many criticize his methodology.[14]

Also, Huntington's theory comes from a uniquely Western perspective. He basically asks, what will be the next challenge to the West now that the Cold War is over? It is not hard to see how he could have concluded that Islam, among other "civilizations," will be a principal threat to the West. Yet it is arguable that if this threat exists, it is not new to the post-Cold War era. Islamic groups have been challenging Western groups for some time. For example, the proportion of ethnic conflicts involving Islamic groups in general and of those involving Islamic vs. Western groups has changed little with the end of the Cold War.[15] Thus, Huntington's theory has much in common with those who see a return of the importance of religion when, in all probability, religion never ceased to be important.

Be that as it may, the vigorous nature of this debate over Huntington's theory underscores the influence many scholars believe identity, including religious identity, has on political behavior. This is particularly important given that many believe religion to be one of the most important influences on identity (Laustsen and Waever, 2000).

Despite all the criticism of Huntington's theory, the argument that the end of the Cold War has influenced the nature of conflict has merit. It is reasonable to argue that the end of the Cold War has removed many systemic restrictions on religious conflict. States no longer have as much of a need for a superpower sponsor, which is likely to restrain their actions and support them in struggles against religious groups within their borders. The conflict in Bosnia is a good example of a conflict that was extremely unlikely to occur during the height of the Cold War.

Summary of the Counter-Arguments Against the False Predictions of Religion's Demise

Current events have contradicted the argument that religion has become, or ever was, epiphenomenal. This argument is also contradicted by a large and well documented body of literature. While the three counter-arguments to the modernization/secularization thesis are distinct, they complement each other to form an even stronger counter-argument. This counter-argument is founded on the well-supported claim that religion has never ceased to be a factor in politics and society. It has always been inseparable from politics and society and will remain so for the foreseeable future.

While this argument alone suffices to counter the modernization/secularization thesis, those who argue against it add that modernization, the very factor that is supposed to cause religion's demise, has in fact contributed to a resurgence or revitalization of religion. The failure of modernization and the Western ideologies associated with it to provide the political freedom, justice, and prosperity that its prophets promised has led to a crisis of legitimacy in many parts of the world for these ideologies. This has led to a return to more traditional ideologies, including religion. In addition, modernity has led to a considerable amount of social and personal dislocations, as well as the breakdown of traditional society. This has led to a traditional/religious backlash to preserve the essence of what has been lost in these dislocations and societal breakdown. The tools of modernized society, including but not limited to modern communications, have facilitated the worldwide organization of groups seeking to restore the role of religion in society. Finally, the end of the Cold War has removed many of the restraints the international system had placed upon the use of religious ideologies in politics and society as well as in conflict.

These counter-arguments to the modernization/secularization thesis are strong and convincing. Furthermore, they are backed up by current events. Accordingly, it is safe to argue that the modernization/secularization thesis' arguments notwithstanding, there is considerable justification for engaging in the study of religion and conflict. The counter-arguments regarding religion and modernity also provide a better understanding of religion in our times. While modernity did not make religion disappear, it did alter many of the ways it interacts with society, politics, and conflict.

The Debate Continues

While political scientists seem to have reached a consensus that modernization theory's predictions of the demise of religion and ethnicity were premature, there are still many sociologists who continue to defend secularization theory. The debate among sociologists has coalesced into two main arguments. The first is over the definition of secularization. Some define secularization as the demise of religiosity, that is, the extent to which people are religious, while others define it as the decreasing influence of religion on public institutions and behavior, in other words, the transfer of religion from the public to the private sphere. The second argument is over the extent to which both of these processes have occurred.

The argument that people are becoming less religious is strongly opposed. For instance, Stark (1999) argues that people are actually more religious now than they were in the past. U.S. church attendance has tripled in the past 150 years and there is no measurable decline in European church attendance. Most prominent historians agree that there never was a Golden Age of faith and that there were always many who were irreligious. For instance, in medieval times, the Church settled for nominal support by the masses and there was actually less belief in the supernatural than there is today. Swatos and Christiano (1999) similarly argue that the belief that people were more religious in the past is exaggerated. Voye (1999) argues that while religiosity is declining, it has not gone away. Science may have replaced religion's role as a belief system to some extent, but religion is still necessary to deal with many issues of ethics, morality, and identity. However, Lechner (1991) defends the notion that people are becoming less religious. He argues that secularization theory does not depend on a Golden Age of religion followed by a decline in religiosity. Furthermore, the true definition of secularization is not that people are becoming less religious but, rather, that religioun has lost most of its power in society.

As noted above, this final argument is also controversial. Those who oppose it generally argue that while the exact nature and role of religion has changed in modern times, it still has a strong influence. For instance, Beyer (1999) argues that although modernity may have altered the nature of religion's influence on society and public institutions, that influence remains strong. Religion remains an important influence even if its dominant influence was in the past. Swatos and Christiano (1999) argue that while pluralism and competition, both among religions and between religion and other institutions, has altered the role of religion in society, that role is still a strong one. Lambert (1999) argues that while people are more autonomous from religion than they have been in the past, religion still remains a significant influence. Finally, Voye (1999) argues that while religiosity is declining, religion still influences society. Science may have replaced religion's role as a belief system, but religion is still necessary to deal with many issues of ethics, morality, and identity.

Lechner (1991) argues that this is not the case: arguments such as those described above admit that religion's influence on society is weaker than it was in the past and this is, in fact, the definition of secularization. Dobbelaere (1999) takes this a step further and argues that the decline in religious influence has occurred to such an extent that this influence is no longer important. Religion, which was the dominant system in the past, has been relegated to being a subsystem among many other subsystems in a society dominated by a rationalism which has replaced many of religion's functions. Bureaucratic rules and laws have replaced the role of morality in regulating behavior, and religion has been restricted to the private sphere of life. Religion is now an individual choice in a plural society that offers people many choices, and religious institutions no longer have the ability to enforce their beliefs.

Others make similar arguments. Yamane (1997) argues that secularization theory does not predict that religion will disappear, but that it will transform into a less influential form. Thus, the concept of secularization is best understood as the declining scope of religious authority structures. What needs to be assessed is not individual belief and behavior but the orientations individuals have toward religious authority structures. In a similar vein, Chaves (1994) argues that "secularization is best understood not as the decline of religion, but as the declining scope of religious authority." This decline in religious authority has three elements. The first is laicization, where secular institutions gain autonomy from religious institutions. The second is internal secularization, which describes a process where "religious institutions undergo internal development towards conformity with the secular world." The third is religious disinvolvement, which is the "decline of religious beliefs and practices among individuals."

Beyer (1994: 70-86) argues that secularization is the privatization of religion, meaning that religion is becoming primarily the concern of individuals and is losing much of its public relevance. He takes this argument one step further by positing that it is not enough for private beliefs to be translated into public action for religion to be considered publicly influential. Rather, institutions must have some form of direct control, such as the control of some essential public service like health professionals or political leaders. This privatization has occurred because of the process of globalization, which removes obstacles to communication between societies. In such a multicultural climate, religion can only order the lives of individuals, not the workings of society as a whole.

According to Beyer (1994: 86-94) even those influences religion does have on society are more secular. This is because religion today deals with social problems that are not religious in origin and thus shapes itself to greater society. There are two types of responses to such problems. The "liberal option" treats evil in abstract fashion because evil cannot be "clearly localized and personified." In fact, to do so leads to intolerance and particularistic ascription, which are the source of evil. Thus, this option discourages the particularistic ascriptions associated with traditional religion and encourages a more universal identification will all peoples. The "conservative option" of returning to traditional religion despite modernity is also a reaction to secular issues and problems that is used when secular responses to these problems fail. This "conservative option" is the only thing that is making religion visible in the world today and is a minority view that "finds itself in conflict with the dominant trends in global social structure." It is still privatized, but has holistic emphasis and concentrates on community solidarity. In any case, in a global society, it is unlikely that one cultural outlook will prevail. Therefore, some religions have focused on particular territories. These attempts may "stem the tide" of modernization for a while, but cannot "negate the fundamental structure of global society."

Furthermore, even the "conservative option" will use modern structures to enforce its will and will look more and more like any other legal system, with laws that can be interpreted, changed, and repealed. This is because religion in a modern system must structure itself like other institutions. Because religion deals with ultimate meaning, it is "generally relevant in all situations but specifically relevant in comparatively few." In primitive societies, this made religion important for everything but these functions have been usurped by secular institutions in modern society. Furthermore, because religion is so broad and nonselective of its function, it has a hard time competing with other functional subsystems. Due to this, those functions that religion does serve tend to be those that the dominant systems do not address or cause without solving (Beyer, 1994: 93-94, 101-104).

While this argument is interesting, its central claim that religion is losing its influence on societal-level behavior is contradicted by events in the real world. These events include the Iranian revolution, the Islamic revolutions and opposition movements throughout the Islamic world, and the influence of the religious right in the United States to name a few. It is also contradicted by the rise of the level of ethnoreligious conflict since 1945 documented by Gurr (1993a, 1993b, & 2000), as well as evidence that is presented in chapter 4. Beyer's arguments that religious institutions actively address social problems that other social institutions cannot or will not address also implies that religion has social significance. Even if these problems are not religious in origin, the attempts by religious institutions to address them at a societal level are by definition an aspect of attempts to influence society and be politically relevant. Also, it is difficult to understand Beyer's argument that individual religious beliefs that translate into public action do not constitute a religious influence on society. If the collective actions of individuals guided by their religious beliefs succeed in influencing a society, how can this not be considered a way in which religion influences society?

Perhaps the reason that many of the defenders of secularization theory fail to see the influence of religion on society is that they tend to focus on religion in the United States and, occasionally, will also address religion in western Europe. While, as many sociologists argue, religion is an important factor in the United States, its influence is probably less apparent than in the non-Western world. This is because of the constitutional separation of church and state in many Western states. However, if one looks more closely one can find many religious influences on society and politics in the West. The role of the religious right in the anti-abortion movement in the United States is but one example. Furthermore, an examination of the role of religion in many non-Western states, Islamic states in particular, makes it hard to argue that religion's influence has been limited to only individual behavior.

Thus, it is fair to argue that if one were to defend the secularization thesis, one would be forced to concede that religion continues to influence politics and society, although this influence has declined substantially. This would constitute a redefinition of the term secularization to mean the decline of the influence of religion rather than its disappearance. This is a clear retreat from claims that religion is becoming "epiphenomenal," and it opens up a series of difficult questions. These questions include: What constitutes a religious influence? Are influences on public institutions the only relevant influences or are influences in the private sphere and on individuals also considered? How does one measure these influences both in the present and in the past? What is considered a decline of religious influence, as opposed to change in the nature of that influence? To what extent must the influence of religion decline for this decline to be called secularization?

To some extent, the arguments described above by the defenders of the secularization thesis do make the argument that secularization is the substantial decline in religion's influence. The debate between them and those who disagree with the thesis revolves precisely around this definition and the questions presented above. Given this, it is fair to conclude that there are few who argue that the influence of religion has disappeared. However, there are some who argue that this influence has decreased substantially. This backing away from the argument that religion is becoming an "epiphenomenal" force in society is a significant, perhaps even a revolutionary, retreat. Yet even the argument that religion's influence in society is declining is questionable. The combination of factual evidence and the multiple scholarly arguments that religion continues to influence society and politics provides considerable evidence that this is not the case. This is especially true given that many argue that modernity has made religion even more important. Also, that most in the discipline of political science have rejected the argument that modernity has made religion less relevant (and it is only some sociologists who continue to make this argument) shows that the majority of the academic community believes religion has not gone away.

In any case, it is clear that even sociologists agree that religion still has some influence on society, even if some feel that this influence has declined significantly. They also agree that modernity has changed the nature of religion's interaction with society, even if they do not agree on the specifics of these changes. Finally, as will be seen in later chapters, the debate over the truth of secularization/modernization theory roughly coincides with an increased interest by scholars in how religion influences conflict. That is, in order for the study of the influence of religion on society, politics, and conflict to begin to flourish, as it arguably has in recent times, the dominant paradigms that considered religion a thing of the past had to be successfully challenged.

Notes

1. While the focus of modernization theory is clearly on ethnicity, Appleby (1994: 7-8), Haynes (1994: 21-23), and Sahliyeh (1990: 3-4) make the argument that it is also meant to apply to religion. Also, most definitions of ethnicity include religion (for example, see Gurr [1993a: 11]).

2. For a survey of the literature on modernization, see, among others, Almond (1960), Apter (1965), Deutsch (1953), Foster-Carter (1985), Halpern (1964), Kautsky (1972), Lerner (1968), Randall and Theobald (1985), Rostow (1959), Smith (1970, 1971, and 1974), and Sutton (1963).

3. For a further survey of the literature on secularization, see, among others, Beckford (1985), Bell (1971), Berger (1969), Cox (1965), Glasner (1977), Martin (1978), and Wilson (1966 and 1976).

4. For a further survey of the literature on dependency and globalization, see, among others, Cardoso and Faletto (1978), Cockcroft (1972), Foster-Carter (1985), Frank (1971), Randall & Theobald (1985), and Wallerstein (1974a, 1974b, and 1983).

5. The data she uses is taken from the ISSP survey (International Social Survey Program) from 1991 using data from the United States, Great Britain, Norway, the Netherlands, West Germany, East Germany, Northern Ireland, and Italy.

6. These issues include abortion, working women, capital punishment, confidence in institutions, and support for religion in politics. The analysis controls for gender, current marital status, education, age, and employment

7. Their data comes from the World Value Survey of 22 countries from 1981-1983.

8. For an analysis and criticism of Olson's rational actor theory, see Rule (1988).

9. Rabbi Haym Soloveitchik is a prominent and respected Talmudic scholar. His observations do not constitute a systematic study of the topic but, rather, reflect his opinions based upon anecdotal evidence and personal observations as well as his knowledge of the evolution of *Halakhah*, the body of orthodox Jewish religious law.

10. See for example, "U.S. Official Calls Muslim Militants a Threat to Africa" *New York Times*, 1/1/92, 3; "Mahatma vs. Rama" *Time*, 6/24/91, 35; Benjamin J. Barber, "Jihad vs. McWorld" *The Atlantic*, 1992, 269 (3), 53-55, 58-62, 64-65. "Ethnic Strife Succeeds Cold War's Ideological Conflict" *Washington Post*, 12/18/94, 36.

11. Italics added for emphasis.

12. Eisenstadt (2000: 616), Lausten and Waever (2000: 705), Smith (2000: 791), and Tibi (2000: 844) similarly argue that Huntington's definition of civilizations is mostly based on religion.

13. See for example Fox (2001), Gurr (1994: 356-358), Russet, Oneal, and Cox (2000), Henderson (1998), and Henderson and Singer (2000)

14. Hassner (1997a) and Pfaff (1998) accuse Huntington of oversimplification. Beedham (1999), Pfaff (1998), Smith (1997), and Tipson (1997) question Huntington's assessment of what the world's civilizations are. Ikenberry (1997) similarly argues that the features that Huntington feels make the West unique are, in fact, not cultural factors nor are they unique to the West. Heilbrunn (1998) notes that Huntington, in his various writings, contradicts

himself. Gurr (1994) and Halliday (1997) note that Huntington's evidence is completely anecdotal, leaving room for many to cite counter examples. Similarly, Senghass (1998), Rosecrance (1998), and Walt (1997) argue that Huntington provides no systematic analysis of the link between civilizational controversies and political behavior. That is, a quantitative, or at least a more systematic, analysis of Huntington's work is necessary before it can be properly evaluated.

15. Fox (2001: 464) shows that Islamic civilizational conflicts constituted 23.2 percent of all civilizational conflicts during the Cold War and 24.7 percent after the Cold War. Islam vs. West conflicts constituted 5.6 percent of all civilizational conflicts during the Cold War and 6.9 percent after it. Also, conflicts between two Islamic groups constituted 12.0 percent of all ethnic conflicts during the Cold War and 13.8 percent of all conflict after it.

Chapter 4

Is Religion the Symptom or the Disease?

Even if, as is contended in the previous chapter, the modernization/secularization thesis is flawed, there remains another school of thought which argues against the relevance of religion to politics and conflict. This second school of thought, known as functionalism, basically posits that religion is a symptom, not the disease. That is, when it appears that religion is influencing politics and society, other more basic factors are the true original cause and religion is only the medium through which they act.

The Functionalist Argument

It is clear that the functionalist school of thought has for some time been a very influential, if not the dominant, school of thought in the sociology of religion. Functionalists argue that religion can be explained by its social functions. That is, rather than being a force in society that must be reckoned with, religion is one of the manifestations of other, more basic and fundamental, forces in society. Although it may appear that religion has a strong influence on politics and society, it is really those fundamental forces working through religion that are actually causing this influence. The functions that religion serves in society are determined by needs created by these more basic influences. Therefore, it is not religion which is important and must be studied but, rather, the societal and political forces which stand behind it.

This means that even if, as is contended here, the arguments against the modernization and secularization theses are correct, the study of the role religion plays in society is irrelevant. This is because, according to the functionalists, any role that religion appears to play is in reality a manifestation of more basic forces in society. Thus, according to the functionalists, whether religion has always played a role in society or is in a phase of resurgence due to the imperatives of modernization or the end of the Cold War is beside the point. If this argument is correct, any study based on the assumption that religion can and does play a role in politics and conflict would also be irrelevant. Furthermore, unlike the modernization/secularization thesis, current events cannot provide a counter-argument to the functionalist argument. This is because a functionalist would argue that despite the apparent role religion seems to be playing in conflict, it is really acting as a front for more fundamental social and political forces.

Turner (1991: 109) lists three social functions of religion, according to various sociologists from the functionalist school of thought: the social cement which bonds potentially antagonistic individuals; the social opium which suppresses conflict between social groups; and the source of social control in social relationships. He also describes the functionalist trends in the early influences of sociology. He argues that, according to Weber, "the historical origins of religion resided in the search to control the empirical world for entirely secular and instrumental purposes"(Turner, 1993: 16).

Latin (1978: 564-565) makes a similar assessment and adds that Weber argued that certain types of groups and classes tend to be attracted to certain types of religious doctrines. Latin goes on to say that

> Weber argued that, while priestly answers to the problems of evil or of salvation were related to sociological, economic, cultural and political "needs" of the people, as well as to the different prophetic messages, the reformulated and routinized answers took on a sociological reality, and could themselves influence the behavior of future generations (Latin, 1978: 565).

Thus, although it is clear that Weber believed most religions have functional origins, it is not clear that he believed that once they come into being they do not play an independent role in society and politics. In fact, Beckford (1985: 347) notes that the British version of the Weberian tradition argues against the functionalist argument.

There are many who believe that Durkheim gives religion a functionalist role in his sociology (Wilson, 1982; Hannigan, 1985). More specifically, Durkheim believed that "religion can only be understood by concentrating on its social role in uniting the community behind a common set of rituals and beliefs" and "that the real, objective phenomenon behind religious symbolism is not God but society" (Turner, 1991: 15, 47).

It is easy to see how one would come to this conclusion. Durkheim did argue that religion is intertwined with society and what religion does is done by society. Furthermore, he believed that society is the basis of religion and religion is the product of social consensus. For Durkheim, the formation of an ideal "is a natural product of social life." Also, the "collective ideal which religion expresses" is a reflection of society's ideals, and it is through the society that the individual learns to conceive of ideals (Durkheim, 1964: 418-425).

However, Pickering (1984: 300-301) argues that although Durkheim used functionalism to describe religion, it was only one aspect of his explanation of religion. He admits that Durkheim did influence later functionalists but should not be identified with "the hardened and more logically extended functionalism which began to emerge in the 1920s." Thus, as is the case with Weber, it is not clear in Durkheim's writings that he believed that religion does not play an independent role in society.

The functionalist argument is less ambiguous in Marxist writings. Turner (1991: 75-75, 110-114) discusses Engels's beliefs that religion is no more than a linguistic cloak for class struggles and that religion is used by the bourgeois for the purposes of political control. According to Engels the "role of ideology in society, especially religious teaching on sexuality and family life, is to secure the social conditions under which this reproduction of human bodies can take place." Thus, religion helps to support an economic system based on the family.

A more modern version of the functionalist argument is offered by Wilson. He argues that

> the science of society [sociology] was regarded as emerging in order to dislodge the religious conceptions of man and the world by which mankind had previously governed social affairs. Thus, there persisted a certain animus against religion, whilst, at the same time, the claim was made that sociologists viewed society with detachment and according to the cannons of value-freedom (Wilson, 1982: 5).

Furthermore, "functionalism remains one of the dominant perspectives of sociology" (Wilson, 1982: 7). This is at least partially due to the fact that "functionalism makes sense of arbitrary, empirically unprovable teachings (myths), and of equally arbitrary prescribed practices (rituals)" (Wilson, 1982: 7-8).

He continues that religion serves a variety of latent functions in society. These latent functions include providing social cohesion; legitimizing the social order/social control; accounting for (or allowing people to discount) the physical universe; legitimizing the "purposes and procedures" of society; conferring identity on individuals and groups; and acting as an "agency for emotional expression and regulation." This approach allowed sociologists to explain the endurance of non-rational behavior through its latent and rational uses, as well as giving sociologists the "gratification" they generally derived from "debunking."

However, according to Wilson, in advanced societies, most of these latent functions are no longer served by religion: they have been replaced by secular institutions and norms. Thus, the functionalist school of thought is closely related to the secularization thesis. It argues that not only is religion actually a manifestation of more basic societal and political imperatives, the role that it did play in society is now filled by secular institutions.

Friederichs (1985: 361-362) makes a similar argument. Like Wilson, he believes that religion is "an essentially universal (though culturally relative) and primarily communal phenomenon explainable by–and thus reducible to–more fundamental social scientific factors." Also, like Wilson he argues that the functions claimed for religion in this paradigm "are being taken over by the natural and social sciences, medicine and psychiatry, and the secular largess of the welfare state." However, unlike Wilson, he argues that these secular disciplines have been "stripped of their certitude" making them also, to an extent, dependant on faith. Thus, for Friedrichs, modernization has resulted in what can be called a new form of faith.

Geertz (1973: 201-209) discusses the functionalist school of thought with respect to ideologies. He discusses what he calls the two main approaches to the social determinants of ideology. The first, which he calls interest theory, is basically the argument that ideology is really the tool of other forces in society and especially in the "struggle for advantage." The second is what he calls strain theory. Strain theory posits ideology as a chronic effort to correct socio-psychological disequilibrium. This is necessary because no social arrangement can be completely successful in coping with the functional problems it inevitably faces. These functional problems include insoluble antinomies like liberty vs. social order, stability vs. chaos, effectiveness vs. humanity, precision vs. flexibility, etc.; the discontinuity between norms in society; and discrepancies between goals in different sectors of society. However, Geertz is somewhat skeptical about these functionalist arguments and asserts that it is the absence of a theory or analytical framework to describe symbolic behavior that has reduced sociologists to describing ideology as an elaborate cry of pain or a mask for interests.

Although this brief survey of the functionalist argument is by no means complete, it does make clear where the advocates of this school of thought stand. However, even within the functionalist school of thought there is some ambivalence over the argument's validity. For example, it is unclear whether Durkheim and Weber, considered by many to be among the first members of the functionalist school, actually believed in functionalism. Also Geertz, one of the more prominent advocates of this school of thought, seems ambivalent over his support of functionalism.

Be that as it may, the functionalist school of thought poses a direct challenge to any study of religion and conflict. A functionalist would argue that any theory positing that religion plays a role in politics or conflict as an independent force is false. Furthermore, any results from an empirical study which seem to indicate that religion does play a role actually represent the hidden effects of other more basic social forces.

Religion as an Independent Factor in Society and Politics

As can be inferred from this ambivalence among the functionalists, there are many who disagree with the functionalist school of thought. For instance, Beckford

(1985) argues that there has always been a healthy skepticism of functionalism, at least outside of North American sociology. He cites the British version of the Weberian tradition and French rationalism or historical materialism as examples. However, because of the primacy of the functionalist school of thought in the discipline, the sociology of religion has been relegated to a position of inferiority. This has resulted in functionalists explaining away religion with other phenomena and religion being treated as one of many forms of functional meaning-systems created in the course of social interaction. Also, the primacy of secularization theory has gotten to the point where sociologists ignore other interpretive frameworks. This has resulted in a failure of the sociology of religion to "take serious account" of religion and its capacity to "influence social processes in distinctive ways" (Beckford, 1985: 353). He goes as far as to say that the functionalists in the sociology of religion have succeeded in "concealing the social significance of religion from non-specialists" (Beckford, 1985: 351).

Chaves (1994: 751) and Coleman (1990: 336) harshly criticize the functionalist school of thought, calling it the functionalist fallacy. They strongly differ with the functionalist assumption that if a religion serves a social function, it must be subordinate to that function. They argue that the functionalists fail to show how the need for a particular institution or norm results in its establishment. There is no reason to assume that religion, or any other social institution for that matter, does not exist independently even if it is used to fulfill social functions. That is, religion is a social institution that is the original source of many social influences, as well as serving social functions that may be influenced by other social forces.

Robertson (1985: 356) similarly argues that functionalism serves more as a legitimating myth rather than the central orientation of the sociology of religion. Functionalism, according to Robertson, while important, is but one dimension of sociology. To focus on it exclusively would be "throwing out the baby with the bath water." He asserts that "much damage has been done to our endeavors by the functionalist orientation, but that does not mean that all the work performed under the rubric of functionalism . . . is now to be regarded as suspect on its face." Be that as it may, he still believes that the fundamental assumption of functionalism is flawed. This is clear from his statement that

> it is distinctively implausible to think that one factor or dimension of human life can be used in order to account for another. Specifically, religion cannot be explained–nor can a specific religious phenomenon be explained–by another factor; nor, on the other hand, can religion itself–or a specific religious phenomenon–explain another religious factor (Robertson, 1985: 367).

One influence religion has on society for which the functionalist explanation of religion does not fully account is change in religions. If the social functions of religions remain, more or less, constant, why then is religion so often an agent of change? (Pickering, 1984)

In all, those who argue against the functionalist school of thought do not dismiss it out of hand. They admit that other societal and political forces do have an influence on religion. However, they do not agree that is all religion is. Even after controlling for those societal and political imperatives that the functionalists argue are religion's true sources, religion has a significant independent influence on politics and society.

This debate is echoed in the literature on ethnic conflict. The instrumentalist school of thought mirrors that of the functionalists and argues that ethnic political activity is explainable by the desire for political and material gains and any invocation of ethnic identity is really a method to achieve those gains. Those who argue against the functionalists are mirrored in the ethnic conflict by the primordialists. The primordialists argue that ethnicity does have meaning above and beyond any immediate political or material goals and that this meaning derives from a primordial sense of ethnic identity.[1] Gurr (1993a: 124) and Gurr and Harff (1994: 79) argue that the two schools of thought are compatible. While an instrumental desire for political gain may motivate ethnic political action, it is far easier for ethnic group leaders to make use of such motivations if a strong ethnic identity, as described by the primordialists, already exists.[2]

These counter-arguments are strong and convincing. More importantly they provide a justification for engaging the study of the role of religion in politics and conflict.

Is Religion Relevant to Ethnic Conflict?

While the above arguments demonstrate that religion continues to have an impact on society, politics, and conflict, few of them directly address ethnoreligious conflict. As already noted, Gurr (1993a, 1993b, and 2000) documents a rise in the level of ethnoreligious conflict since 1945. However, this is part of a general rise in ethnic conflict, so it is unclear from this data alone whether the rise in ethnoreligious conflict has anything to do with religion or is simply part of the larger trend.

As shown in chapter 2, religion is an aspect of ethnicity, with its importance varying over time and place. While it can be the single most important factor in some ethnic identities, it can have little relevance to others. The key factor which determines whether religion will be salient is the perception of the group itself. Accordingly, the definition of ethnicity used here is based upon this view of ethnicity by Gurr and Horowitz. An ethnic group is considered an ethnic group if its members believe themselves to be an ethnic group. Any conflict between two such groups is considered an ethnic conflict. Ethnic conflicts are considered here to be potential ethnoreligious conflicts if the two groups that are in a conflict are primarily of different religions.

This argument that religion is an aspect of identity is not intended to obscure the fact that not in all cases is religion associated with ethnicity, nor are all ethnicities associated with a religion. Rather it is intended to show that religion can contribute to an ethnic identity. Nevertheless, in practice, the distinction between religion and ethnicity is often unclear. The two forms of identity can be "intertwined and mutually reenforcing" (Appleby, 2000: 61). Religion is often used to justify ethnic aspirations, and ethnicity can often give rise to religious traditions.

While all of this makes clear that religion can potentially become an important factor in ethnic conflict, it does not address how often this actually happens. In other words, how often is religion actually relevant to ethnic conflict? This is not an easy question to answer because most ethnic conflicts involve a whole range of issues other than religious ones. These include issues of political, economic, and cultural discrimination as well as issues of autonomy and self-determination. In addition, they can be complicated by other factors. Whether a state is democratic or autocratic is strongly associated with the level of repression against ethnic minorities. The process of democratization is associated with a level of political, social, and economic instability that makes ethnic conflict more likely. Political activities among ethnic minorities in one state can inspire similar activities in another. Finally, international support for an ethnic movement can facilitate its activities.[3]

Accordingly, when considering the importance of religious issues to an ethnic conflict, one must consider not only whether the two groups involved are of different religions, but whether religion is an issue in the conflict and, if so, how important are religious issues compared to other issues. As shown in figure 4.1, of the 268 ethnic minorities in the Minorities at Risk dataset,[4] 105 are ethnoreligious minorities and 163 are not religiously distinct from the dominant group in their state. Religious issues are not at all relevant to 28 ethnoreligious minorities, marginally relevant to 38, relevant but less so than other issues for 27, and at least as important as other issues for 12. This means that religious issues are more than marginally relevant in slightly more than 37 percent of ethnoreligious conflicts or about 14.5 percent of all ethnic conflicts. Furthermore, religious issues are among the dominant issues in only 11.4 percent of ethnoreligious conflicts or 4.5 percent of all ethnic conflicts. While these results show that religion is not as important to ethnic conflicts as often as one would expect, they also show that religious issues are very important to a significant minority of ethnic conflicts.

In fact, the relevance of religion to the conflict has a profound influence on the dynamics of ethnoreligious conflicts. Governments engaged in religious conflicts employ disproportionally high levels of discrimination, including political, economic, and cultural discrimination. Some examples of ethnoreligious minorities engaged in conflicts with their governments in which religion is among the most important issues include the Bahai minority in Iran, the Christians and animists living in the southern regions in Sudan, and the Muslim Arab minority in Mynmar. All of these groups suffer from almost double the mean of political discrimination, more than double the level of economic discrimination, and about triple the level of cultural discrimination as the average ethnoreligious minority.[5] On the other

Figure 4.1: The Salience of Religious Issues[6]

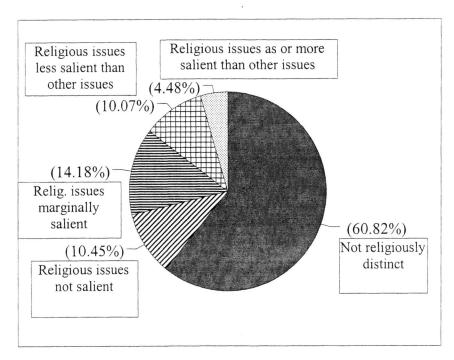

hand, the minorities like the Scots in Britain, the Jurassians in France, and the Quebecois in Canada, who are involved in conflicts where religion is not at all an issue, suffer from no political, economic, or cultural discrimination.[7] One possible explanation for this trend is that those states in which religion is more relevant to the conflict tend to be more autocratic and those states in which it is not tend to be more democratic.[8] It is a well known fact that autocratic governments are generally more discriminatory than democratic ones. However, even accounting for this, economic, political, and cultural discrimination still, on average, increase as religion becomes more relevant to ethnoreligious conflicts.[9]

The relevance of religion to the conflict also affects the level of protest and rebellion engaged in by an ethnoreligious minority. As the relevance of religion goes up, the level of protest and rebellion also tends to rise.[10]

Ethnoreligious minorities as a whole differ from other ethnic minorities in several respects. First, they tend to suffer from higher levels of political and cultural, but not economic, discrimination.[11] Second, grievances expressed by ethnoreligious minorities over all types of discrimination are higher than those expressed by other ethnoreligious minorities.[12] Finally, ethnoreligious minorities are more likely to have had some form of autonomy in the past than other ethnic minorities and, consequently, express more grievances over autonomy issues.[13]

Thus, while religion is important in only a minority of ethnoreligious conflicts, when it is an important issue it clearly affects the dynamics of these conflicts. Also, whether religion is relevant or not, there appears to be some general differences between ethnoreligious conflicts and other ethnic conflicts. The details of this religious influence on ethnoreligious conflicts are discussed in more detail in later chapters.

Conclusion

Despite the predictions and arguments made by the modernization/secularization and the functionalist schools of thought, religion plays an important role in society and politics as well as in violence, conflict, and revolution. The predictions of the various forms of the modernization/secularization school of thought that religion would become an epiphenomenal force in society were premature. Religion has continued to play an important role in politics and society. In fact, this role seems to have been reinforced by the very imperatives of modernization that were supposed to have caused religion's demise, as well as by the freedom of action created by the end of the Cold War. This role has been made increasingly apparent by recent events including, but by no means limited to, the ethnoreligious conflicts of the 1990s. Also, the role that religion plays in politics and society is not, as the functionalist school of thought argues, merely a manifestation of other more basic forces. While religion is affected by other political and social forces, it nevertheless plays a role in politics and society that is independent of those forces.

This argument is crucial to any study of the role religion plays in politics and conflict. Should the modernization/secularization thesis be correct, there would be nothing to study. Should the functionalist argument be correct, the results of any such study would be irrelevant.

In addition to providing the justification for studying religion and politics, the debates over the validity of these two schools of thought are also important tools in understanding both the role religion plays in society and the academic study of that role. The debate over the modernization/secularization school of thought brings out the point that religion must be studied in context. That is, religion cannot be divorced from the political, economic, and social environment in which it exists. For instance, modernization has had a strong influence on religion in the twentieth century. The literature on fundamentalism, which describes fundamentalism as, among other things, a reaction to modernization and a more secular world, is but one example of this.

The debate over functionalism brings out a similar point. Religions do play a role or serve functions in most societies, and most religions cannot be fully understood unless this role is taken into account. The exact nature of this role will be discussed in later chapters. However, religion is not the slave of these functions that it serves. That is, while religions do play a functional role in most societies and are influenced by this role, their influence in society is not limited to the imperatives of this role. Religions are not merely social tools serving a social function and only serving that function. Rather, while they do serve a social function, they also have considerable influence on people's behavior above and beyond the social functions that they serve.

Finally, both the modernization/secularization and the functionalist schools of thought provide considerable insight into the study of religion and conflict. It is argued here that, surprisingly, no comprehensive and dynamic theory of religion and conflict has been developed. The preoccupation of the study of religion and politics with the debate over whether religion is actually at all relevant to politics goes a long way toward explaining this. It is likely that this debate has discouraged many academics from studying the subject. It is also likely that many who were not discouraged spent much of their time and effort arguing that religion *is*, in fact, relevant to politics rather than attempting to discover *how* it is relevant. Thus, a large portion of the resources of social scientists have been diverted away from the study of religion and politics and much of those resources committed to the study were used not to study the phenomenon itself but to defend the validity of studying it at all. Given this drain on resources actually devoted to the study of religion and politics, it is not surprising that the field lacks a comprehensive and dynamic theory.

Notes

1. For examples of the primordialist argument see Geertz (1973) and Isaacs (1975). For a review of both primordialism and instrumentalism see Connor (1972) and Comaroff and Stern (1995).

2. For a further discussion of instrumentalism and primordialism see Comaroff and Stern (1995).

3. For a full examination of the influence of these issues and factors, as well as others, on ethnic conflict see especially Gurr (1993a, 1993b, and 1997) as well as Carment and James (1996, 1997a, 1997b, and 1998) and Regan (1998).

4. For a description of the Minorities at Risk dataset see appendix A.

5. In 1994-1995, these three groups measured an average of 7.67 on the political discrimination index used in this study (ALLPD94), 8.33 on the economic discrimination index (ALLED94), and 5.5 on the cultural discrimination index (CULRES94) as compared to means for all ethnoreligious minorities of 3.89 for political discrimination, 3.57 for economic discrimination, and 1.84 for cultural discrimination.

6. A version of this table previously appeared in Fox (1997: 10).

7. In 1994-1995, all groups where religion was not relevant to the conflict measured an average of 2.32 on the political discrimination index used in this study (ALLPD94), 3.04 on the economic discrimination index (ALLED94), and 0.68 on the cultural discrimination index (CULRES94) as compared to means of 5.83 for political discrimination, 4.09 for economic discrimination, and 3.33 for cultural discrimination for those minorities where religion is one of the most important issues in a conflict.

8. Those states in which religion is not relevant to the conflict measure an average of 1.82 (out of 10) on the autocracy index (NAUT94) and a 5.86 (out of 10) on the democracy index (NDEM94). Those states in which religion is one of the most important issues average 5.08 on the autocracy index and 2.75 on the democracy index. The average level of autocracy and democracy for all the cases in this study are 2.79 and 4.70 respectively.

9. For details on this trend, as well as a more in-depth analysis of the effects of the relevance of religious issues on ethnoreligious conflicts, see Fox (1997).

10. When religion is not relevant to the conflict, protest among ethnoreligious minorities averages 1.08 on the protest index for 1995. This goes up to 1.51 when religion is a marginal issue, and 1.70 when religion is an important issue but not as important as other issues, but drops to 1.48 when religion is one of the most important issues in the conflict. When religion is not relevant to the conflict, rebellion among ethnoreligious minorities averages 0.54 on the rebellion index for 1995. This goes up to 0.97 when religion is a marginal issues, 0.96 when religion is an important issue but not as important as other issues, and 1.25 when religion is one of the most important issues in the conflict.

11. The mean level of political and cultural discriminations against ethnoreligious minorities in 1993-1994 are respectively 2.97 and 2.01. Against other ethnic minorities these levels of discrimination are respectively 2.57 and 1.12. Economic discrimination is 3.57 against ethnoreligious minorities and 3.58 against other ethnic minorities.

12. The mean levels of economic, political, and cultural grievances in 1992-1993 expressed by ethnoreligious minorities are respectively, 2.56, 3.10, and 2.47. The mean levels for these variable for other ethnic minorities are 2.11, 2.69, and 2.13.

13. Ethnoreligious minorities score a mean of 0.32 on the lost autonomy index (AUTLOST) and a mean level of 2.10 on the autonomy grievances index for 1992-1993 (AUTGR93). Other ethnic minorities score respectively 0.25 and 1.45 on these indexes.

Chapter 5

Previous Approaches to the Study of Religion and Conflict

While there is a large body of literature dealing with the issue of religion and conflict, no comprehensive and dynamic theory on the subject has been developed. As noted in chapters 3 and 4, one possible explanation for this is that so much energy has been devoted to the debate over whether religion is relevant to conflict, or politics and society at all for that matter, that few resources have been left for the study of the actual relationship between religion and conflict. However, this is not to say no theories of religion and conflict have been developed.

There are five types of theories and an additional approach that are discussed in this chapter. They deal with religion's relationship with violence, conflict and, revolution. The first type of theory deals with the nature of religious ideologies and doctrines. It hypothesizes that certain types of religion are more likely to dispose their adherents toward violence and conflict than others. The second type looks at environmental factors. The third type takes a structural view of the relationship. The fourth type is what is called here the "laundry list" approach, which lists several ways in which religion affects conflict but does not put these effects into a coherent conceptual framework. The fifth are those studies which examine the influence of religion on a specific type of sociopolitical phenomenon to the exclusion of all others. Finally, the case study approach to the study of religion and conflict is discussed.

While these theories and approaches are informative, none of them constitute an adequate theory of religion and conflict. As will be recalled, it is argued here that an adequate theory of religion and conflict should be both comprehensive and dynamic. A comprehensive theory should describe most, if not all, of the ways in which religion becomes involved in conflict. A dynamic theory should address the interrelationships between the various propositions contained in the theory, placing them in a more dynamic framework.

Category #1: Some Religions Are More Conflict Prone than Others

The first category of explanations, as already noted, includes those theories that assert that some religions are more likely to promote various forms of conflict than others. This type of explanation is based on the assumption that some religious doctrines and ideologies are more conducive to violence than others. An example of this is Weber's belief that "religions with world accepting ideologies are more likely to take part in revolution than those with world rejecting ideologies" (Weber 1968 in Kowalewski and Greil 1990: 516). Another example is Lewy's (1974: 548) assertion that religions that endorse "patterns of subservience," such as the concept of a divine king or India's caste system, are less likely to support rebellion. Similarly, many argue that Islamic doctrine is more conducive to violence than the doctrines of other religions.

Although it is true that some religions incorporate beliefs that seem to be more prone to violence than others, it seems to be a widely accepted truism that all religions have the potential to inspire violence. For instance, Rapoport (1991a: 118-123, 1991b: 446) maintains that while some religions have higher propensities for violence than others, all major religions have enormous potentials for creating and directing violence. Nothing surpasses religion's ability to inspire commitment and emotions, creating an intensity of feeling that makes it harder to reconcile religious conflicts and invites violent solutions. He cites examples of this, including that religion is the principal justification for contemporary terror, that wars of religion tend to be more violent and difficult to resolve, and that virtually all of this century's genocides had a religious element. He also notes that an examination of encyclopedias on religion shows that there are five times as many articles on war as there are on peace. In fact, fundamentalists can exploit the violent potential a religion contains even when that religion is rarely perceived as having violent potential.

For example the Sinhalese Buddhists in Sri Lanka have developed an interpretation of Buddhist doctrine that justifies violence despite the fact that most perceive Buddhism as being inherently pacifist. They believe Buddha charged them with preserving the true Buddhism, known as Therevada Buddhism, and gave the Island of Lanka to the Sinhalese to create a "citadel of pure Buddhism." This interpretation is based on a chauvinistic interpretation of a Buddhist text called the Mahavamsa. The result of this interpretation is a claim for Buddhist rule in Sri Lanka. The pretext of protecting the Sinhalese Buddhism from perceived dangers inspired violent, murderous riots in 1956, 1958, 1977, 1981, and 1983, and massacres of the island's Tamil minority by extremists within Sri Lankan security forces since then, including the murder of about 40,000 Tamils by death squads between 1987 and 1990. It should be noted that many Buddhist purists have, to say the least, doubts about whether some of the religious and political practices of Buddhist extremists are consistent with Buddhism. In addition to opposing the violence as against Buddha's principles, they accuse Sinhalese Buddhists of incorporating outside elements into Buddhist religious practice. They include Hindu practices as well as rites incorporating "black magic, demons, astrology, sorcery, trance-like states, and so forth." However, proper or not, many Sinhalese, with the support of elements within their clergy, have interpreted Buddhism, a religion that is generally perceived as being pacifist, in a way that justifies extreme violence (Manor, 1994).

Similarly, Buddhists in Tibet have, despite a tradition of pacifism, on occasion, violently opposed the Chinese occupation. Guerilla groups known, among other things, as "defenders of the faith" were formed in the 1950s in response to the Chinese occupation. This opposition eventually led to the Lhasa uprising and the exile of the Dalai Llama and 50,000 of his followers in 1959. Religious ceremonies among Tibetian exiles include commemorations of this uprising. Since the uprising, there have been sporadic protests, some of them violent, protesting the Chinese rule. Many of the protests have been led by young Buddhist Monks (Kolas: 1996).[1] Also, the Bahai, who are doctrinally pacifist, actually began as a violent messianic movement and later reverted to pacifism (Rapoport, 1988: 204).

According to Rapoport (1991a: 125-136) and Girard (1977) one reason for the intimate link between religion and violence is that religion has its origins in violence. They argue that the original purpose of religion is to keep violence outside the community. In doing so, religions create a special kind of violence to prevent more violence.[2] One of the reasons for the creation of the state was religion's failure to sufficiently limit violence. Accordingly, it is not surprising that the basic reasons we associate the state with violence are also reasons we associate religion with violence. These include violence against foreign communities, violence against domestic upheaval, efforts to reconstitute the social order, and the use or abuse of religion and/or the state by those who have ulterior motives. Rapoport also notes that religion can also inspire violence by adherents who wish to reestablish what they believe to be the ideas of their religion's founding community.

Juergensmeyer (1991) similarly argues that religions by their very nature incorporate "notions of sacrifice and martyrdom" which are "so integral to religion that without them many religious concepts would be almost unthinkable" (Juergensmeyer, 1991: 102). Based on this, it is not surprising that the "rhetoric of war" can be found in most religious traditions. This includes the idea of the hero sacrificing himself for the interests of the religion which is found in Judaism, Christianity, and Islam as well as in Sikhism and Hinduism

In addition to having the ability to promote conflict, all religions also have the potential to deter it. That is, all religions have elements which encourage peace, cooperation, and accommodation. Lewy (1974:3, 550-55) admits this when he states that religion is a "double edged sword" that can be used to both support the government and revolt against it and that the determining factor may be the social and political interests of various actors in society. In fact, while there is no denial of religion's violent tendencies it is, for the most part, agreed upon in the literature that all religions have within them what Keddie (1985) calls "quietist" tendencies, the potential to be peaceful and support the status quo. One reason for these dual and opposite tendencies is that most long-established religions have ideologies and doctrines that are so diverse and complex that justification for both quietism and violence can be found within their traditions. Greely (1982: 134) makes a similar argument when he states that "in some circumstances religious stories and religious groupings validate and confirm the dominant social perspective. In other circumstances religious stories and religious groupings are at odds with the dominant perspective, and they can even attempt to destroy it."

Little (1996a) develops a classification system for religious intolerance and tolerance. The most violent face of religion is violent intolerance. "Religions appear invariably to make room for violence as a legitimate means of defense." That is, violence is often justified in cases where there is a perceived threat against a religion, combined with the belief that violence can remedy that threat. A less violent face of religion is what Little calls civic intolerance. This is when religious activists try to follow their agenda through the ballot box, using "legitimate violence" to enforce their beliefs. The peaceful face of religion is called nonviolent tolerance. Little sites Jesus, Gandhi, and Martin Luther King Jr. as examples of this. Little's final category, civic tolerance, can be described as religiously inspired violence for a good cause. This category includes the use of "legitimate violence" to enforce human rights and tolerance. This classification system implies that one can expect more violence when religious groups are threatened, have a higher propensity to perceive threats against them, have a greater reliance on violence for problem solving, and/or are in situations where all options other than violence have been blocked or exhausted

Haynes (1994: 13-14) also classifies the violent and quietist potential of religions. He argues that there are three different types of movements within the recent resurgence of fundamentalist movements. First, religiopolitical movements are "those . . . whose leaders utilize religious ideologies . . . to attack the socio-political legitimacy and economic performance of incumbent governments." Such groups include Algeria's Islamic Salvation Front, Iran's Islamic Republican Party, and al-Nahdha in Tunisia as well as others elsewhere. These are mostly Islamic movements whose aim is to set up an Islamic state based on Islamic religious law, known as Sharia. Haynes also considers the liberation theology movements in Latin America to be examples of religiopolitical movements.

Second, religious revivalist movements are those which are "dedicated to society's moral re-awakening and at times have a national and political dimension" (Haynes, 1994: 14) but in general do not focus on the state. These groups are often labeled as "fundamentalists" and include "conservative Protestant sects and churches which seek to reform and produce 'new' Christians" (Haynes, 1994: 14). Such sects, which can be found in Europe, North and Latin America, Sub-Saharan Africa, and the Pacific Rim, do not seek to establish a religious state but rather, "to establish communities of right-minded people to do God's will on Earth" (Haynes, 1994: 14). These groups do involve themselves in politics. The campaigns against abortion and for religious teaching in U.S. schools during the 1980s and 1990s are an example of such political activity. However, such activity tends to be peaceful.

Third, syncretic hybrids are movements with a mixture of different elements of

Christian or Islamic religious beliefs and traditional practices which may or may not be politicized. This category seems to be more properly described as an "other" category in which Haynes places groups that do not quite fit either of the previous two categories. In any case, Haynes' categorization of fundamentalist movements is consistent with the argument that there are both violent and quietest tendencies among recent fundamentalist movements.

Keddie (1985: 158-161) discusses this with respect to two central Shi'i Muslim concepts. The first is the belief that the "messianic" Mahdi will return and dissemi-nate justice and equity. This belief has been used to fuel messianic revolts with the belief that the Mahdi would return to "overturn [a] disliked social system and bring justice to the earth." This belief, according to Keddie, fueled early Shi'i messianic revolts in the seventh and eighth centuries as well as in some later periods of Shi'i messianic revolt, especially in times of social stress. Yet this concept has also been used as a justification for the status quo when Shi'i-supported governments came to power. This was true when, in the tenth century, adherents of the Ismaili (also known as "Sevener") branch of Shi'i Islam came to power in Egypt and north Africa. A doctrine of quietism also developed among the "Twelver" branch of Shi'i Islam based on the indefinite wait for the twelfth Imam (religious leader/successor to the prophet Mohammed). It is believed by Twelver Shi'i

> that the Eleventh Imam, who some said died without a successor, in fact had an infant son who disappeared, but who remains alive on earth and will return at an unknown future time as Mahdi. . . . High ranking Abassid officials . . . seem to have promoted the doctrine of disappearance and occultation, largely to remove any potential conflict between theoretically infallible Imams and temporal rulers. In time Twelver Shi'is became accustomed to and indefinite wait for the Mahdi . . . and so the Mahdi became more a source of vague comfort about an indefinite future than an incitement to revolt. Indeed, he was made to discourage revolts or efforts to bring him back before his time (Keddie, 1985: 160).

The second such Shi'i concept Keddie describes is the Martyrdom of Hussein. This "central event in Shi'i thought and ritual" has inspired the widespread violent practice of self-flagellation in Iran on the anniversary of Hussein's death. Also, during the Iranian revolution, Hussein was seen as a courageous and heroic figure "leading a battle against odds in order to establish justice" and as such was considered a role model for the Iranian people. Yet, in times of peace Hussein plays the more spiritual and quietist role of interceding with God for the people. In fact, Haynes (1994: 46) argues that the martyrdom of Hussein has traditionally been interpreted as an allegorical representation of the suffering and martyrdom of the Shi'i, that is, as an example of how to peacefully bear one's situation. It was not until recently that Khomeini recreated the myth as a model of how the Shi'i should "stand up and combat oppression and political marginalization." Esposito and Voll (2000: 637-638) similarly argue that Islam is not monolithic, and the voices of violence are joined by those of dialogue and cooperation.

Another example of a religion with both quietist and revolutionary/violent aspects is Christianity. From the early Middle Ages until the Protestant Reformation, Catholicism was the ultimate religion of the status quo. It was the official state religion for European states and its theology legitimized those states' systems of government. It is also clear that there is a strong tradition of pacifism within Christianity that Catholicism does not reject. Yet Catholic institutions also participated in the Crusades and the Inquisition. The current international law scholarship on the concept of just war has its origins in Catholic theology dating back to St. Augustine.[3] Also, liberation theology, which interprets Catholic theology in a revolutionary manner, is a movement within the Catholic Church. Liberation theology combines traditional Catholicism with modern, often Marxist, social analysis in order to develop a theological foundation for often violent forms of political action in order to effect human liberation from social injustice (Pottenger: 1989). An example of such an interpretation of Catholic doctrine is that Jesus was killed by the establishment and his resurrection is a triumph over that establishment (Berryman 1987: 156).

Judaism also has both violent and quietist tendencies. While in the diaspora, Jewish doctrine generally counseled a pacifistic acceptance of the often violent discrimination against the Jewish minorities in Europe and the Arab world. However, the concept of holy war can be found throughout the Old Testament. For example, Deuteronomy: 25-19 contains the commandment to "wipe out the remembrance of [the nation of] *Amalek* from under heaven." The extent of this commandment is clarified in Samuel I: 15-3 where the prophet Samuel relates to King Saul God's command to destroy *Amalek* to the last "infant and suckling, ox and sheep, camel and ass."[4] The Jewish concept of holy war was used to justify the Bar Cochva rebellion against the Romans two thousand years ago.[5] Jewish doctrine is also used today in Israel by several religious groups to justify various forms of violence.[6] Thus, the Jewish concept of holy war seems to be activated mainly by Jews living in the land of Israel. This phenomenon has both ideological and practical explanations. The ideological connection between reclaiming or defending the holy land and violence is readily apparent.[7] On a more practical level, the pacifism of Jews in exile can be explained by their lack of ability to effectively use force against a more powerful and often hostile ruling population.[8] Be that as it may, it is clear that Jewish doctrine contains within it the potential to justify both quietism and violence.

On a more general level, Weigel (1992) argues that the Judeo-Christian religious tradition, which none would argue does not have its violent aspects, has helped to shape the West's "preference for legal and political, that is, nonviolent conflict resolution" (Weigel, 1992: 174). He backs up this assertion with a survey of the contributions of religion to peace across the globe in recent years.

An example of empirical research that has shown a single religion, at different times, to result in differing levels of militancy are the works of Marx (1967a and 1967b) and Alston et al. (1972). Marx found, based on a 1964 survey of attitudes among blacks, that even when controlling for education, age, region, sex, and denomination, low religiosity among blacks led to heightened levels of militancy. It is easy to conclude from this that, in 1964, religion among blacks in America had a quietist influence. However, based on a 1969 survey, Alston et al. found, after taking methodological differences with Marx into account, that the association between low levels of black militancy and high levels of religiosity had considerably weakened. Thus, in the space of five years the quietist tendency of religion among blacks in America was considerably weakened.

Nielson and Fultz (1995), based on survey data, find that the key factor in determining whether a religion will inspire violence or quietism in an individual is whether that individual's religiosity is intrinsic or extrinsic. A person whose religiosity is intrinsic considers religion an end in itself, but someone whose religiosity is extrinsic considers religion as a means to other ends. Intrinsic beliefs tend to lead to lower levels of conflict, but extrinsic beliefs tend to lead to more conflictive behavior.

All of this describes a paradox where most religions are interpreted by their adherents as the bearers of peace as well as the bearers of the sword. The ambiguities of life lead to ambiguities in the sacred. That is, in life we often need justifications for both violence and peace and this leads to the multiple interpretations of religious doctrine known as "internal pluralism" (Appleby, 2000: 25-55). This can be alternatively described as an "ambivalence" over religious doctrine which leads to "divergent interpretations" (Lewy, 1974: 555-556). While the violent aspects of religion tend to be more often emphasized, or at least more often recognized, the peaceful aspects can be an important tool for conflict resolution (Gopin, 2000). Thus, religions have multiple traditions and religious leaders must choose between them. As is discussed in more detail in chapters 6 and 7, this role of the leadership can be crucial in determining which element of religion will be emphasized at a given time and place.

Are Muslims More Conflict Prone than Followers of Other Religions?

Despite the fact that all religions appear to have the potential for both violence and quietism, the question of whether or not some religions are more conflict prone than others is an issue that should be addressed. For example, it is commonly believed in the West that Islamic groups tend to exhibit violent tendencies more often and more intensely than others. *It is important to emphasize that this author is not endorsing this stereotype.* However, it must be acknowledged that, right or wrong, the stereotype does exist, which begs the question of whether there is any truth behind it.

The stereotype of the Islamic militant has become prevalent in the West especially since the late 1970s. The Islamic revolution in Iran was one of the major impetuses for this stereotype. The daily drama of young Islamic militants holding Americans hostage for reasons barely understandable to the American public created a vivid impression. The stereotype has been perpetuated by the continuing behavior of Iran's theocratic government, as well as the demonization of the Iranian government by U.S. politicians and the Western media. Other events have added to the perpetuation of this stereotype. These include, but are by no means limited to: the Islamic involvement in rebellions and violent conflict in Afghanistan, Algeria, Egypt, and the Kashmir province of India; the sectarian war in Lebanon; the rebellion by the Muslims in Chechenia against Russia; the violent Palestinian campaign against the state of Israel followed by the violent resistance of Hamas and other Islamic militant groups to the Palestinian-Israeli peace process; the various conflicts in the former Yugoslavia; the bombing of the World Trade Center in New York by a small Islamic militant group; the bomb attack on U.S. troops in Saudi Arabia, apparently by Islamic militants; and the various activities supported by Islamic extremist Usama Bin Laden including the events of September 11, 2002.

This violent image has also merged with the image of nationalist terror movements by Arab groups in the 1970s and 1980s, despite the fact that many of these nationalist groups do not profess to be particularly religious. This stereotype has become prevalent in Western media, policy-making, and academic circles.[9] There is even some empirical evidence to support these claims.[10] Some other religious groups evoke a similar violent stereotype, among these: Christian fundamentalists who violently oppose abortion; Jewish "settlers" living on the West Bank and in Gaza; and the conflict between Catholics and Protestants in Northern Ireland. However, it is clear that no other religious group is perceived in the West to exhibit more violent tendencies than Islamic groups. Whether this is an accurate perception of reality is an open question.

A question of this nature cannot be answered by anecdotal evidence. Those who perceive Islamic groups to be more conflict prone and those who disagree with this stereotype can cite numerous examples. The debate surrounding Huntington's (1993 and 1996) contention that "Islam has bloody borders" is an excellent example of this.[11] Only a more objective quantitative analysis has any hope of shedding some light on this question. The data from this study can help to assess this question using a large-n, cross-sectional analysis of ethnoreligious groups. Because this study deals only with ethnoreligious conflict, it has some limitations. The most serious of these limitations is that it focuses only on ethnic conflict and does not deal with other types of conflict, including conflicts between the secular and religious elements of a society. For example, the conflict between the Coptic minority and the Muslim majority in Egypt is included, but the conflict between the country's Islamic fundamentalists and its more secular government is not. Even with these limitations, this study does provide an objective means for comparing certain types of religious conflicts and, as such, can shed light on the questions of whether religion is more important in conflicts involving Islamic groups and whether these groups are more conflict prone.

The three major religious groupings analyzed here are Christianity, Islam, and all other religions. While there are clearly major divisions within both Christianity and Islam, not to mention many the different religions within the "other" category, these more general categories have been selected so that each category has a sufficient number of cases for meaningful statistical analysis. The analysis looks at the characteristics of ethnoreligious conflict based on both the religion of the minority group involved in the conflict as well as the religion of the dominant group involved in the conflict.[12]

There are 105 cases in this study. For each case there is a minority group and a majority group. There are 40 Islamic minorities, of which 35 are Sunni, 4 are Shi'i, and 1 is coded as "other Islamic sect" (the Ahmadis in Pakistan). There are 29 Christian minorities, of which 7 are Catholic, 7 are Protestant, and 15 are coded as "other Christian sect."[13] There are 36 minority groups coded as "other." These include 19 animist minorities, 6 Hindu minorities, 4 Buddhist minorities, 4 minorities that have members of more than one religion, and one each of Sikhs, Bahai, and Druze. There are 35 Islamic majority groups, 25 of which are Sunni, 8 are Shi'i, and 2 are coded as "other Islamic sect."[14] There are 48 Christian majority groups, of which 12 are Catholic, 7 are Protestant and 29 are coded as "other Christian sect." There are 22 majority groups coded as "other." This includes 11 Buddhist groups, the 6 cases in India, which has a Hindu majority, the 3 cases in China which is coded as having a secular majority, and the 2 cases in Israel which has a Jewish majority. For a full listing of the groups in this study, see appendix A.

There are three aspects of ethnoreligious conflict compared here. The first is the comparative importance of religion to the conflict. The second is the comparative level of the conflict itself; that is whether Islamic groups, in fact, engage in higher levels of conflict than Christian and other groups. The third is the nexus between religion and democracy. According to the stereotype, Islamic groups should be involved in conflicts in which religion is more important, the level of the conflict is higher, and be associated with more autocratic states.

The findings with regard to how important religion is to conflicts support this stereotype. There are two variables used here to measure this. The first is the relevance of religion to the conflict, which measures the importance of religious issues in comparison to other issues including economic, political, cultural, and autonomy issues. As shown in table 5.1, whether controlling for the religion of the minority or of the majority ethnoreligious group, religious issues are more important for Islamic groups than the other categories. In addition, Christian majority groups are considerably less likely to be involved in conflicts in which religion is important than all other types of groups. The second variable "combined religious factors" measures the absolute level of religious factors in the conflict, including religious discriminations, religious grievances, and religious legitimacy. The results for this variable, as shown in table 5.1, are similar to those for the first variable.

Another way to examine this data is to look not only at the religion of the majority or minority group separately but to look at the interaction between majority and minority groups. In table 5.2, the relevance of religion is assessed based on whether none, one, or both groups involved in the conflict are Muslim and whether none, one, or both groups involved are Christian. These results show that as the number of Islamic groups goes up, so does the relevance of religion to the conflict

Table 5.1: The Impact of Religion Controlling For Religion Type

	Minority Group			Majority Group		
	Islamic	Christian	Other	Islamic	Christian	Other
Relevance of Religion 1990s	1.58	1.37	1.19	2.00	0.79	1.41
Combined Religious Factors 1994-95	7.58	5.59	5.36	9.09	3.78	7.20

Table 5.2: The Impact of Religion Controlling for the Number of Islamic and Christian Groups

	Islamic Groups			Christian Groups		
	None	One	Both	None	One	Both
Relevance of Religion 1990s	0.64	1.57	2.83	1.94	1.10	0.25
Combined Religious Factors 1994-95	3.33	7.23	13.79	9.25	5.03	0.23

and as the number of Christian groups increases, the relevance of religion to the conflict decreases. The results for the "combined religious factors" variable, as shown in table 5.2, are similar. Thus, with regard to ethnoreligious conflict Islamic groups do, in fact, tend on average to be involved in conflicts in which religion is comparatively more important. In addition, Christian ethnoreligious groups tend to be involved, on average, in conflicts where religion is comparatively less important.

The next step is to assess the comparative level of ethnoreligious conflict between religion types. The first aspect of ethnoreligious conflict examined here is nonreligious grievances expressed by the minority group and nonreligious discrimination expressed by the majority group. It is important to note that these variables measure the type of discrimination and grievances involved, not their motivation. That is, these variables focus on whether the discrimination involves economic, political, or cultural restrictions and grievances expressed over these issues, but do not address whether the motivation for this discrimination is religious or not. As shown in table 5.3, Islamic minorities express the most nonreligious grievances, followed by "other" religious minorities and Christian minorities in that order. Muslim majority groups engage in more nonreligious discrimination than Christian majorities but not as much as "other" ethnoreligious majorities.

Table 5.3: Non-Religious Conflict Variables Controlling for Religion Type

	Minority Group Characteristics				Majority Group Characteristics	
	Grievances 1994-95	Protest 1995	Rebellion 1995	Democ. 1994	Discrim. 1994-95	Democ. 1994
Christian	4.29	1.17	0.90	4.45	6.77	6.67
Muslim	6.11	1.82	1.00	4.83	7.73	2.29
Other	5.44	1.49	0.72	4.78	9.11	4.27

The second aspect of ethnoreligious conflict examined here is the actual amount of conflict, as measured by protest and rebellion by ethnoreligious minorities in 1995. As shown in table 5.3, Islamic minorities engage in the most protest, followed by "other" religious minorities and Christian minorities in that order. Islamic minorities also engage in slightly more rebellion than Christian minorities and "other religious groups" engage in the lowest level of rebellion.

The one common factor that can be found when examining all of these aspects of ethnic conflict shown in table 5.3, is that Islamic groups consistently score higher on all ethnoreligious conflict variables than Christian groups. This is important to the stereotype of the Islamic militant because this stereotype is a Western stereotype. When Westerners see Muslims as violent, they are in fact seeing Muslims as violent in comparison to themselves. Since most Westerners are Christian, that Muslims consistently score higher on various measures of ethnoreligious conflict is probably an important element of the stereotype. However, it should be noted that some of the differences between Christians and Muslims, including the levels of rebellion and nonreligious discrimination, are not very large.

The final point of comparison between religious groups is the level of democracy of the state in which they live. As shown in table 5.3, while there is almost no difference in the level of democracy when controlling for the religion of the ethnoreligious minority, there is a considerable difference when controlling for the religion of the majority. Islamic majorities on average rule, by far, the least democratic states and Christian majorities rule the most democratic states. This opens the question of whether the finding that religion is more important in conflicts involving Islamic majorities is due to something inherent in the religion or whether it is due to the autocratic nature of regimes in Islamic states. That is, these results indicate that autocracy may provide an alternate explanation for the differences between Islamic and other regimes, especially Christian regimes.

Table 5.4: Religious and Ethnic Conflict Factors Controlling for the Level of Democracy in 1994

	Religious Relevance 1990s	Combined Religious Factors 1994-95	Non-Religious Grievances 1994-95	Non-Religious Discrim. 1994-95
Less Democratic (0-5)	1.57	7.39	8.09	4.51
More Democratic (6-10)	1.11	5.34	7.13	6.14

This alternate hypothesis is tested in table 5.4 by assessing the differences between religious relevance, the "combined religious factors" variable, nonreligious discrimination, and nonreligious grievances controlling for the level of democracy. The results show that the less democratic regimes score higher on all of these variables except nonreligious grievances. These results clearly show that the autocratic nature of Islamic governments can explain much of the significance of religion to ethnic conflicts in which these regimes are engaged.

However, this alternate explanation is problematic for several reasons. While the comparative democratic nature of governments can explain the behavior of majority groups, it cannot explain the behavior of minority groups. The average level of autocracy and democracy of the states in which all types of ethnoreligious minorities live is nearly the same, yet religion is, on average, a more important issue in conflicts involving Islamic minorities. Even among majority groups, the level of democracy can only explain part of the differences. The differences between Muslim and Christian majorities in relevance of religion to the conflict and "combined religious factors" are greater than the differences between the more and less democratic governments. Also, the interaction between majority and minority show differences in the levels of religious relevance to the conflict and "combined religious factors" for which the level of democracy cannot account. However, the differences in the level of nonreligious discrimination between Islamic and Christian governments and between more and less democratic governments are about the same. Thus, the level of democracy may be able to explain the comparatively high level of repression engaged in by Islamic majorities, but it cannot fully explain that religion is more important in conflicts involving Islamic groups.

Despite this, even if one accepts the explanation that it is the nature of the regime that is responsible for religion being an important issue and the comparatively high level of repression by Islamic majorities, one must still answer the question of why Islamic regimes are less democratic. That is, if there is some connection between Islam and the lack of democracy, one can not use democracy to explain away the differences between the behavior of Islamic and non-Islamic majority groups. To do so simply changes the question of why is religion more important to Islamic regimes and why do they engage in more repression to one of why are Islamic regimes less democratic, thereby causing them to discriminate more as well as causing religion to be more an important issue?

In all, as far as ethnoreligious conflicts are concerned, there is some justification for the stereotype of the Islamic militant. This is especially so when the differences between Christians and Muslims are taken into account. However, these differences are less marked in the absolute level of conflict than in the importance of religion to the conflict. That is, while religion is considerably more important an issue in ethnoreligious conflicts involving Muslims, the differences in the actual level of the conflict are relatively small. Also, it is clear that there are many Muslim groups involved in conflicts where religion is not particularly important. For instance, the conflict between the Islamic Lezghin minority in Azerbaijan, an Islamic majority republic, has little to do with religion and focuses mostly on issues of protection of their ethnic identity and demands for some form of autonomy. Similarly, there are conflicts that involve Christian groups in which religion is important, including the Christian minorities in Iran and Egypt. In other words, despite a tendency by Islamic ethnoreligious groups to involve religion in conflicts and a tendency by Christian groups to avoid such involvement, it cannot be said that Islamic groups always involve religion in their conflicts and Christian groups never involve religion in theirs.

Thus, it is clear that religious doctrine by itself is not an explanation for when and why religion inspires conflict or quietism. Such a conclusion would be completely illogical in light of the fact that in many cases, the same doctrine has inspired both violence and quietism at different times and places. While the likelihood of religiously inspired violence may vary from religion to religion, the possibility for both violent and quietist behavior still exists. Even if the probability that any given religion would inspire violence were known, we would know only how often that religion would inspire violence, but not when. That is, it could tell us which religions would be more likely to inspire conflict but not when that conflict would occur. Accordingly, it is necessary to look for factors outside of the specifics of religious doctrines and ideologies to explain when and why religion inspires conflict. Thus, the pertinent question is not one of comparative theology but, rather, it is one that asks what is it that causes the adherents of a religion to use their doctrine to support violent or quietist activities?

Given this, it is clear that the theories which predict that some religions are more violent than others are neither comprehensive nor dynamic. They are not comprehensive because they only look at which religions tend to be more violent, but not when that violence surfaces and when it does not. They are not dynamic because, since such theories have only the one proposition that for whatever reason some religions are more conflict prone than others, there is no possibility of relating that proposition to other propositions.

Category #2: Environmental Theories

Environmental theories posit that some change in the international environment is responsible for the recent rise in religious conflict. These theories are discussed in more detail in chapter 3, in the context of why many believe that there has been a recent resurgence of religion. One such theory is Huntington's (1993 and 1996) argument that the end of the Cold War has contributed to the rise in religious conflict.

Another example of an environmental theory is Juergensmeyer's (1993) argument that the loss of faith in secular nationalist ideologies in the Third World has led to religiously based opposition to secular nationalist governments. As will be recalled, Juergensmeyer cites several reasons for this loss of faith. First, secular nationalism promised political freedom, economic prosperity, and social justice but many governments which have subscribed to this ideology have failed to fulfill these promises. Second, secular nationalism is perceived by many in the non-Western world as a foreign ideology imposed from outside without any local authenticity or legitimacy. Third, the imposition of secular nationalism by governments in former colonies has led to the accusation that the leaders of these former colonies are perpetuating colonialism through their espousal of secular nationalism. Fourth, secular nationalism has been associated with cultural colonialism, which is said to erode the traditional aspects of society along with the influence of religion in society. According to Juergensmeyer, the loss of faith in secular nationalism caused by these four factors has resulted in a resurgence of religious ideologies. Although his arguments deal mostly with the non-Western world, many of them also apply in the Western context.

Juergensmeyer's arguments are part of a larger body of literature, also discussed in chapter 3, which argues that the imperatives of modernization have led to a resurgence of religion. In addition to Juergensmeyer's argument that secular ideologies are losing their legitimacy, religion is experiencing a resurgence because: modernization has failed to provide the economic prosperity that many expected it to provide; modernization has led to many unsettling consequences, including the alienation of those left out of the process and the breakdown in community values, both of which have led to a religious backlash; modern technology has allowed religious institutions to extend their influence; greater political participation has led to the participation of those with religious agendas; communications technology has allowed for greater international coordination of religious efforts; and greater religious freedom and more individual choice in selecting a religion has led to greater individual interest in religion.

These environmental theories provide considerable insight into why there is religious conflict in the current political, social, and economic environment. They also provide some general information on the nature of that conflict and the issues over which there is religious conflict. However, they cannot predict which religious group will engage in religiously inspired violence and which will not. That is, these theories can predict whether the aggregate level of religious conflict in the world will rise or fall, but they do not do well at predicting the specific conflicts that will occur. Huntington's "clash of civilizations" thesis argues only that the end of the Cold War removed systemic restraints on conflict. Juergensmeyer's argument predicts that any Third World state which has a government guided by a secular nationalist ideology is at risk of a religiously based rebellion. However, he provides inadequate means to determine which governments are most at risk. The argument that modernization has contributed to religious conflict is insightful, but sheds little light on why one religious group rebels and another does not. Thus, this body of theory cannot be called comprehensive because it looks only at systemic factors. In addition, these propositions are not arranged into a dynamic framework.

Category #3: Structural Theories

The third type of explanation, structural theories, takes a more institutional approach. This type of theory tends to focus on the relationship that the clergy and religious institutions have with government institutions, elite groups, and opposition groups. While this type of approach is excellent at highlighting the interactions of political and religious elites and institutions, it tends to ignore other factors.

Kowalewski and Greil (1990) provide an example of this type of theory. They believe that it is the structure of the relationship between religious and political elites that determines church participation in rebellion. Specifically, the relevant factors are "(1) the degree of tension in the social contract forged by state official-dom and the church hierarchy; and (2) the configuration of social relations among political and religious elites in religious bodies" (Kowalewski and Greil, 1990 515). When the social contract between the political and religious elites is strong and mutually beneficial, the church will generally support the regime. Such a mutually beneficial social contract usually consists of an official or unofficial agreement between the religious and political elites in which the religious elites use the church to support the regime in return for noninterference or support by the state. Also, participation by the political elite in the church will lessen the religious elite's support for revolution.[15]

Gill and Keshavarzian (1999) paint a similar picture of the relationship between religious and political elites. The relations between religious and secular actors are not "conceived exclusively in ideological terms." Rather, these relations are based on their interests and strategic calculations. Religious elites have an interest in increasing their membership and enforcing their belief. The best way to do this is early socialization, which can be achieved through privileged access to education systems as well as using government power to eliminate or marginalize rivals. Political actors primarily want survival, which means eliminating or marginalizing their rivals. Religious leaders can provide the support of their constituents. Thus, church-state conflict is most likely when either of the two sides feels secure enough that it does not need the other or when one side feels that the other cannot provide the security it needs. In other words, conflict between religious and political elites occurs when either one side does not need the social contract between them, or one side is not able to fulfill its half of that social contract.

Lincoln (1985: 268-281) takes a similar structural view of religion and revolution. He discusses three types of religions: religions of the status quo; religions of resistance; and religions of revolution. A religion of the status quo is basically a mutually beneficial social contract between religious elites and the state, similar to that described by Kowalewski and Greil, with the addition that such religious elites have the goal of ideological hegemony. That is, the religious elites want their religious ideology to be the primary or only accepted ideology in their society. A religion of resistance is, in short, any religion other than the dominant one. Such religions tend to challenge the ideological hegemony of the dominant religion because, by definition, they usually advocate a religious ideology other than the dominant one. The main goal of the adherents of these religions is survival, and they usually do not attempt to spread their influence outside of their own geographical and social milieu. A religion of resistance becomes a religion of revolution when the objective conditions in society worsen and its adherents "successfully articulate a new theory of political legitimacy." This poses a challenge to the legitimacy of the dominant religion and allows the advocates of the religion of revolution to recruit new members from the adherents of the dominant religion. If successful, a religion of revolution becomes the new religion of the status quo. Although Lincoln does not discuss it, his theory can be extended to ideologies. That is, secular ideologies can also be used to articulate theories of political legitimacy and compete with religions in the marketplace of ideas.

Stark and Bainbridge (1985: 506-530) outline a structural theory similar to Lincoln's. They argue that for a religious monopoly to exist it must be backed by the coercive power of the state. The only reason the state would provide this support is if the religion, in turn, provides the state supernatural sanctions for its power. Thus, any political dissenters automatically become religious dissenters and are forced to either support another religion or oppose all religion. They also note that opposition movements aspiring to unattainable goals will usually seek religious/supernatural support for their movement because such support makes the attainment of impossible goals believable.

Billings (1990: 4-8) takes a more evolutionary or dialectical approach. He argues that religious beliefs and practices are often out of touch with the real conditions of people's lives. As a result, the old religion is juxtaposed with the current mass beliefs and opinions. The outcome is a new and progressive religion that is often blunted by contradictions and incoherence.

Durham (1996) describes the relationship between the type of support a government provides for religious institutions and the level of religious freedom within a state. He describes seven categories for this relationship: (1) regimes with established or official churches endorsed by the government; (2) regimes with endorsed churches–"regimes that fall short of formally affirming one particular church . . . but acknowledge that one particular church has a special place in the country's traditions" (Durham, 1996: 20); (3) cooperationist regimes in which certain religions benefit from state patronage but no religion is officially endorsed; (4) accommodationist regimes which have separation of church and state but the government behaves with a benevolent neutrality toward one religion; (5) separationist regimes where there is separation of church and state and a slightly hostile government attitude toward religion; (6) regimes that behave with "inadvertent insensitivity" toward religion by making little distinction between the regulation of religious and other types of institutions and; (7) regimes that are hostile to religion and engage in overt persecution against it.

The relationship between these types of regimes and religious discrimination is a U-shaped relationship. That is, those governments with the strongest and the weakest affiliations with religion tend to be the most discriminatory, while those in the middle tend to be the most tolerant. Governments which strongly affiliate with a single religion, such as those with official churches, tend to be intolerant of all other religions. Aggressively secular regimes tend to be hostile to all religions. The most tolerant tend to be accomodationist regimes which are neutral with respect to religion. As Durham notes, an important implication of this is that aggressive separation of church and state can become hostility toward religion.

These structural theories, while informative, are limited. They focus mostly on the direct relations between religious and state institutions and elites. For Kowalewski and Greil, as well as for Gill and Keshavarzian, the only important factor is the relationship between church and state elites. Durham only looks at the level of state endorsement for religion. Lincoln's theory focuses on conflicts between religious institutions for control of the state and the minds of the people. Stark and Bainbridge focus on religion as a legitimizing force. Unlike the rest, Billings arguments do not focus on the elites and rather focus on the evolution of mass beliefs. However, it is also limited in that it focuses only on this evolution.

Thus, while this type of theory may be dynamic it is generally not comprehensive. The existing structural theories include several propositions that are related to each other in a dynamic framework. That is, the predictions made by each proposition in the theory are dependent upon or somehow connected to the predictions made in the other propositions. However, the existing structural theories tend not to be comprehensive in that they look at only one aspect of the involvement of religion in conflict. Kowalewski and Greil focus on religion as an institution, Gill and Keshavarzian focus on elite interests, Lincoln, as well as Stark and Bainbridge, focus mainly on religion as a source of legitimacy, Billings focuses on mass beliefs, and Durham focuses on the level of state sponsorship for religion. Also, structural theories of religion and conflict are not comprehensive in that they tend to ignore the general theories of conflict developed by social scientists.

Category #4: Laundry Lists

The laundry list approach is in many ways the opposite approach to that taken by structural theorists. This approach, which consists of a list of several propositions positing relationships between religion and conflict, is often comprehensive due to the length of the list. However, this approach is rarely dynamic because little attempt is made to relate these propositions to each other or to any general theory on conflict.

Lewy (1974: 539-41, 585-6) takes the laundry list approach and lists several ways that religion can manifest politically in support of a rebellion:

- Revolutionary messianism, the struggle for earthly paradise, can result in revolts when there is social or political distress or disorientation without a clearly perceived cause.

- Militant religious nationalism materializes in "situations of awakening national consciousness," where "religion supplies a sense of national identity." Such a situation is likely to occur in the context of an anti-colonial struggle.

- "The leaders of religious bodies with a developed ecclesiastical organization support a revolutionary upheaval because they are sympathetic to the aims of this revolution, or because they are protecting the interests of the religious institution."

- "Individual theologians or laymen support a revolutionary movement to give a concrete social and political meaning to the transcendent elements of their faith."

- Religion can be manipulated for political purposes.

It should be noted that, as Lewy points out, these manifestations of religious support for rebellion are not mutually exclusive. It is theoretically possible for religious nationalism to manifest itself with the support of church leaders in the form of messianism, which gives "concrete social and political meaning to the transcendent elements of [the people's] faith" and that this movement will be manipulated for political purposes.

A more blatant example of the laundry list approach is the list of the factors that contribute to the materialization of religion in politics provided by the United Council of Churches (in Williamson, 1990: 246)

- religion as a component of nationalism, especially ethnonationalism,

- religious factors exacerbating tensions or conflicts whose root causes are sociopolitical and economic,

- religious factors and sentiments being deliberately used to heighten tensions,

- religious notions of state transforming political institutions and leading to conflicts,

- religious fundamentalism or fanaticism influencing state policies substantially,

- erosion of the secular and the identification of the secular with the West,

- use of religion in political processes and in influencing policies of governments

- growing lack of confidence in governments in many parts of the world by minorities, leading to opposition and conflict, and making use of religion,

- tensions resulting from new financial power acquired (from outside) by previously marginalized sections,

- religious conflicts used by outside forces to destabilize countries.

This laundry list approach used by the United Council of Churches and, to a lesser extent, Lewy, can be called comprehensive in that the lists hit upon most of the important factors in the relationship religion has with rebellion and violence. However, this approach cannot be considered dynamic in that it does not do a good job of putting these factors into perspective. That is, the laundry lists identify many pieces to the puzzle but do an incomplete job of putting that puzzle together. Some of the items on these laundry lists can be contributing factors to others, such as a religious notion of nationalism leading to "religious notions of state transforming political institutions." Some, such as a lack of confidence in a government and church leaders using this situation to further their own interests, can combine to have an additive affect on the level of rebellion and violence. Also, some, like "religious conflicts [being] used by outside forces to destabilize countries," can only come into play when rebellion or violence has already started. To be fair, Lewy does discuss the items on his list in considerable detail but he does not do a very good job of integrating them. If Lewy, the United Council of Churches, or other authors using the laundry list approach made such connections in their discussions of religion and conflict, their theories would be considerably more dynamic. To become truly dynamic, however, the laundry list approaches would also have to take into account the general body of theory on conflict.

Category #5: Theories on Specific Types or Aspects of Conflict

Many who study religion and conflict do so while looking at only one type of conflict or one social or political phenomenon that impacts on conflict. One of the most prominent categories of conflict associated with religion is terrorism. Many aspects of religious terrorism are posited to be different from other types of terrorism. First, for secular terrorists, violence is a means for achieving a political end, but for religious terrorists it can be the end itself. Second, secular terrorists usually use violence to influence an audience other than themselves, but religious terrorists often care about no audience other than themselves. Third, secular terrorists often see themselves as fighting to change a political and social system. But religious terrorists generally wish to replace the system altogether. Fourth, secular terrorists tend to focus on creating a new future, but religious terrorists tend to focus on the past and try to recreate what they believe to be the conditions that existed at the founding time of their religion. Fifth, secular terrorists can change their goals, but religious terrorists tend to be restricted in this by their doctrines. Sixth, religious concepts of martyrdom make suicide attacks more likely. Seventh, both the timing and targets of religious terrorists usually have religious significance. Eighth, religious terrorists who believe that a messianic event is imminent can use this to justify greater violence than most secular beliefs (Hoffmam, 1995; Kennedy, 1999; Martin, 1989: 356-357; Ranstorp, 1996; Rappoport, 1988 and 1999).

Other specific social and political phenomena which have been posited to be influenced by religion include international conflict (Hendnderson 1997), genocide (Fein, 1990: 49), ethnic cleansing (Osiander, 2000: 785), international diplomacy, (Johnston, 1994), Democracy (Midlarsky, 1998; Oomen, 1994), the family (Hardacre, 1993), environmentalism (Taylor, 1998), perceptions of the nature of human rights (Van der Vyver, 1996), public school policy (Wayland, 1997), nationalism (Smith, 1999 & 2000), the origins of the Westphalian state system (Philpott, 1999), the process of globalization (Beyer, 1994), political culture (Latin, 1978), personal wealth (Schbley, 2000), and economic policies (Kuran, 1991; Rosser, 1993).

This type of literature is perhaps the second most common type of study on religion and conflict and the most common that usually has theoretical content that can easily be applied to many different cases. However, these types of theories, while sometimes dynamic, are by definition not comprehensive because they examine one social or political phenomenon at the expense of all others.

Category #6: Case Studies

The final, and probably most common, type of approach to the study of religion and conflict is the case study approach. The prohibitive size of the case study literature on any one of several conflicts alone, much less this literature in its entirety, makes a review of this literature difficult if not impossible. Accordingly, the discussion presented here of the case study literature is limited to some general comments about this type of approach.

The ability to discern the details and nuances of a specific case is the major advantage of the case study approach. The ability to look into the details of a case allows for the discovery of variables and relationships that were not thought to exist. For this reason, the case study approach is useful for asking the questions of what happened? and why did it happen? in instances where there is no coherent theory to answer these questions. In other words, case studies are often the sources of hypotheses and theory building.

The major drawback of the case study approach is in the area of generalizability. The case study approach rarely uses more than a few cases and most such studies are limited to a single case. Although the conclusions drawn from this approach can be stated in general terms which can be tested elsewhere, such results cannot, in and of themselves, support a general conclusion. That is, just because some religious factor appears to be important in Algeria, for instance, that does not mean it will be important in Sri Lanka. In addition, it is often the case that different observers using the case study approach will come to immensely different conclusions about the same case, thus making this approach even more difficult to use as the basis of generalization.

The nature and implications of this drawback are discussed in detail by Deutsch (1963: 53):

> Introspection, intuition [and] insight [are] processes that are not verifiable among different observers. . . . But even though we can understand introspectively many facts and relations which exist, it is also true that we can understand in our fertile imagination very many relations that do not exist at all. What is more, there are things in the world that we can not understand readily with our imagination as it is now constituted, even though we may be able to understand them . . . in the future, after we have become accustomed to the presuppositions of such understanding. We can, therefore, do nothing more than accept provisionally these guesses or potential insights. . . . If we want to take them seriously, we must test them. We can do this by selecting . . . data, verifying them [and] forming explicit hypotheses as to what we expect to find. . . . And we then finally test these explicit hypotheses by confrontation with the data. . . . In the light of these tests we revise our criteria of relevance, we get new and revised data and we set up new methods of testing.

What Deutsch is basically saying is that the introspections, intuitions, and insights derived from case studies are unreliable and, therefore, more scientific methods are needed to test them. Such scientific methods would include a large-n aggregate data approach. Similar arguments are made by Brecher (1999: 224-227). However, this author knows of no study using such an approach toward religious conflict in general, much less religious ethnic conflict, except for a very few studies, such as those of Henderson (1997) and Rummel (1997), which examine if conflict

98   *Chapter 5*

is more likely between certain religions or if the religions of the groups involved in the conflict are different. Thus, there has been no attempt to scientifically test the different and often contradictory theories of religion and conflict, other than a few studies which ask if religious differences alone are correlated with more conflict. While these studies are interesting and do reveal that when religious differences exist, conflict is more likely and more intense, they do not constitute the testing of theories that describe how religion influences conflict. They only note that it probably does.

Be that as it may, it is clear that the case study approach cannot be comprehensive. Looking at only one or a few cases and excluding all others, by definition, can not be comprehensive. Also, while case studies have the potential to be dynamic within the context of the case in question, the dynamism of the case study literature varies greatly.

Thus, the existing theories and literature on religion, violence, and revolution are all lacking. Some explanations are dynamic but are limited to various aspects or instances of the relationship between religion and violence and revolution. Others are comprehensive, having extensive lists of factors contributing to religious violence and revolution, which may or may not cover all aspects of this phenomenon, but fail to tie them together in a dynamic framework. Few, if any, of these theories take into account the general body of theory on conflict. Also, none of these existing theories has been tested beyond the case study level. Thus, a theory that is more generalizable, dynamic, and coherent as well as testable by scientific methods is needed.

Conclusion

Although questions of when, why, and how religion plays a role in ethnic conflict have not been answered, these questions have been placed in the proper context to evoke meaningful answers. In chapter 2, the nature of religion and its role in society, politics, and conflict are defined. The intellectual environment in which the existing theories on religion, politics, society, and conflict evolved are described in chapters 3 and 4. Those chapters also address the major theoretical objections to engaging in such a line of enquiry. In this chapter, the existing body of theory is assessed and found wanting. In doing so, several important conclusions have emerged.

First, despite the predictions of the various forms of the modernization and secularization schools of thought, religion has not at any time become an epiphenomenal force. Rather, it has continued to play an important role in politics and society. This role has been made increasingly apparent by recent events. However these schools of thought have influenced the study of religion and conflict, mostly by stifling it for a considerable period of time. Also, the debate over these theories has demonstrated that modernity has profoundly influenced the interaction between religion and society.

Second, the role that religion plays in politics and society is not, as the functionalist school of thought argues, merely a manifestation of other more basic forces. While religion is affected by other political and social forces, it nevertheless plays a role in politics and society that is independent of those forces.

Third, the role religion plays in society includes providing a framework with which individuals and groups are able to comprehend the world. Such a framework usually includes a code of behavior and the impetus for the creation of institutions. Both of these serve to link individual actions with the framework. Such a framework is also capable of legitimating governments as well as oppositional movements.

Fourth, the fundamentalist movements which have received so much recent attention do not represent any basic change in the role of religion in politics and society. Rather, they represent a particular form of religious framework. The fundamentalist framework emphasizes the proper modes of behavior that must be adopted in private life as well as the imperative to use the political system to enforce these standards. These standards of behavior derive from what is considered to be an authentic and literal interpretation of original religious scriptures and doctrines. However, fundamentalism is a uniquely modern phenomenon in that it is a rejection of the secular values inherent in modernity, and because fundamental- ist movements make extensive use of modern technology and techniques.

Fifth, religious frameworks, especially those based upon long-established religions, tend to have diverse and complex traditions that can and have been interpreted in order to support both violent and "quietist" actions. Thus, anyone in search of an explanation for the connection between religion and violence must look beyond religious ideologies and doctrines for that explanation.

Sixth, the existing body of theory on religion and conflict is lacking in several ways. The failures of this body of theory basically boil down to the lack of a general, coherent, dynamic, and comprehensive theory of religion and conflict which has been integrated into the general body of theory on conflict. Also, no such theory has been tested using scientific methods based upon the large-n cross sectional approach.

Finally, other than case studies, there have been few studies of ethnic religious conflicts. However, this literature does make it clear that religion is an aspect of ethnicity whose salience toward ethnic identity and ethnic conflicts varies over time, along with shifting perceptions of ethnic identity by ethnic groups and by those with whom they interact.

All of these points are crucial to the study of religion and conflict. Some are necessary to justify engaging in any theoretical or empirical work on the subject and some are necessary to provide the proper foundation and/or context for any such work. In the following chapters, this foundation is used to develop and test a more comprehensive and dynamic theory of religion and conflict in the ethnic context.

Notes

1. For more details on the Buddhist opposition to China in Tibet see the Minorities at Risk webpage at www.umd.edu/cidcm/inscr/mar.

2. Weber similarly argues that "the historical origins of religion resided in the search to control the empirical world for entirely secular and instrumental purposes" (Turner, 1993: 16).

3. For a discussion on religious perspectives on just war from the perspective of several religions see Smock (1992). For a more general discussion of the concept of just war see Walzer (1977). For a discussion of St. Augustine's views on war, see Deane (1963: 154-171).

4. For a more detailed discussion of the nation of *Amalek*, see the *Encyclopedia Judaica.*

5. For a discussion of this rebellion and its religious aspects, see Rapoport (1984).

6. For a discussion of religiously inspired violence in Israel, see Sprinzak (1991).

7. For more details on this ideology, see the discussion in chapter 6 of this work.

8. For a discussion between Jewish ideological radicalism and the exile, see Don-Yehiyah (1992).

9. See for example, "U.S. Official Calls Muslim Militants a Threat to Africa" *New York Times,* 1/1/92, 3; "Mahatma vs. Rama" *Time,* 6/24/91, 35; Benjamin J. Barber, "Jihad vs. McWorld" *Atlantic Monthly,* 1992, 269 (3), 53-55, 58-62, 64-65; "Ethnic Strife Succeeds Cold War's Ideological Conflict" *Washington Post,* 12/18/94, 36; and Huntington (1993 and 1996).

10. Ibrahim (1998) documents that the Middle East, a mostly Islamic region, while constituting only 8 percent of the world's population, accounted for about 25 percent of the world's conflicts since 1945. Also, Midlarsky (1998) found that Islamic governments are more likely to be autocratic.

11. Huntington (1993 & 1996) claims that "Islam has bloody borders," meaning that Islamic groups are more often in violent conflict with their non-Islamic neighbors than any other religious group. Islam is, in particular, expected to be in conflict with the West. Huntington's arguments concerning Islam and the West are, to say the least, not uncontroversial and there are several opposing arguments. First, some, like Ajami (1993) Bartley (1993), Esposito (1995), Fuller and Lesser (1996), and Monshipouri (1998) argue that Huntington mistakes conflicts caused by economic, national, political, cultural, psychological, post-colonial, modernity, and strategic issues with civilizational conflict. Second, some argue that Islam is not the threat many believe it to be. Third, others, like Kirkpatrick et. al. (1993) and Mahbubani (1993) argue that rather than rejecting it, the West is being embraced by other civilizations. Fourth, others, including Beedham (1999), Kader (1998), and Monshipouri (1998), argue that conflicts occur more often within the Islamic civilization than between it and other civilizations. Fifth, Hunter (1998) adds that the rise in Islamic fundamentalism is not unique to the Islamic civilization and furthermore, the enthusiasm for Islamic fundamentalism is waning.

On the other hand, many like Gregg (1997), Gungwu (1997a and 1997b), Hardjono (1997), Harris (1996), Lewis (1993), Murphey (1998), Naff (1998), Seamon (1998), and Walid (1997) agree with Huntington's arguments. Even some of Huntington's critics, like

Hassner (1997) and Heilbrunn (1998), believe that there may be something to Huntington's arguments with regard to clashes between the Western and Islamic civilizations.

What all of these scholars have in common is that they cite anecdotal evidence. Thus both sides of this argument are easily able to find examples that support their side even though it is clear that both sides cannot be correct.

12. For a more detailed statistical analysis on the relationship between specific religions and ethnic conflict, see Fox (2000a).

13. The groups coded as other Christian sect include members of Orthodox Christian churches, groups whose members are of several Christian denominations, and cases where it was difficult to determine the minority's denomination.

14. Both of these cases occur in Nigeria where the coders were unable to specify to which sect of Islam the majority group belongs.

15. Kowalewski and Greil (1990: 515) also provide a checklist to evaluate the religious role in a revolution: use of religious symbols and ideas to justify rebellion; use of religious gathering sites as foci and sanctuary for rebels; religious funding, intelligence, and support; interpersonal and organizational ties between religious elites and rebellion; and direct participation by the church.

Chapter 6

A More Comprehensive Theory of Religion and Conflict

In chapter 5, it is argued that there is no adequate theory of religion and conflict. However, despite this lack, the building blocks for such a theory exist. These building blocks can be found in the general list of the properties that religion and ideology have in common, which was constructed and discussed in some detail in chapter 2. Four of the five items on this list describe the various social functions of religion:

- Religion provides a meaningful framework for understanding the world.

- Religion provides rules and standards of behavior that link individual actions and goals to this meaningful framework.

- Religion links individuals to a greater whole and sometimes provides formal institutions which help to define and organize that whole.

- Religion has the ability to legitimize actions and institutions.

It is argued here that the role religion plays in ethnic conflict is defined by these four social functions. That is, whenever any aspect of religion becomes involved in ethnic conflict, or, for that matter, becomes involved in most aspects of politics and society, it is as a direct result of one of these four social functions of religion. While this may appear to be simply another form of the laundry list approach, which is criticized in chapter 5, a discussion of the role that each of these social functions of religion plays in ethnic conflict will help to relate these propositions to each other as well as to the general conflict theory literature. Thus, these social functions of religion, in addition to providing a comprehensive understanding of the role of religion in conflict, can also be placed in a dynamic framework.

The focus of this chapter is to develop a generally applicable theory of religion and conflict. In the next chapter, this theory will be applied to the more specific case of ethnic conflict.

Social Function #1: Religion as a Meaningful Framework for Understanding the World

Human beings need some sort of belief system or framework in order to comprehend the world around them. This includes the need to understand the nature of the physical universe, how it was created and how it functions. It also includes more philosophical questions like, among others, why are some more fortunate than others? what is the nature a of man's soul? why does evil exist? is there life after death? and if so, how do we get there?

This basic human need is often, but by no means always, filled by religious frameworks. That is, religious frameworks provide their adherents with a basis for understanding reality which enables these adherents to comprehend the real world and to function in it. Thus, religious frameworks constitute an essential part of the psyche of their adherents. Accordingly, when a religious framework is challenged in any way, its adherents are also challenged at the most basic levels. In other words, an attack upon a religious framework also constitutes an attack upon an essential element of each individual adherent's very being. In a sense, such an attack constitutes an attack on the foundations of the adherent's physical and spiritual universe. Given this, it is not hard to argue that such a challenge is very likely to provoke a defensive reaction among the adherents of the challenged religious framework and that this defensive reaction is likely to be conflictive in nature. This is because they are not only defending their religion, they are also defending their personal and communal identities.

This argument is presented eloquently by Wentz. He argues that human beings are more than just biological creatures who simply process physical sensations and react to them. They are also open to the possibility of transcending their biological roots, attempting to understand the ultimate order, and finding meaning in their existence. In fact, they have a need to seek such understanding and meaning. Religion is one of the ways in which humans achieve this goal. Thus, religion is a tool for transcending biological existence and telling a story about ultimate order and meaning. For this reason, Wentz argues that "religiousness"[1] is fundamental to human nature (Wentz, 1987: 13-21).

For Wentz, religion has to do with one's place in the world and the manner in which the world is meaningfully put together. In fact, he believes that religion is, among other things, the ordering of space and time. Such beliefs and values concerning the ultimate order and the meaning of existence, according to Wentz, are by definition political. He describes them as the walls of religion. People build a psychological wall of religion around themselves and their religious communities in order to deal with reality, and they are prepared to defend it (Wentz, 1987: 35-36).

According to Wentz, some people will do anything to preserve the frameworks which they use to make sense of ordinary existence. For this reason, violence is frequently justified when these frameworks are threatened. Fanatics, as Wentz calls them, are not worried about their personal identities but, rather, are worried about the identities and social solidarity that their religious frameworks provide. For this reason many are often willing to sacrifice themselves for the sake of these communal identities and social solidarity. People need the security of absolutes that many religious frameworks provide and are willing to fight to protect them (Wentz, 1987: 53-70).

Geertz makes a similar argument in his discussion of "symbol systems," a concept very similar to that of religious frameworks, when he states that

> the thing we seem to be least able to tolerate is a threat to our powers of conception, a suggestion that our ability to create, grasp, and use symbols may fail us, for were this to happen we would be more helpless . . . . Man depends upon symbols and symbol systems with a dependence so great as to be decisive for his creational viability and, as a result, his sensitivity to even the remotest indication that they may prove unable to cope with one or another aspect of experience raises within him the gravest sort of anxiety (Geertz, 1966: 13-14).

Thus, like Wentz, Geertz argues that a threat to a religious framework, or as he calls it a "symbol system," will provoke a reaction from those who depend on it for their understanding of reality. Geertz further posits that three types of challenges to such frameworks exist: explaining natural events, explaining suffering, and explaining evil (Geertz, 1966: 14-24). However, Geertz does not take the next step and include challenges posed by other groups.

Little (1991: xxi) does consider challenges by other groups to constitute challenges to religious frameworks that can provoke a reaction. He describes three categories of such challenges to religious frameworks: an unorthodox belief, which is "a religious or ideological belief perceived as intolerable from the point of view of the orthodox belief system"; a political belief, which is "a religious or ideological belief perceived as threatening the existing polity simply by virtue of recommending an alternative government structure or character"; and a seditious belief, which is "a religious or ideological belief perceived as constituting incitement against an existing government." Gopin (2000: 14-16) argues that while religious belief systems can be a source of violence, they can also be used to oppose it.

Laustsen & Waever (2000: 719-725) also focus on how religious beliefs can lead to violence. They argue that "religion deals with the constitution of being as such." Accordingly a threat to a religion is an attack on one's identity and is therefore, by definition, a security issue. Furthermore, religious threats by others are seen as more threatening. It is harder to find room for compromise with enemies who are guided by faith and not power gains. The faith of these enemies also makes them unpredictable and dangerous, even ready to sacrifice themselves. Their faith can also make them more violent. This is because if they believe that they are at war, violent acts are deemed appropriate, even if others, who believe the world to be peaceful, see these acts as terrorism.

In another version of the argument linking religious frameworks and defensive violence, Seul (1999: 558-562) links religion to the concept of identity. He argues that "No other repositories of cultural meaning have historically offered so much in response to the human need to develop a secure identity. Consequently, religion often is at the core of individual and group identity." These religious identities are more resistant to change than other aspects of identity and thus contribute to social stability because they provide a world view to their adherents. This world view is a source of love, affirmation, and self-esteem and defines an ultimate reality for those who believe in it. Accordingly, denying that reality can lead to conflict. Kabalkova (2000) describes how such identities are linked to faith. Believers of faith-based world views are discouraged from subjecting their beliefs to scientific scrutiny. Truths are to be accepted on faith, protected by sanctions, and they define one's identity and understanding of the world.

The discussion in chapter 3 on the school of thought which argues that the imperatives of modernization, as well as other systemic factors, have led to a revitalization or resurgence of religion is also consistent with this argument. The proponents of this school argue that the processes associated with modernization and other systemic factors have encroached upon the understandings of reality advocated by many religious frameworks. This has caused many adherents of these frameworks to feel threatened and has provoked a response from them. This response includes what is being called the revitalization or resurgence of religion in the political arena. Thus, the provocation posed by modernization to the religious frameworks of many people has led to a defensive reaction that has contributed to the current resurgence or revitalization of religion.

Juergensmeyer (1997) makes this argument with regard to religious terrorism. He argues that most international terrorism in the 1980s and 1990s is based on combining religious frameworks with politics. For Juergensmeyer religion is

> not just an ethnic religious identity–such as Irish Catholic or Tamil Hindu–but the appropriation of an ideology of transformative significance, the sort of religious and political vision that transformed Iran after the Islamic revolution of 1978. Such an ideology . . . provides the vision and commitment that propels an activist into scenes of violence, and it supplies the ideological glue that makes that activist's community of support cohere (Juergensmeyer, 1997: 17).

The motivation for this violence is a rejection of secularism. "In their vision of a world gone bad, what most of us regard as ordinary politics–the secular politics of modern civil societies–is viewed as the enemy of religion." The targets of religious terrorists are symbols this enemy. These include: the 1994 nerve gas attack on Japanese subways by Aum Shineikyo's cult; the abortion clinics attacked by pro-life activists in the United States; tourist boats and hotels in Egypt because they were considered "impositions from a foreign culture"; the Shrine of the Patriarchs in Hebron, which was attacked by Baruch Goldstein in 1994 as symbolic of the Islamic occupation of the Jewish state; and "the World Trade Center and Oklahoma City federal building, along with airplanes, subways, and public houses," general symbols of "the power and stability of society itself."

In addition, it is important to note that previous empirical studies on the association between religiosity and violence are mixed. Rummel (1997) found that the more religious an ethnic group involved in an ethnic conflict, the more intense the violence. Nielson and Fultz (1995) found that those who believe religion is a means to another end are more likely to engage in violence. However, others, like Ellison (1999) and Marx (1967a and 1967b), found that increased religiosity leads to lower levels of violence.

In sum, religious frameworks are intimately connected with conflict because when these frameworks are challenged, their adherents are likely to react in their defense, often in a conflictive manner. This is true regardless of the position of these adherents in the sociopolitical hierarchy. That is, members of ruling elites being challenged from below and religious minorities whose religious frameworks are being challenged by the government or by other nongovernmental groups are similar in that they are likely to react in a conflictive manner to defend their challenged religious frameworks. This is because this aspect of the connection between religion and conflict is not political or economic. Rather, it is based on the role religion plays in individual frameworks of belief. Because everyone, regardless of their social standing, has such a framework (even if it is not always based on religion), an individual's position in the social, economic, and political order is only relevant to the extent that it provides him with the resources to actualize his desire to defend his belief system.

This argument can be summarized in the following proposition:

- *Proposition 1*: Any challenge to a religious framework is likely to provoke a defensive and often conflictive response from the adherents of that religious framework.

Social Function #2: Providing Rules and Standards of Behavior that Link Individual Actions and Goals to a Religious Framework

Religious frameworks usually provide rules and standards of behavior for their adherents. That is, religious frameworks usually include some sort of instructions guiding the behavior of their adherents. It is argued here that these rules and standards of behavior are often interpreted in a manner which requires the adherents of a religion to engage in behavior which is likely to provoke a conflict. There are two ways in which this can happen. First, the required actions are in and of themselves conflictive. Second, the required actions are likely to infringe upon another group's religious framework, forcing the second group to defend their beliefs.

That religious frameworks can inspire their adherents to engage in conflictive acts is not a difficult assertion to prove. All three of the Abrahamic religions have within them the concept of holy war, which has at times been put into action.[2] The same can be said for many other religious traditions. Haynes (1994: 14) makes an argument consistent with this assessment when he describes what he calls religio-political movements. He defines such movements as those movements "whose leaders utilize religious ideologies . . . to attack the sociopolitical legitimacy and economic performance of incumbent governments."

However, this is not the only way that the rules and standards of behavior contained in a religious framework can contribute to conflict. These rules and standards of behavior are often interpreted by the adherents of a religion as requiring actions which infringe upon the religious framework of those who adhere to another religion. That is, religions often inspire their believers to engage in actions which are likely to provoke conflicts with nonbelievers or the followers of another framework. Such provocative actions can consist of anything from outright holy war to attempts to impose a religiously inspired social, economic, and/or political agenda upon those who do not agree with that agenda. Thus, the first way in which religious rules and standards of behavior can contribute to conflict is included in the second. A holy war is a conflictive act in and of itself and often constitutes a challenge to the religious frameworks of other groups.

Haynes (1994: 30), in defining the characteristics of religiopolitical movements, implicitly agrees that such movements, by definition, attempt to impose their religiously inspired agenda upon others. These characteristics include seeking to transform the prevailing socio-religious situation; seeking power and influence; seeking to put religion into practice through political means; using religious myths and symbols to influence the political process; and espousing both religious and secular goals.

While Haynes is referring to organized movements, Little (1991) argues that the actions of ethnic groups are also influenced by their religious frameworks regardless of whether or not these groups also constitute organized religiopolitical movements. He notes that "religion or similar beliefs often play an active and prominent part in defining group identity and in picking out and legitimating particular ethnic and national objectives" (Little, 1991: xx). He also discusses what he calls a "warrant," which he defines as "a belief held by the dominant group that is taken to entitle that group to act intolerantly toward others" (Little, 1991: xxi). It is a small leap of logic to infer that such intolerant actions inspired by beliefs, which are often religious, are likely to provoke a conflictive response from the target of that intolerance.

Greenwalt (1988: 30) makes a similar argument at the individual level. His basic argument is that "religious convictions of the sort familiar in this society bear pervasively on people's ethical choices, including choices about laws and government policies." Thus, even in the absence of any organized group, religious frameworks can still independently inspire their individual adherents to make political choices which are likely to provoke those who disagree with the views advocated by these frameworks. Wayland (1997) provides some examples of how this has occurred in specific situations including the French opposition to the wearing of headscarves by Muslim women in schools, and the Canadian resistance, which was eventually overcome, to the wearing of ceremonial daggers in schools by Sikhs.

Several survey-based studies also find that religious affiliation influences political attitudes and behavior. For example, Hays (1995) finds that those who are religious tend to be more politically conservative than those who are not religiously affiliated. Miller (1996) finds that Christians and Jews group political issues into categories differently. Ellison, Bartkowski, and Anderson (1999) demonstrate that, in general, religiosity is inversely related to domestic violence, but men who have more conservative religious views than their partners are more likely to engage in domestic violence.

The arguments here can be summed up in the following set of propositions:

- *Proposition 2*: Group actions influenced by that group's religious frameworks and affecting groups which do not subscribe to the same religious framework are likely to infringe upon those other groups and provoke a conflictive response.

- *Proposition 3*: The rules and standards of behavior included in religious frameworks are often interpreted as requiring actions, such as a holy war, which are in and of themselves conflictive in nature.

This argument that religious frameworks can inspire behavior that can provoke other groups into conflict is closely related to the argument regarding the first social function of religion discussed earlier. Actions taken by one group, inspired by their religious framework, are likely to infringe upon the religious frameworks of other groups. That is, actions taken by adherents of one religion are likely to be perceived as a challenge to the religious framework of another group. Such a challenge, as discussed previously, is likely to provoke a conflictive response by the challenged group. Nielson and Fultz (1995) make this argument when they demonstrate that the use of religion as a means to other social ends is positively related with conflict.

Accordingly, these propositions are basically the other side of the coin to *proposition 1*. This is because, as noted earlier, the actions taken by groups which are inspired or mandated by their religious frameworks are likely to infringe upon the religious frameworks of other groups, thus invoking the conflictive responses described in *proposition 1*. However, it should be noted that this relationship between religion and conflict is not deterministic. As is discussed in greater detail in chapter 5, religious doctrines can be interpreted very differently at different times and in different places. These rules, often the very same doctrine, can inspire both conflict or quietism depending upon the situation. Thus, while religious frameworks and rules and standards of behavior define how religion becomes involved in conflict, their existence does not guarantee that it will.

Religious Frameworks and Fundamentalism

In theory it is easy to distinguish between the defense of religious frameworks against outside challenges (social function #1) and the effect of religious rules and standards of behavior on conflict (social function #2). However, in practice it is often difficult to distinguish where one begins and the other ends. The modern phenomenon of fundamentalism provides an example of this.

There seems to be a considerable amount of agreement within the scholarship on fundamentalism that it is a defensive reaction to modernity. For example, Marty and Appleby (1991: 3), in their landmark study of fundamentalism, argue that contemporary fundamentalists feel themselves to be threatened by many aspects of modern society and are acting to defend themselves. These fundamentalist individuals and movements manifest themselves

> as a strategy, or a set of strategies, by which beleaguered believers attempt to preserve their distinctive identity as a people or group. Feeling this identity to be at risk in the contemporary era, they fortify it by a selective retrieval of doctrines, beliefs, and practices from a sacred past. These retrieved "fundamentals" are refined, modified, and sanctioned in a spirit of shrewd pragmatism: they are to serve as a bulwark against the encroachment of outsiders who threaten to draw the believers into a syncretistic, areligious, or irreligious cultural milieu.

Ammerman (1994b: 155) also discusses the defensive origins of fundamentalism:

> So long as the tradition is in place, there is no need to organize and defend it. But when the external boundaries and the internal structures of the communities that have sustained the traditions can no longer make them matters of habit and assumption, one of the responses is likely to be a fundamentalist movement that seeks to restate those traditions in ways that take account of the new circumstances.

In a similar vein, Kuran (1991: 290-291) argues that fundamentalist economics is largely a reaction to perceived injuries in existing economic systems and to transformations engendered by the Industrial Revolution, the expansion of modern government, and the information revolution. That is, modernization has corrupted individuals, torn apart societies, compartmentalized human knowledge and replaced the fundamentalist atmosphere of premodern society with ruthless competition in the marketplace and over public resources. Thus, fundamentalist economics is a defensive reaction against the threats to religious frameworks posed by modernity.

Williams (1994: 798-799) argues that this defensive reaction can take two forms. Some fundamentalists attempt to cut themselves off from the modern world, claiming they are "free from any obligation to allow public institutions or norms into their world." Others engage in activism to make public institutions accountable to religious standards. However, Marty and Appleby (1994: 5-6) note that while fundamentalism is a reaction to modernity it is not necessarily reactionary. Some movements are formed by newly empowered peoples who wish to carve out a place for themselves in the modern world.

Frykenberg's (1994: 593-596) list of the eight essential elements of fundamentalism provides a good summary of the nature of fundamentalist frameworks, why fundamentalists perceive the need to defend them, and how they do so. (1) *The truth* is how he refers to fundamentalist frameworks themselves. The truth was brought to our attention by (2) *the messenger,* who "embodies or personifies the truth." Those who follow the truth are (3) *the community,* who are the elect and, thus, separate and distinct from unbelievers. This community shares a belief in their (4) *destiny,* which includes "their certainty of a utopian future." The community is also threatened by (5) *evil,* which mostly consists of "corruption and danger of pollution from outside" the community. One reaction to this evil is (6) *radical conversion,* the call for "drastic and complete action against evil." Another reaction is (7) *revivalism,* the efforts to restore vitality to the religion by reviving its past. A final reaction is (8) *separatism*, alienation from the outside world.

While, perhaps, the origins of fundamentalism are to a large extent defensive, the form it takes in many societies are guided by fundamentalist rules and standards of behavior. Furthermore, it is often an essential element of these rules and standards of behavior that they be enforced not only on believers, but on society as a whole, usually through the formation of a religious state. Appleby (1994: 15) sums up this synthesis of the first two social functions of religion when he argues that the term "'fundamentalist' connotes a certain kind of believer who wishes to form or defend a state based in some explicit way upon sacred history, laws, customs, traditions, and/or moral obligations."

Marty and Appleby (1991: 3-4) similarly argue that the renewed religious identity created by fundamentalist frameworks becomes the basis for a recreated political/social order oriented on the future and that fundamentalists seek to make this order a reality. Boundaries are set, enemies identified, converts sought, and institutions created and sustained to accomplish the fundamentalist movement's goals. They further argue that when the state is controlled or influenced by fundamentalists, these fundamentalists are encouraged or empowered to spill over their natural borders and permeate the larger society. That is, fundamentalists attempt to impose the views advocated by their religious framework on the entire state, regardless of whether everyone in the state agrees with those views. Marty and

Appleby also argue that, because the state regulates many aspects of social existence and it is the goal of most fundamentalists to do just that, fundamentalists inevitably become involved in modern politics. In sum, fundamentalist movements almost inevitably attempt to impose the rules and standards of their frameworks on others and consider the powers of the state a useful tool to achieve this goal. This makes conflict between them and those who adhere to incompatible frameworks almost inevitable.

Marty and Appleby (1991: 3) further argue that fundamentalists attempt to impose the views advocated by their frameworks in the most intimate zones of life. These intimate zones include marriage, sex, family life, child rearing, education, morality, and spirituality. Hardacre (1993: 129) argues that fundamentalists pay special attention to pursuing social programs intended to shape the family in accordance with their values. This is because the family is the primary unit for most fundamentalist interpretations of religion. It is the most fundamental source and place for religious observance. It is the primary place where religious education and the transmission of religious knowledge from one generation to the next occurs. It is also often considered a microcosm of universal moral order.

It should be noted that, obviously, this emphasis on morality and family values is not limited to fundamentalist approaches to religion. Most religions do consider these issues to be important. However, what distinguishes fundamentalist movements in the modern era is their determination to impose their version of morality and family values on others. More traditional religious movements tend to be more content to focus their energies on maintaining the morality of their own members.

Kuran (1991: 295-297) argues, with respect to Islamic fundamentalism, that fundamentalists often seek to curb demand with morality. That is, they seek to control individual economic behavior by advocating an interpretation of their religious framework which regulates such behavior. The futility of removing unsatisfied wants gives fundamentalists irremovable justification for demanding moral reform. Furthermore, when eliminating wants does not work, fundamentalists use this as an excuse to engage in education, repression, and redistribution as well as redefining as moral and permissible the actions that were formerly considered immoral and prohibited.

Certain aspects of modernity make it almost inevitable that fundamentalist frameworks and rules and standards of behavior will lead to conflict. The increasing power of the state in the modern world, as well as the widening scope of its authority, means that the state must deal with fundamentalists either by repressing, co-opting, or appeasing them. In extreme cases, the state itself is the reward for fundamentalist political action. In addition, the pluralism found in many modern civil societies has provided legitimacy to ways of life that are at odds with fundamentalist frameworks. "Only in societies where there are competing options is it necessary to declare so vigorously that there is only one correct choice." For this reason fundamentalists also often challenge conventional ecclesiastical authorities, who are seen as having gone too far in accommodating the modern secular state and the pluralist mode of thought (Williams, 1994: 799-807).

However, Marty and Appleby (1994: 3) note that

With a few important exceptions, fundamentalists have enjoyed the greater success in reclaiming the intimate zones of life in their own religious communities than in remaking the political or economic order according to the revealed norms of the traditional religion. Yet they persist in making forays into the outside world; they persist in activism designed to either protect or expand the borders of their enclave or to transform some aspect pf the environment which threatens to undermine their hold on values and lifestyles they find essential to their identity.

Marty and Appleby (1994: 6-7) note that this fundamentalist activism is in some ways problematic for fundamentalist movements. This is because "it seems that in order to defend tradition, fundamentalists must constantly reinterpret it or select from among its diverse teachings the appropriate prescription for the particular needs of the moment." As a result, fundamentalists "face an additional challenge of having to justify ideological shifts, and the programmatic changes accompanying them, to members who base their loyalty in part on the assumption of both consistency and immutability in the fundamental doctrine and goals of the movement."

Similarly, Williams (1994: 788, 819-822) argues that as society changes, social movements must adjust their ideologies along with it, which poses a problem for fundamentalists who must be "both timeless and timely." This problem occurs because, as movements clash with other ideological frameworks in plural societies, institutional goals tend to replace value-driven ones. As a result, fundamentalists become vulnerable to compromise politics and/or limit themselves to more quantifiable goals. Also, when fundamentalists attain some success in shaping the public realm, they tend to become less oppositional because there is less to oppose. They start to make accommodations with other elements of the "pluralist mix" of their society, thus moving them even farther from the ideological ideals with which they began.

In all, the two characteristics that define fundamentalism are its origins as a defensive reaction to modernity and the attempt to impose fundamentalist rules and standards of behavior on society as a whole in order to actualize this defense. Given this, it is not surprising that it is difficult to determine whether it is this defensive reaction or these rules and standards of behavior which define the role of fundamentalism in conflict. It is, in fact, a combination of the two. Modernity poses a threat to the religious frameworks of fundamentalists because it has begun to create a society where it is considerably easier to live at odds with traditional religious frameworks. As is discussed in chapter 3, modernity has brought science, which gives man an alternate explanation for the world, and political ideologies that provide alternate ways to organize individual lives and society. In other words, modernity has given man the ability to choose a set of secular rules and standards of behavior. Fundamentalists react to this by trying to reassert what they believe to be the original rules and standards of their religion. Thus, the defensive reactions of fundamentalists originate in a threat to an environment where their rules and standards of behavior can be practiced most freely and result in attempts to impose these rules and standards of behavior on society as a whole. This intimate connection between the defense of fundamentalist frameworks and those framework's rules and standards of behavior make it difficult, if not impossible, to separate the effects of these two factors on the role of fundamentalism in conflict.

This overlap between religious frameworks and rules and standards of behavior can be seen in most instances of fundamentalist violence. Many, such as Rapoport (1991a: 127-132; 1991b: 429-430) make the argument that all fundamentalist violence, no matter how aggressive it appears, can be considered defensive in nature. While Rappaport makes this argument in general, Sprinzak (1991) makes it in the specific case of Jewish fundamentalists in Israel. However, upon closer examination, it becomes clear that this defensive reaction is intertwined with fundamentalist rules and standards of behavior.

Sprinzak (1991) notes that "the main sources of Haredi [Jewish ultra-orthodox] militancy are animosity, fear, and suspicion of Zionism in particular and modern secular culture in general" and discusses two types of violence prevalent in the Haredi community. The first is enforcement violence within the Haredi community. He compares the Haredi lifestyle to a totalitarian system in which there is little freedom for individuals to decide their own lifestyle. The rules and standards of behavior of the Haredi framework are absolute. Members of the community who are even rumored to violate them can be subject to brutal retaliation. Enforcement violence is the most prevalent form of violence within the Israeli Haredi community for two reasons. First, because it is believed within the Haredi community that there is little hope of positively affecting the powers that be in Israel at this point in history and therefore efforts are best focused on maintaining what they have. Second, the external threat to the Haredi community by secular elements of Israeli society requires strict uniformity within the community as a defense.

The rarer occurrences of Haredi violence against those outside the community are usually based on one of two motivations, which can also be described as defensive. First, there is violence directed at the perceived sources of threat to the Haredi lifestyle: Christian groups in Israel who attempt to convert Jews to their faith, thereby representing the historical threat Christianity has presented to Judaism, and Israel's aggressive Jewish secularists. Second, any change for the worse, from the Haredi perspective, in the "status-quo" relationship between the secular and the religious in Israel can provoke often violent protest.

Thus, most, if not all, Haredi violence in Israel can be considered defensive of the purity of the community. The threats can be internal nonconformity or perceived external infringement. In both cases, that which is perceived to be at risk, and accordingly defended, is the Haredi rules and standards of behavior. This intertwining of the first two social functions of religion with regard to their affect on violence makes it difficult to separate them when discussing the motivations for that violence.

Haredi violence is not the only form of Jewish religious violence in Israel. The religious Zionist movement has also, at times, used violence. Sandler (1996: 138-140) argues that a major aspect of this movement is the concept that reclaiming the land of Israel is a holy pursuit that can actually facilitate the coming of the Messiah. Even Jews who are not observant contain a divine spark, and their efforts to establish and defend the Jewish state can contribute to this process.[3] Until the peace process that began with Camp David, secular Zionism was sanctified by virtue of its efforts to establish a Jewish state. Camp David marked the beginning of the process where land that had been so redeemed was to be given away. As a result, many religious Zionists believed, and still believe, that any effort to return land must be opposed. Thus, the return of land is both an attack upon the belief that the land of Israel must be redeemed, and it invokes rules and standards of behavior regarding actualizing that redemption.

These rules and standards of behavior are inherently fundamentalist because they are based on a reinterpretation of Jewish sacred texts in response to modernity. In addition, they are based on a doctrine of Rav Avraham Kook's that historical events reflect God's plan and, when properly interpreted, can provide instructions for behavior. For instance, as noted above, secular Zionists are part of this historical process and their participation in it will bring them closer to the religion. Also, the Holocaust reflects evil of non-Jews, shows that the Jewish people must return to Israel, and that foreign states cannot be trusted with the safety of the Jewish people (Don-Yehiyah, 1994: 267-271).

Given this, it is not surprising that the Camp David Accords provoked violent actions by some religious Zionists in the late 1970s and early 1980s. In signing the Camp David Accords, Israeli Prime Minister Begin not only provided the framework for returning the Sinai to Egypt, he also recognized the "legitimate rights of the Palestinians" and pledged to give them autonomy. This resulted in a legal movement to oppose the withdrawal from the Sinai as well as an illegal movement, which became known as the Jewish Underground. The latter movement was responsible for attempts to destroy the Dome of the Rock Mosque, the attack on the Islamic College, the maiming of Arab mayors with bomb attacks, and terror attacks against the National Guidance Committee.[4] However, these activities were considered radical by the majority of religious Zionists and were condemned by the movement's leaders (Sandler, 1996: 143-146; Don-Yehiyah, 1994: 275-286).

The more recent peace process, beginning with the Oslo Accords, has also resulted in a violent reaction from elements within the religious Zionist community. Legal demonstrations against the creation of the Palestinian authority and the ceding of power to it have often turned violent. There have also been a few incidents of lethal violence. Unlike the Jewish Underground of the previous decades, however, the most notorious acts of violence have been at the hands of individuals acting alone. The first of the most notorious of these acts was on February 25, 1994, when a U.S.-born Israeli, Dr. Baruch Goldstein, opened fire on Muslim worshipers in the cave of the Patriarchs in Hebron, killing 29 people and wounding over 100 more. Goldstein was then beaten to death by Palestinians in the Mosque. Goldstein was a supporter of the late Rabbi Meir Kahana, who formed the Kach party, which is based on a radical interpretation of religious Zionism and has been outlawed in Israel for its racist views. It is believed that Goldstein acted alone and was mentally unstable.

The second such incident was the assassination of Prime Minister Yitzchak Rabin by Yigal Amir on November 4 1995. Amir, like Goldstein, acted alone or, perhaps, with the support of one or two others. Sandler (1996: 148-149) argues that his religious framework was a combination of the religious Zionist opposition to returning land to the Palestinians and the Haredi denial of the legitimacy of the secular state. Amir is also believed to have been affected by rumors that "some national religious rabbis had charged Prime Minister Rabin with being a *rodef* (one whose actions endanger the lives of others), an accusation that sanctioned his execution."

In a less known incident, on January 1 1997, Noam Friedman, an off-duty Israeli soldier, opened fire with his M-16 automatic rifle on a crowded Hebron market wounding seven. Juergensmeyer (1997: 23) describes his justification for this act as follows: "he claimed that he had been on a mission from God. 'Abraham bought the Cave of the Patriarchs for four hundred shekels of sliver,' Friedman said, referring to the Hebron shrine that all three Abrahamic faiths–Judaism, Christianity, and Islam. 'And', he added, 'nobody will give it back.'" This justification is also consistent with the religious Zionist doctrine of reclaiming the land of Israel.

Messianism is another element of the religious framework of the religious Zionist ideology that influenced Goldstein, Amir, and Friedman that must be taken into account. Rapoport (1988: 197) defines messianism as the "faith that there will be a day in which history or life on this earth will be transformed totally and irreversibly from the condition of perpetual strife which we have all experienced to one of perfect harmony that many dream about." He argues that "holy terror" is usually linked to messianism. While most religions contain some messianic elements, there are six factors that make messianic beliefs come to the fore and inspire violence. It is argued here that many of these elements are present within the religious Zionist movement and probably influenced the actions of Goldstein and Amir.

The first, and probably most important, such factor is imminence, or the belief that the time of redemption is near and that its coming can be influenced by the actions of men.[5]

> Once a sense of imminence takes root, some believers must find it psychologically impossible to regard their actions as irrelevant. . . . At the very least, they will act to secure their own salvation. And, once the initial barrier in action has been overcome, it will only be a matter of time before different kinds of action make sense too. Soon they may think they can shape the speed or timing of the process" (Rapoport, 1988: 201).

The religious Zionist belief that the physical act of reclaiming the land of Israel will contribute to the coming of the Messiah clearly fits this definition. The Palestinians and the peace process can both be considered obstacles to the reclaiming of Israel, the Palestinians being alternate claimants to the land and the peace process actually giving them some of it. Accordingly, actions against the Palestinians and against Rabin, an advocate of the peace process, could easily be considered means to further the religious Zionist goal of reclaiming the land and, in so doing, bringing the redemption closer.

The religious Zionist ideology of the reclaiming of the land of Israel is also consistent with two more of the elements described by Rapaport as contributing to the "holy terror" inspired by messianism. One is whether the "holy terrorist" believes that he must "force the end" of the struggle. That is, unless the "holy terrorist" takes action, the redemption will not take place. The belief that the land of Israel must be physically reclaimed by Jews fits this description. Reclaiming the land is not a passive action. Actions against those who are seen to oppose or obstruct this reclamation could be considered necessary to actualize the Jewish reclamation of Israel. The other such element is that there are believed to be "signs and portents" that the messianic time is coming. The very act of reclaiming Israel can be considered to be such a portent.

The fourth element described by Rapoport is the belief by the "holy terrorist" that his actions are moral and justified. Amir has continued to assert that his actions were moral and justified, and it is hard to believe that Goldstein did not consider his actions justified. Don-Yehiyah (1994: 273-274), argues that it is this aspect of radical religious Zionist messianism that distinguishes it from other forms of Jewish messianism which have been present throughout the history of Judaism. That is, the radicalization of Jewish messianic beliefs to the point that anything is justified to bring the messiah closer that is unique to radical religious Zionism. Thus, while Jews have always prayed for the coming of the messiah, some religious Zionists feel anything is morally justified to cause that event to occur.

This moral justification is closely associated with the fifth element described by Rapoport which is the belief that there is divine participation or assistance in the "holy terror." God acts as the great equalizer. Even when you are outnumbered, you cannot lose with God on your side. Once one believes that his actions are moral and justified under divine law, it is not a great leap to assume that there is divine assistance. This belief is an element of the Jewish faith and can be found in prayers commemorating Jewish victories in the past. For instance a prayer said by all Orthodox Jews on the holiday of *Hannukah*, commemorating a Maccabean victory over Assyrian-Greek oppressors reads:

> ... when the evil Greek empire rose up against your [God's] nation Israel to make them forget your Torah [the Old Testament] and to turn them from the statutes of your will. And you, in your great mercy, stood up for them [the nation of Israel] in their time of distress. You fought their struggle, judged their judgement, avenged their wrong. You delivered the strong into the hands of the weak, the many into the hands of the few, the wicked into the hands of the righteous, the defiant sinners into the hands of those who study your Torah. . . .[6]

This prayer clearly contains elements of the concept of divine aid to the righteous in the pursuit of a moral cause. The final element described by Rapoport is that the "holy terror" is seen by the "holy terrorist" as a means to demonstrate his faith. It is not clear whether this element was present in the acts of Amir, Goldstein, and Friedman.

The actions of Goldstein and Amir have been venerated by a small fraction of the religious Zionist movement. For example, Jewish extremists who support Goldstein's actions after the fact have constructed a monument to him at his grave in Kiryat Arba, a Jewish town near Hebron.[7] However, these actions are condemned by the vast majority of religious Zionists. Be that as it may, the violent actions of these two men were clearly inspired by their religious frameworks. Their actions were most likely a result of their desires to both defend their concept of religious Zionism against what they perceived to be an overt threat and to follow the rules and standards of behavior of their interpretation of the religious Zionist movement which deal with the reclaiming of the land of Israel. Like the case of Haredi violence, it is difficult to determine where defending the religious Zionist framework ends and following the ideology rules and standards of behavior begins.

Social Function #3: Religion as a Link Between Individuals and a Greater Whole and Sometimes as a Provider of Formal Institutions Which Help to Define and Organize That Whole

While the first two social functions of religion characterize how religions can cause conflict, this and the next social function characterize how religions can facilitate conflict processes that have other causes. As noted in chapter 2, the third social function of religion is that adherents of religious frameworks tend to build formal institutions around their frameworks. There are two opposing ways in which religious institutions can affect conflict. They can be a very useful resource for mobilizing their adherents for political action, thus facilitating conflict. However, they can also be strong supporters of the status-quo and deter conflict. The former tendency will be considered first.

As long as a group adheres to a common religious framework which is associated with formal institutions, those institutions become a convenient meeting place, means of communication, and basis for organization. Such an infrastructure is likely to be useful in mobilizing and organizing group action regardless of the grievances that originally motivated that action. That is, religious institutions are capable of facilitating mobilization regardless of whether or not the basic causes of that mobilization are due to challenges to the group's religious framework or motivated by the rules and standards of that framework. This is because organizations tend to organize people. Groups that are already organized in some sort of institutional or organizational framework are easier to mobilize for political action than groups that are not organized under such a framework. Religious organizations usually have places to meet, scheduled meetings, leaders, membership lists, and formal and informal communication networks. Announcements can be made at prayer sessions as well as through the various communications networks. The formal meeting places provide a base of operations as well as a place to meet. All of this can facilitate organizing a group of people for political action regardless of the motivations for that action.

It should be noted that the level of formal organization associated with a religious framework does not need to be very high for it to facilitate mobilization. Even a group of informal meeting places that have no connection with each other than the fact that they are used by adherents of the same or similar religious frameworks can provide such facilitation. Such a group of meeting places can still make the tasks of organization and communication far simpler than it would have been had no such infrastructure been available.

Gurr, in his discussion of the mobilization of ethnic minorities for political action, makes a similar argument when he notes that

> political organization is essential to the formulation and expression of group interest. . . . Sustained collective action and political influence depend on the articulation of a believable set of demands and a strategy of action that mobilizes a substantial group of people. Such demands and strategies can be provided only by political organizations that represent and pursue group objectives. The organizational fabric for group mobilization can come from preexisting clan or *religious hierarchies*[8] (Gurr, 1993a: 68-69).

Thus, although Gurr does not deal with religious issues except as an aspect of a whole range of social issues, it is clear that he would agree that religious institutions can provide the infrastructure for mobilizing a group regardless of whether or not those grievances are religious in nature.

There is considerable support for this argument in the literature on religion. Sahliyeh (1990: 13) argues that organized religion can provide a framework for mobilization. He also notes that churches, mosques, and temples provide places to meet. These institutions also provide social services at little cost to the beneficiaries of these services which also serves to facilitate mobilization.

Johnston and Figa (1988: 35-38) discuss in more detail how a church can facilitate mobilization. They make several points in this regard. First, the material resources of a church are especially effective in the mobilization process due to the fact that they often have a protected status. That is, it is often safer to organize within the context of religious institutions because such institutions are less likely to be targeted by the opposing group or government. One reason for this is that the church is often the only legal place to organize, thus making it the logical place for groups to meet. Second, church access to media is often extensive and important for an opposition group. In fact, the church media is often the only uncensored media in authoritarian regimes. Third, the more a regime has a need for legitimacy, the more likely church organizations are to play a catalyzing or facilitating role in developing opposition.[9] Fourth, in more economically developed and socially differentiated societies, the role of the church in mobilization lies in broadening and bridging effects. That is, it can create a common ground for discussion between the classes and an ideological and symbolic bridge between divergent class interests.

Rubin (1994: 24-32) makes a similar argument in a discussion why Catholic bishops, priests, and nuns have played important roles in nationalist, revolutionary, and pro-democratic movements. First, like Johnston and Figa, he argues that their association with the Church makes them more difficult targets. Second, the international connections they gain through the Church give them international support. Third, the Church is in many ways a de facto political party with information and educational networks. In fact, the Church is often the strongest institution in states with weak governments. Accordingly, its presence and influence among the people make them an excellent alternative basis for mobilization.

The literature on religion and conflict also discusses how religious organizations can become involved in conflicts whose bases are not religious. Hadden and Shupe (1986) argue that religious ideas can become mobilizing ideologies among those who are alienated and dispossessed. Sahliyeh (1990: 11-14), in a similar vein, argues that religion is often the only vehicle for the articulation of grievances. He also argues that political, social and economic hardships often lead the clergy to assume the leadership of a political protest movement.

Many scholars of fundamentalism argue that institutions and mobilization are essential elements of fundamentalism. For instance, Ammerman (1994a: 15) argues that "fundamentalist ideas do not . . . exist in the cultural stratosphere. They are generated and supported in concrete social institutions." While the formation of institutions alone does not make fundamentalism different from other social movements, the institutions that fundamentalists establish tend to be distinctive.

Marty and Appleby (1991: 630) note that fundamentalist leaders are effective at exploiting ideological inconsistencies and policy failures of secular governments in order to mobilize their adherents. They are also effective at mobilizing large numbers of people in the short term, as well as maintaining a smaller number of loyal workers to maintain the organization over the long term.

Williams (1994: 810-813) argues that fundamentalist organizations' ability to recruit and mobilize adherents is based, to a great extent, on their ability to be seen as representing transcendent authority. However, this characteristic of fundamentalist organizations also creates some limitations on their ability to recruit and mobilize. First, in order to maintain the ideological purity of the rank and file members, religious organizations must establish visible boundaries between members and nonmembers, like modes of speech, distinctive clothing, and special rituals. As these demands on the membership increase, the ability of the organizations to recruit new members and retain the old ones decreases. As a result, fundamentalist movements must provide a broad range of social and economic supports to keep their membership in the fold, thus adding to the institutional burdens of the organization. But, this does have the advantage of increasing the loyalty of those who remain in the fold because "those willing to pay the costs hold the membership dear." Second, the enforced ideological homogeneity of fundamentalist movements mean that incorporating different social groups into a movement can be ideologically impossible or, if possible, can dilute the ideology of a movement. This is because members coming from backgrounds other than the one in which the fundamentalist movement originated will generally have worldviews that are harder to reconcile with the fundamentalist framework of belief.

Williams (1994: 813-818) also argues that the fact that many fundamentalist movements are, at the beginning, based on charismatic leaders is also an obstacle to the long-term survival of these movements. Charisma tends to be organizationally unstable. The movement can be subject to the whims of the charismatic leader. The leader has problems delegating authority and is often overwhelmed by his responsibilities. Also, charisma is hard to transfer to the next generation of leaders. The solution to this problem of organizational survival is to institutionalize the movement. There are three ways to do this. First, create a "charisma of office" where it is the office and not the one who holds it that has the charisma. Second, create a "legal-rational authority" where certain rules and procedures are given legitimacy. Finally, professionalize the religion by developing the expectation "that representatives of the religious organizations, including but not restricted to the clergy, will accept their vocation as a full-time occupation and will have the training to perform organizational roles." This leads to the development of "standards, ethics, behaviors, and knowledge deemed appropriate to–and the more or less exclusive property of–the profession."

While the Catholic Church is not generally considered a fundamentalist movement, it provides a good example of a religious organization that has successfully used all three of these practices. The office of the Papacy clearly has a "charisma of office" independent of its officeholder. The Catholic Church has developed a large and complicated body of rules and procedures that are considered legitimate by Catholics and followed rigorously. Finally, the Catholic clergy meet the professional standards described above.

There is also some support for this argument in the general literature on mobilization. Tarrow (1989: 7) argues that "social protest movements" are "groups possessing a purposive organization, whose leaders identify their goals with the preference of an unmobilized constituency, which they attempt to mobilize in direct action in relation to a target of influence in the political system." This description could easily fit religious leaders using religious organizations to mobilize their flock for political action.

McArthy and Zald (1976: 1217-1218) define a social movement as "a set of opinions and beliefs in a population which represents preferences for changing some elements of the social structure and/or the reward distribution of a society." Such preferences could easily be those advocated by a religious framework. Furthermore, McArthy and Zald define a social movement organization as "a complex or formal organization which identifies its goals with the preferences of a social movement or countermovement and attempts to implement those goals." It is not difficult to see that a religious organization could constitute such a formal organization.

McAdam (1982: 43-47) argues that indigenous organizational strength is one of the factors that facilitates mobilization. He argues that a conducive environment for mobilization only provides the opportunity; resources are needed to take advantage of it and organizations already in place help to provide those resources. Thus, mobilization is far easier for previously organized groups. Such groups tend to have communications networks in place and well known leaders who can lend their prestige and organizational skills to the mobilization effort. Such previously organized groups also find it easier to establish a structure of solidarity incentives to help mobilize and maintain their movement. It is clear that religious organizations can and often do constitute exactly such indigenous organizational strength.[10]

As noted earlier, the other side of the coin to the argument that religious institutions facilitate mobilization is that they support the status quo. This argument is not a new one and needs little elaboration. That religions support the status quo is a basic element of Marxism. The discussion in chapter 5 on the violent and quietist tendencies of religions also assumes that religions can and often do support the status quo. Also, many of the scholars who discuss the more violent aspects of religion also explicitly note that religious institutions can support the status quo.[11]

It is clear that both of these opposing arguments have a basis in fact. That is, under some circumstances religious institutions will facilitate mobilization for political actions and conflict and in other cases they will inhibit it. The structural theories discussed in chapter 5 can provide an explanation for when religious institutions support opposition as opposed to the status quo. Most of these theories focus on some form of elite interest. Thus, it is logical to argue that religious institutions can be used for mobilization unless the elites in control of those institutions have an interest in maintaining the status quo. This argument can be summed up in the following proposition.

- *Proposition 4*: Any type of grievance among any type of group can lead to the use of religious institutions in the mobilization of that group, thus facilitating conflict, unless the elites in control of the institution have a greater interest in supporting the status quo.

Social Function #4: Religion's Ability to Legitimize Actions and Institutions

One of the few truisms in the study of politics that seems to have near universal acceptance is that religion can bolster the legitimacy of both governments and opposition movements, as well as just about any political activity. This truism can be found in textbooks[12] and in the behavior of politicians worldwide. Even Marxist governments, which ideologically reject religion, accept the fact that it is a powerful legitimating force, calling it the "opiate of the masses." Perhaps this power comes from the fact that the moral authority of religion is acknowledged even by many who are not religious. In addition, it allows those who invoke it align themselves with what is considered good and moral while at the same time to present themselves as disinterested parties "involved in politics only out of a sense of righteousness, not personal gain" (Williams, 1994: 795-796).

The basic argument here is twofold. First, when a state, for whatever reason, suffers from a crisis of legitimacy, so too does the ideological framework which guides that state. This leaves the state, and the ideological framework which guides it, vulnerable to attacks by the adherents of opposing frameworks, including religious frameworks. Second, regardless of the legitimacy of a state, religious frameworks are capable of providing legitimacy both to the state and to its opposition. For that matter, religious frameworks are capable of providing legitimacy to just about any group or individual action, including violent activities such as terrorism.[13]

There seems to be considerable agreement among scholars that religion can act as a legitimizing force in society for both governments and those who oppose them. As will be recalled, chapter 5 cites the body of literature which argues that secular governments have been suffering from a crisis of legitimacy. The secular frameworks guiding these governments, which have fallen into disrepute have, in turn, contributed to what many call the recent resurgence or revitalization of religion. Scholars like Appleby (1998: 41), Haynes (1994), Juergensmeyer (1993), Marty and Appleby (1991 and 1993), Sahliyeh (1990), and Shupe (1990) have all made similar arguments. Their lists of the factors which have caused this crisis of legitimacy for secular ideologies contain mostly nonreligious causes including failed promises of freedom, economic prosperity, and social justice; secular nationalism being perceived as a foreign and illegitimate ideology as well as being connected with the issues of colonialism and cultural colonialism by the West; the unsettling social and economic consequences of modernization; and the facilitation of religious movements by modern mass communication technology. Thus, it is clear that religious frameworks can give legitimacy to movements based on grievances that are not religious in origin. For this reason, if a secular state is suffering from a crisis of legitimacy, it is likely that a religious framework will be used to provide legitimacy for the opposition to that state.

Kokosalakis (1985: 368-371) argues that there is a dialectical relationship between power and religious legitimacy. Reflecting the discussion in chapter 5, Kokosalakis notes that political and economic modernization create an alternative basis for legitimation in society. Yet, political processes like constitutional separation of church and state do not mean that religion has no role in power and legitimization. Furthermore, even though the current justification of state power usually rests on ideologies like nationalism, the pursuit of democracy, and humanitarian values, a "strong residual element of religion, which clearly exists even in Western societies, can still perform basic legitimizing or oppositional functions within such ideologies." In fact, the "immense complexity of power and economic structures and the very inequalities of power, wealth, and status as well as the social cleavages of race, gender, etc." that are associated with modernization create some of the problems of legitimacy exploited by religious groups. Geertz (1977: 267-268) similarly argues that "thrones may be out of fashion and pageantry too; but political authority still requires a cultural framework in which to define itself and advance its claims, and so does opposition to it."

Turner (1991: 178-198) engages in a detailed discussion of Christianity and the legitimation political power. This legitimacy historically came from a descending theory of legitimacy in which power descends from God to the rulers, known as the doctrine of divine right. Based on this doctrine, people have no right of resistance and no power over their ruler. This form of legitimacy was the theological justification provided by the Catholic Church for the monarchies in Europe. However, over time, perhaps due to the decline in the power and influence of the Catholic Church since the Reformation, the Western world has switched to an ascending theory of legitimacy in which power comes from people, thus giving them a right of resistance. A classic early example of this form of argument is found in Hobbes's *Leviathan.* In this work, Hobbes justifies the power of the monarchy not as an extension of divine right but as being based on a social contract to protect people from the state of nature by maintaining order. Later social contract thinkers, like Locke and Rousseau, developed the concept further, advocating a direct rule by the people through some form of democracy. Like Kokosalakis, Turner argues that this secular basis for legitimacy has not been completely successful in legitimating modern governments. He attributes the current "crisis of capitalism," in part, to "the inability of legal formalism to provide a system of normative legitimation" (Turner, 1991: 197).

Billings (1994: 175) argues that there has been a similar shift in the United States from religion supporting the status-quo to also supporting opposition movements. They argue that, in the United States there has been "a shift from earlier conceptions of religion as a legitimator of the status quo to one that emphasizes its directly combative stance vis-a-vis both secular legitimations and religiously based but compelling moral visions of a good society."

Little (1991: xx) also considers religion important to political legitimacy. He argues that "religion or similar beliefs often play an active and prominent part in defining group identity and in picking out and legitimating particular ethnic and national objectives." This is because of the human need to "elevate given political and economic arrangements in reference to sacred or cosmic standards." Luttwak (1994: 17-18) uses this principle on a more practical level when he argues that conflict resolution can be facilitated by making concessions seem like deference to religion, thus reducing the vulnerability of leaders to accusations of weakness.

Lincoln (1985: 268-281) addresses the ability of religion to legitimate political movements and governments in his discussion of three types of religions. What differentiates these three types of religion is what type of movement they legitimate. Religions of the status quo legitimate established regimes, religions of resistance legitimate religious minorities, and religions of opposition legitimate opposition movements.[14] Lincoln's categories are also consistent with the argument that religion can legitimate both governments and opposition movements.

Mcneil (1993: 561-563) argues that "The basic reason for supposing that religiously inspired movements may be gaining momentum in our times is that perceptions of inequality–and the tangible realities that provoke those perceptions–are on the increase." He also argues that the discontents felt by peasants and ex-peasants are an important cause of fundamentalist movements. In addition, he notes that the majority of humankind fits into these categories, which makes their reactions to the harsh conditions in which they live very important.

In all, as is the case with religious institutions, religious legitimacy can be used to legitimate both governments and opposition movements. This leads to the following set of propositions on the role of legitimacy in religious conflict:

- *Proposition 5*: Religious frameworks can be used to legitimize grievances and mobilization efforts that are not religious in nature.

- *Proposition 6*: Religious frameworks can be used to bolster the legitimacy of governments and other ruling elites and institutions.

Religious Elite Interests and the Role of Religious Institutions and Legitimacy

Just as the first two social functions of religion are intimately intertwined, so are the second two. Religious institutions and religious legitimacy, while conceptually distinct, are in practice difficult to separate. When religious organizations and institutions involve themselves in political activities, they implicitly give these activities an aura of legitimacy. What religious institution would allow itself to be used for a purpose of which it does not approve? For instance, when the Southern Christian Leadership Conference was formed in 1957 to mobilize the civil rights movement in the south, and when the Reverend Martin Luther King Jr. gave his famous "I Have A Dream" speech on the Mall in Washington D.C. in 1963, it was clear that many of the southern black religious institutions supported the cause.

Conversely, when secular causes gain religious legitimacy, it is often through the aegis of the clergy and other religious elites. The clergy are among the most visible and authoritative arbiters of religious legitimacy. It is they who generally hold many, if not most, of the important positions in religious institutions and are among the most authoritative interpreters of religious doctrine. Thus, the same people who control many of the religious institutions are also in the best position to determine what should and what should not be granted the aura of religious legitimacy. Additionally, other religious elites who have influence over religious organizations and institutions may also have the ability to confer religious legitimacy by virtue of their influence in those organizations and institutions. For instance, there are numerous examples of the Catholic clergy in South America championing the economic and human rights of the people.

Williams (1994: 793-799) makes this argument, noting that those with religious authority have control over the symbols of religion which have considerable legitimacy in the eyes of adherents. This is especially so in modern times, where various aspects of society have been "compartmentalized," with religion gaining control over many of the moral aspects of society. However, he also notes that the use of religious legitimacy can be available to even nonclergy, where religion has a generalized legitimacy. In fact, once religious symbols are released into the public discourse, they can take on a life of their own, leading to consequences never intended by those who first introduced them. He cites the violence in Sri Lanka and the attempts to Islamize Pakistan as examples.

This connection between religious institutions, religious legitimacy, and religious elites can perhaps provide an answer to the question of which element of society, if any, is granted political legitimacy and the use of religious institutions. Since the religious elites to a great extent control the religious institutions and, consequently, the ability to grant religious legitimacy, they have considerable control over these sources of political support. Thus, which side of a conflict and which elements of society gain the use of religious institutions and the support of religious legitimacy are, to a great extent, determined by the interests and con-sciences of the elites who control those religious institutions.

For example, that the Catholic Church in feudal Europe generally supported the monarchies and nobility of the time can be explained by the fact that the religious elites came mostly from Europe's noble class. However, in modern Latin America, liberation theology, which is based in part on Catholic theology, legitimizes opposition to governments despite the opposition to this movement by many in the upper levels of the Catholic hierarchy. The leaders of this movement are the grass roots Catholic clergy and lay persons who mostly come from the region's lower classes. Given this, it is not surprising that this alternative religious elite identifies with the struggle of Latin America's poor to eke out a living in dismal economic conditions and in the face of government indifference or oppression. Gill (1998) notes that these movements, as well as the growth of Protestant movements in the region, have influenced the behavior of Catholic elites in Latin America. The Catholic Church generally supports the state unless there are successful competing religious movements in the state, in which case the Church supports the masses in order to avoid losing members.

The importance of religious legitimacy is also reflected in the dispute between the Chinese government and the Dalai Lama, Tibet's spiritual leader, over the designation of Tibet's second most important religious figure, the Panchen Lama. The Dalai Lama has opposed the Chinese invasion and rule in Tibet since the 1950s, granting the opposition a considerable amount of religious legitimacy. However, the most recent Panchen Lama, whose most recent incarnation died in 1989, supported the Chinese government. Buddhists believe in the transmigration of souls from life to life. Thus, major religious figures, including the Dalai Lama and the Panchen Lama are reincarnated after their deaths. The naming of the new

Panchen Lama has considerable implications for the control of religious legitimacy in the conflict over Tibet. The Chinese need the continued support of the Panchen Lama to maintain whatever religious legitimacy they have in Tibet, and the Dalai Lama and other supporters of Tibetan independence want all of the religious legitimacy for themselves. Also, the new incarnation of the Panchen Lama will also have a say in determining the next reincarnation of the Dalai Lama. In 1995, the Dalai Lama determined that Gehun Choekyi Nyima, a six-year-old boy, was the reincarnation of the Panchen Lama. The Chinese government opposed this decision, detained Gehun Choekyi Nyima, and enthroned a different six-year-old boy, Gyaincain Tashi Lhunpo, as the tenth reincarnation of the Panchen Lama.

The case of the Islamic opposition to Egypt's government provides an example of different elements within the religious elite supporting different sides of a conflict. Militant Islamic fundamentalists have been carrying out an intermittent but violent campaign against the Egyptian government throughout the 1990s. The group Gama'a al-Islamiya is believed to be responsible for much of this violence, but it is only one of the numerous militant Islamic organizations. These rebel groups can be described as underground Islamic institutions headed by a religious elite that are used to mobilize opposition to the Egyptian government and lend religious legitimacy to their cause. However, Egypt's formal Islamic institutions, which include most of the country's mosques and the religious educational system, are controlled and financially supported by the Egyptian government. Given this, it is not surprising that these institutions tend to support the government.

The rational choice or economic approach to religion discussed in chapter 3 may help to provide an explanation for when these elites support governments and when they support opposition groups. As will be recalled, this approach to the study of religion is based on its three fundamental simplifications and/or assumptions. The most fundamental simplification/assumption is that individuals engage in maximizing behavior, otherwise known as using a cost-benefit analysis, in selecting their religions. The other two simplifications/assumptions follow from this one. First, religious "producers" attempt to maximize "members, net resources, government support, or some other basic determinant of institutional success. The actions of church and clergy are thus modeled as rational responses to the constraints and opportunities found in the religious marketplace." Second, the combined actions of religious "consumers" and "producers" in a free religious marketplace tend toward equilibrium.

For our purposes, the relevant assumption is the second one, which posits that religious "producers" seek to maximize their access to whatever resources they deem most important. To put it more simply, religious elites seek to gain the support of whatever element of society they think will further the interests of the religious institutions they control. If these elites or "producers" seek political and economic support or at least tolerance from the government, a logical way to maximize these resources would be for the "producers" to lend some of their legitimacy to the government.[15] If these "producers" wish to increase their active membership, taking on popular causes, including opposition to the government, would be likely to make their religious product more attractive to the religious "consumers." Religious "producers" would be especially likely to take this course if they have no hope of government support or are actively persecuted by the government. While rational choice theorists do not deal with it, another "good" that "religious producers" can seek to maximize is morality. That is, religious elites can, and often do, support causes that they believe to be moral even if this support puts themselves and their institutions at risk.

Fawcett (2000), in her analysis of the role of religious institutions in the ethnic conflicts in Ireland and South Africa, also makes the argument that religious elites are influenced by the populations which they serve. She argues that religious and other elites seek to occupy the cultural mainstream, which she defines as "the ideas, institutions, and values which have the greatest hegemonic weight and centrality within the public sphere" (Fawcett, 2000: 11). They do this because much of their power comes from the fact that they occupy this cultural mainstream, to the extent that the legitimacy and authority of whoever occupies the cultural mainstream is taken for granted. Thus, religious elites must shift as people's opinions shift. When political and economic power shift, a battle between old and new order also takes place over where the cultural mainstream will be located. This phenomenon is especially strong when ethnic and religious boundaries overlap.

In all, both religious institutions and religious legitimacy can support either governments or opposition groups. This gives them the ability to both facilitate or hinder conflict. The religious elites who control these institutions and, to a great extent, the ability to grant religious legitimacy, are the key to understanding when religious institutions and legitimacy will support the status quo or the opposition to it. Whether they are guided by moral or more worldly interests, these elites control what are in a sense political commodities, religious legitimacy and the use of religious institutions.

The Overlap between All Four Social Functions of Religion

While the previous discussion highlights how religious legitimacy and institutions can facilitate or hinder conflicts that are not over religious issues, these aspects of religion are not wholly separated from conflicts that involve religious issues. This overlap between the first two and the second two social functions of religion occurs in two ways. First, conflicts involving the defense of religious frameworks and the rules and standards of behavior of those frameworks, by definition, contain elements of religious legitimacy. What could have greater religious legitimacy than defending the religion or following its rules? Ammerman (1994b: 157) makes this argument when she notes that the simple act of cultural critique based on a religious framework refuses legitimacy to both the institutions of the state and society in general. These conflicts also often involve religious institutions because they provide a logical and convenient place to organize and mobilize for religiously motivated conflicts.

Second, conflicts that begin with nonreligious motivations but make use of religious legitimacy and/or religious institutions can be transformed into conflicts over religious issues. This is because once the element of religion is added to a conflict, there is a greater opportunity for issues involving religious frameworks and religious rules and standards of behavior to enter into that conflict. Once religious institutions are being used to oppose a regime, for example, it is likely that the leaders of those institutions will add religious demands to the secular ones that are the original basis for the conflict. Also, when a cause gains religious legitimacy, it is likely to attract a more religious element to its banner, and this element may cause the demands of the cause to become more religious in nature. As these processes continue, there is a possibility that a secular cause can, over time, be transformed into a religious one.

Juergensmeyer (1997) makes this argument. He argues, as discussed earlier, that religious frameworks motivate religious terrorists who are attacking what they see as unauthentic modern, secular, and/or foreign influences in society. He also argues that in addition to this, "The use of religious violence allows a religious group to assert not only its power but also its legitimacy. Challenging the notion that the state holds a monopoly on morally sanctioned violence . . . religious groups can show their moral superiority by sanctioning violence of their own" (Juergensmeyer, 1997: 20). Williams (1994: 790) similarly argues that religious movements

> have a particular interest in ensuring that the new identities of recruits are couched in group terms and are accompanied by an imperative for participation in movement activities. In that sense, the crucial test for movement ideology is whether it can successfully mobilize members to struggle for social change. Mobilization starts with a clear understanding of the conditions the movement is committed to change.

The Transformation from Secular to Religious Conflict in Algeria

The current Islamic revolution in Algeria is a case in point. While Islam has always been legitimate in Algeria, Islamic movements were not able to successfully oppose the government until Algeria's economic conditions worsened. Once this occurred, these movements were able to co-opt the secular dissatisfaction with the country's economic situation and transform it into an effective Islamic opposition.

Islam has always had legitimacy in Algeria. For this reason the FLN party, which has ruled Algeria since its independence, incorporated Islam into the state ideology, despite the party's predominantly secular character. This incorporation is apparent in the oft quoted phrase "Algeria is my fatherland, Arabic is my language, and Islam is my religion." It was clear to the state's founders that Islam was an intrinsic element of the state's culture and national identity in part because Islam was essential to maintaining the cultural identity of Algerians during the

French occupation. For these reasons, among others, Islam had to be incorporated into the Algerian national ideology. Accordingly the government incorporated state reformist Islam into its ideology as the only officially recognized form of Islam, while other forms of Islam, including marboutic Islam, were reduced to virtual insignificance.

However, this official Islam was held tightly under the control of the central state. The religion was institutionalized and organized as a bureaucracy. Through this bureaucracy, the government had absolute power to hire and fire religious leaders, administered all of the state's religious education institutions, administered all of the state's mosques and wakhfs (religious charitable endowments), controlled the publication and distribution of religious books, and censored the Friday sermons in all of Algeria's mosques. Islam was incorporated into the secular state as a cultural component and an identity-forming instrument, but it had no real influence on the state's political structures. Also, the Sharia (Islamic law), which had been undermined by one hundred and thirty two years of French occupation, was not reactivated as a means for organizing society. In fact, the main objective of the state was to relegate Islam into a cultural role which would help to legitimize the state without imposing itself upon the state's secular ideology and to prevent the use of Islamic symbols and organizations against the secular state (Entelis, 1986: 176-183). The secular elites wanted it to be the case that "the intercessor between God and development [would] no longer [be] a [marabout], a prophet or a mufti, but rather, the state apparatus"(Vatin, 1982: 233).

There seems to be a consensus among scholars that the Algerian government's cooptation of Islam did not compromise the state's essentially secular character. According to Mortimer (1991: 577) "although the various party statements always paid homage to Islam, the model of society that they advanced was basically secular." According to Tozy (in Zartman and Habeeb, 1993: 102-103) "a conception of . . . future society was forged that reduced the role of religion to a symbol . . . [and] as a result . . . a balance was established that allowed the state to make Islam the official religion on the condition that [Islam] restrict its activities to civil society." According to Deeb (1992: 55) "Although Islam became the religion of the state . . . the Sharia's, or Islamic law, was not made an integral part of the legal system of the state. . . ." According to Roberts (1988: 562) the FLN "insisted on incorporating the Association [of Reformist Ulema] within its own political structures and thereby deprived it of its autonomy [and] this dependent and subordinate position of the Ulema vis-a-vis the political leadership has endured to this day." According to Reudy (1992: 197) demands "for the inclusion of Islam in political programs . . . received more in verbal than in substantive modifications to secularly inspired programs." Also, according to Layachi and Haireche (1992: 73) "the government monopolized religion . . . and used the egalitarian nature of Islam to promote . . . socialism and to implement vast reform programs. . . . Thus, it appears as if Islam was being secularized."

As long as the economic situation in Algeria was stable, this lip service to Islam was sufficient to stave off any attempts by Islamic fundamentalists to influence government policy. It was only when the government's economic policies began to fail in the mid-1980s that Islamic fundamentalists were able to lend religious legitimacy to the cause of the economically dissatisfied, and, in so doing, mobilize a considerable portion of Algerian society behind their religious agenda for transforming Algeria's government and society. The focus here is on the causes for the development of the Islamic opposition in Algeria in the 1980s. The violent conflict that occurred after the military coup and the cancellation of elections in 1992 is merely the continuation of a historical process that has its roots in the 1980s. That is, the point at which Algeria's Islamic opposition was able to co-opt the economic grievances of many of Algeria's citizens and initiated the conflict with the Algerian government is the relevant factor here, not the violent escalation of the conflict between the two factions once that conflict began.

Algeria's economic problems include urban migration, population growth, housing shortages, mismanagement of the state's agricultural and industrial policies, unemployment, an income gap, international debt, and falling world oil prices. As is generally the case with economic problems, all of these problems are interrelated.

Urban migration contributes to many of the other economic problems in Algeria and is in and of itself a major problem. In order to dissuade the rural population from migrating to the cities, the government decided to refrain from supplying enough housing for potential migrants. This, of course resulted in a severe housing shortage. By 1980 there was a shortage of about one million housing units, creating one of the worse housing situations in the world. This situation has led to problems ranging from annoying inconveniences to serious social dilemmas. These problems include "hot bed" sleeping where people must take turns using beds due to a shortage of places to sleep; overcrowding of existing housing; the lack of places for students to study; crime due to people having no place to go and nothing to do (the idle hands thesis); young couples being unable to marry due to a lack of a place to live; and serious health risks due to the overcrowding and inadequate sanitation facilities.

Another major contributing factor to Algeria's economic woes is population growth. Algeria has done little to dissuade, and has actually encouraged, population growth because, after the revolution, it felt a need to replace the one million lives lost during the revolution.[16] Another reason for this population growth is that Algeria's improved health services have lowered death and child mortality rates. This has exacerbated the problems caused by urban migration, in addition to causing problems of its own.

It is clear that population growth can offset development. If population growth occurs faster than growth in GNP, per capita GNP actually decreases. Growing populations also increase the cost to the government for providing health care, sanitation, education, and other necessary social services. It also increases the amount of resources that must go to food supply and distribution. It increases the size of the work force, often faster than jobs are created, thus increasing the economic drain of welfare programs. All of this also reduces the resources available for investment in economic development. Thus population growth is not the primary source of Algeria's economic problems, but it is a contributing factor to many of them.

In addition, population growth can contribute directly to political unrest. Richards and Waterbury (1990: 94-96) discuss what they call the "politics of young populations." Their thesis is that the disproportionately young population, which is usually the result of high birthrates, results in an age gap between the majority of the population and its leaders. Thus, the leaders and the population have different historical experiences and thus different world views. This results in the two having different goals, which in turn results in political unrest. This can be said to be the case in Algeria. A major basis of the Algerian government's legitimacy is the role that the FLN and many of its present leaders played in the revolution. However, Algeria's young population was not alive or was very young during the revolution and are more interested in their own economic well being and standard of living.

Goldstone (1991) also discusses how population growth can cause revolution. Several factors caused by population growth combine to cause social unrest: increasing pressures on state finances as inflation erodes state income and population growth raises real expenses; intraelite conflicts increase as larger families create an elite too large for the positions available; popular unrest grows due to the competition for land, urban migration, unemployment, declining real wages and the increased youthfulness of the population; ideologies of rectification and transformation become increasingly salient. However, Goldstone's study is based on revolutions between 1500 and 1850 and he notes that, in the twentieth century, government policy can offset these negative effects of population growth. However, the principles he discusses are still relevant and they must be addressed by policies which are not always completely successful. In fact, it is fair to say that the economic and political woes from which Algeria is suffering generally fit this pattern. However, Goldstone, perhaps, goes too far in his emphasis of population growth as the cause of all of these problems, rather that its being a contributing factor.

Another of Algeria's major economic problems is its insufficient agricultural production. Immediately after the revolution in 1962 Algeria was self-sufficient in its food production but by the mid-1980s it was 75 percent dependant on international sources for its food supply (Entelis, 1986: 132). Part of this problem is due to population growth and urban migration, but much of it is due to governmental policies.

A major reason for Algeria's agricultural underdevelopment is the government's policy of favoring industry over agriculture. The government discouraged the intensification of agricultural production in addition to discouraging investment in Algeria's agricultural infrastructure. In fact most government investment went to its industrial program, and it even favored industry in the allocation of Algeria's limited water resources. It kept agricultural prices artificially low, which resulted in a lack of incentives for farmers to produce. Bureaucratic delays and overcentralized decision making merely aggravated the problem (Entelis, 1986: 132-140). To make matters worse as agricultural production was stagnating, population growth increased the number of mouths to feed and urban migration became so rampant that it actually left the agricultural sector with a labor shortage.

This issue of food dependency is a major topic in Third World forums and has considerable potential to undermine a state's legitimacy as well as aggravate its other economic problems. The underproduction of food forces a state to purchase food on the international market. This results in a drain on the state's foreign currency supply, which could have been used for investment in other projects.

This occurred in Algeria to the point where it was forced to borrow money, which led to a debt crisis. When a state has to borrow money to buy food it is in a particularly bad situation because, unlike money borrowed for industrial investment, money borrowed to buy food does not have the potential to bring a return on its investment nor does it address the basic problem at hand. It simply adds to the state's debt and places it in an even more precarious economic situation; the state is left with a larger debt but is still unable to produce enough food for its population. The state is then forced to borrow more money to buy more food, putting it deeper into debt, thus creating a vicious circle that continuously drains the state of the resources it needs to address the basic problem. Also, when a government has trouble feeding its people, problems of legitimacy usually follow.

Despite the sacrifices Algeria made in its agricultural program in order to promote industry, its industrial program was also failing. In the mid-1980s productivity was low–running at 40 percent and lower at some plants (Entelis, 1986: 125). The reasons for this low productivity include: the massive size of the state corporations led to inefficiency; the lack of qualified personnel for mid-level management positions; Algeria's market was not large enough to provide sufficient buying power for an economy of scale; and many of its industries were concentrated in the production of goods for which there was a glut in the world market. To make matters worse, the demands for consumer goods were greater than Algeria's industry could produce, thus contributing to the outflow of currency.

Because of this low productivity, Algeria's industry was not able to provide enough jobs for Algeria's growing and better educated labor force. Since the military and state bureaucracy had already absorbed as much of the labor market as they could, this left Algeria with a considerable unemployment problem. The resentment over this problem was exacerbated by the widening economic gap between the haves and the have-nots.

Although many of these problems were present in the 1970s, high world oil prices allowed Algeria to use its oil revenues to more or less satisfactorily deal with the symptoms. However, when world oil prices dropped in the 1980s, the government's revenues dropped at the same time as the need for them, due to the state's economic problems, increased. This left the Algerian government in a position of having to contract its budget and commit itself to austerity measures at the exact time that it was politically most dangerous to do so.

Accordingly, until about the time of Boumediene in 1979, most Algerians were still benefitting from state programs. Because of this, the government's Islamic critics were unable to use economic issues to undermine the government's legitimacy. Their criticisms during this period mainly consisted of moral attacks claiming that the secular nature of the state was illegitimate and nonindigenous. Islamic fundamentalists attacked the state as being a "Western-oriented secularized elite [that] had confiscated the revolution from the common people who made the revolution in the first place" (Mortimer, 1991: 577). Furthermore, the Islamic fundamentalists attacked "what they saw as the negative moral aspects of modernization–such as alcohol distribution, coed education, and the adoption of Western fashions of clothing by women. They [also] criticized the attempt to link socialism with Islam" (Layachi and Haireche, 1992: 74).

These criticisms were articulated by Islamic fundamentalists before the Algerian government's crisis began but were not in and of themselves enough to cause that crisis of legitimacy. It was only when the government began to fail in providing the economic prosperity that it had promised that these criticisms became salient. As long as they were relatively prosperous, the Algerian people had no reason to question the state's ideology, but once that ideology began to fail in providing the economic prosperity that it had promised, it was open to attack by other belief systems. Islamic fundamentalists articulated a belief system that did exactly that and were able to win over a large portion of the population. As Crenshaw (1994: 267) notes "even Algerians not attracted to the idea of a religious social and political order could sympathise with attacks on bureaucratic inefficiency and corruption."

Islamic nationalism in Algeria was first articulated by Abd el-Kader during the first half of the nineteenth century, during his resistance against the French. Most of the subsequent Islamic nationalist movements in Algeria can trace their roots to Abd el-Kader. Islam was also an important unifying factor in the Algerian revolution and, as previously discussed, it was considered important enough as a source of legitimacy for Algeria's secular government to attempt to incorporate it into their secular ideology.

As also discussed earlier, the government's incorporation of Islam into its ideology did little more than pay lip service to Islam. This was mostly done in order to legitimize the government, unify the people, and prevent religious symbols from being used against the government. However many Algerians were not fooled by this superficial adherence to Islam. Many felt that the government's espoused Islamic principles were not put into practice and that official Islam was sterile and unauthentic. These people believed that other ideologies had failed and only Islamic morality could provide the answers to their society's woes (Entelis, 1986: 83-84).

Thus, at the same time as the government was being deprived of an important potential source of legitimacy, this same source of legitimacy became available to the opposition. As early as 1979 militant Islamic groups making use of Islamic legitimacy were active in Algeria (Reudy, 1992: 241). This newfound popularity of Islam based on its granting of legitimacy to economic grievances was transformed into a challenge of the secular basis of the Algerian state. Arab leaders were accused of ignoring the sovereignty of God.

[This] generated a crisis of ethical standards that . . . led to the acceptance of socialism . . . [which] brought Islamic fundamentalism into open conflict with the political and economic ideologies prevailing in contemporary Muslim countries. [Accordingly,] fundamentalism fiercely opposes nationalism, because the paramountcy granted by this ideology to the nation state, with its secular connotations, clashes with the categorical principles of an immutable divine order. Both secularism and democracy are considered incompatible with the sovereignty of the Koranic principles (Serpa, 1991: 197).

It is probable that this rejection of anything that is non-Islamic, much less secular, has a strong appeal to those who are fed up with what they perceive as a bankrupt dominant secular ideology.

The ability of fundamentalist Muslims to organize and mobilize resources also aided them in their cause to transform Algerian society. In fact, some argue that the militant Islamic movement was the only group sufficiently organized to fill the vacuum created by the government's crisis of legitimacy. Moore (in Zartman and Habeeb, 1993: 63-64) argues that, although the FIS, the major Islamic opposition party, was poorly organized, its unofficial Islamic institutions constituted an organization in place before it became a party. This gave it an advantage over Algeria's other new political parties, which were even more poorly organized and did not have sufficient time to rectify the situation before the 1990 municipal elections. Thus, the FIS was in the best position to take advantage of Algeria's economic crisis.

The Islamic fundamentalists had organizational and mobilizational advantages in that Islam contains the political rules to run a state within it, and they had a network of communication through their mosques and Islamic societies (Wright, 1991: 26-27). Also, during the 1970s, the Algeria government actually encouraged the fundamentalist Islamic movements in order to counter leftist opposition movements. This allowed them the time and freedom to build up an organization that was capable of challenging Algeria's weakened government. This organization included about ten thousand unofficial mosques and the takeover of some of the government sanctioned official mosques. It also included the providing of social services that the government was having difficulty providing. It was upon this base that the FIS (Algeria's official Islamic Party) was founded and was able to successfully challenge the FLN in open elections.

This advantage in mobilization based on Islamic institutions was considerable. Friday sermons by Ali Bekhadj, one of the leaders of the FIS, attracted nearly 20,000 people. Organized FIS demonstrations often had 50,000 attendants (Crenshaw, 1994: 267).

In all, Algeria provides an excellent example of how the use of religious legitimacy and institutions to legitimate secular causes can be transformed into a religious revolution involving religious frameworks and rules and standards of behavior. The desires of the Islamic fundamentalists in Algeria to transform the country's secular government into a more religious one has been constant. However, the movement did not become successful until an economic crisis provided it with the opportunity to co-opt secular dissatisfactions through lending them religious legitimacy and the use of the movement's institutional and organizational network. Once the economic dissatisfactions had been co-opted, the movement was able to transform these grievances into the desire to revolutionize Algerian society.

The transformation of this desire to change Algerian society into open and violent rebellion can be divided into four stages. First, before 1980 fundamentalists wanted to change Algerian society but did not have the political support to do so. From about 1980 until 1988 the economic crisis allowed Islamic fundamentalists to transform economic discontent into support for their cause. From 1988 to 1992, a new constitution, which allowed effective political opposition, allowed Islamic fundamentalists to use mostly peaceful and democratic means to further their cause. This constitutional change was caused by massive riots in 1988 that were widely believed to be due to the country's economic difficulties (Spencer, 1994). The FIS, the Islamic political party, won surprising victories in local elections in 1990, winning control of 854 out of 1541 municipal councils and 32 out of 48 provincial assemblies. They also had considerable success in the first round of national elections in December 1991 and were expected to have enough seats in the national assembly after the second round in January 1992 to hold a governing majority in the National Assembly. This second victory resulted in a military coup in January 1992 and the canceling of the second round of the national elections. As a result, the fourth and most violent stage of Islamic opposition began. This violent opposition is the result of a combination of the desire to transform Algerian society and the dashed expectations of achieving this goal peacefully. Since January 1992, tens of thousands have died in the violent conflict between the government and Islamic fundamentalists.

Summary of the Basic Argument

In all, it is argued here that religion can cause or contribute to conflict in four basic ways. First, religion provides many people with a framework that helps them to understand the world. This fills a basic human need for a tool to organize a chaotic and unintelligible world into an organized and understandable format. In many ways, such religious frameworks do not only interpret reality, but also become a basic part of reality for those who depend upon them. Accordingly, when some outside force somehow challenges a religious framework, those who depend upon that framework understand this challenge as a challenge to their reality. When such a challenge is perceived to occur, it must be met. The reality provided by a religious framework must be defended. This can often lead to a conflictive response by those who use a religious framework, when they perceive it to be challenged.

Second, religious frameworks usually include rules and standards of behavior for the adherents of those frameworks. These rules and standards of behavior are often interpreted by those adherents as to require behavior that can cause conflict. In some cases this behavior is, in and of itself, conflictive in nature, for example the concept of holy war. In other cases, the required behavior may on the surface seem to be peaceful but be perceived by another group as a challenge to their religious framework. For instance, a demand for more religious rights by a minority group in a society has been known to provoke a negative response from the dominant group in that society.

While these first two ways in which religion can become involved in conflict describe how religion can be the initial cause of a conflict, the next two describe how religion can facilitate a conflict that has already started. This facilitation can occur even if the initial cause of the conflict has nothing to do with religion. However, these two factors can also be important elements in inhibiting conflict.

The third way religion can become involved in conflict is through its institutions. Once a conflict has started, groups often need to mobilize for action. Religious institutions can be used to facilitate this mobilization. They constitute a format in which large numbers of people are brought together, and one of the most difficult tasks in mobilization is to do exactly that. Religious institutions can often provide communications networks and access to the media, both of which are useful in the mobilization process. Also, religious institutions are often the safest place to meet, many governments being more reluctant to harass them than other types of social and political groups. Yet often, religious institutions support the status-quo, repressing mobilization against the government.

The fourth way in which religion can become involved in conflict is through its ability to grant legitimacy. Religion can be used to make legitimate acts which would otherwise be unthinkable. Murder can become a holy war and suicide can become martyrdom. When a minority group has political, social, and/or economic grievances, being told by their clergy that their religion demands that they deserve better and should do something about it can grant any conflictive actions that they take an aura of legitimacy far greater than would otherwise have been possible. Yet, in many cases, for example feudal Europe, religious legitimacy is on the side of the government.

The key to understanding when religious legitimacy and institutions will support the status quo or be used to oppose it seems to be the desires and interests of religious elites. These elites have a considerable amount of control over religious institutions and the ability to grant religious legitimacy. Accordingly, their desires and interests greatly influence whether governments or oppositions will be granted the use of these political commodities.

While these four social functions of religion are theoretically distinct, in practice they overlap. Rarely does one find religious frameworks being defended without some sort of invocation of the rules and standards of behavior associated with that framework or the use of religious legitimacy and institutions to buttress that defense. Conversely, using religious legitimacy or religious institutions in support of nonreligious causes runs the risk of transforming a secular conflict into a religious one that involves religious frameworks and rules. This overlap often makes it difficult to tell whether a conflict is truly religious in its origins. Yet, once religious frameworks and rules become involved in the conflict, the question of how they originally became involved is probably academic.

Cleaning Up the Laundry Lists

It has been argued here that all forms of religious involvement in conflict can be traced to one or more of the four social functions of religion discussed here. If this is true, all of the items on the laundry lists of various causes of religious conflict discussed in chapter 5 should fit into one or more of these four categories.[17] The results of this exercise are shown in table 6.1.

Table 6.1: Cleaning Up the Laundry Lists

Item on Laundry List	Framework	Rules	Institutions	Legitimacy
Revolutionary messianism, the struggle for earthly paradise, can result in revolts when there is social or political distress or disorientation without a clearly perceived cause.		√	√	
Militant religious nationalism materializes in "situations of awakening national consciousness" where "religion supplies a sense of national identity." Such a situation is likely to occur in the context of an anti-colonial struggle.	√			√
"The leaders of religious bodies with a developed ecclesiastical organization support a revolutionary upheaval because they are sympathetic to the aims of this revolution, or because they are protecting the interests of the religious institution."			√	
"Individual theologians or laymen support a revolutionary movement to give a concrete social and political meaning to the transcendent elements of their faith."			√	

Continued on next page

Table 6.1—Continued

Item on Laundry List	Framework	Rules	Institutions	Legitimacy
Religion can be manipulated for political purposes.			√	√
Religion as a component of nationalism, especially ethnonationalism.	√			
Religious factors exacerbating tensions or conflicts whose root causes are sociopolitical and economic.			√	√
Religious factors and sentiments being used to heighten tensions.			√	√
Religious notions of state transforming political institutions and leading to conflicts.		√		
Religious fundamentalism or fanaticism influencing state policies.	√	√		
Erosion of the secular and identification of the secular with the West.				√
Use of religion in political processes and in influencing policies of governments.	√	√		
Growing lack of confidence in governments in many parts of the world by minorities, leading to opposition and conflict, and making use of religion				√
Tensions resulting from new financial power acquired (from outside) by previously marginalized sections.		√		
Religious conflicts used by outside forces to destabilize countries.[18]				

Conclusion

As the title of this chapter and the successful attempt at "cleaning up the laundry list" implies, the theory of religion and conflict described here is comprehensive in that it covers most, if not all, of the ways religion is likely to become involved in conflict. It is also somewhat dynamic in the sense that it is demonstrated that the four basic ways religion can become involved in conflict are interrelated. However, this theory is not fully comprehensive or dynamic. While this theory deals with how religion influences a conflict, it does not address nonreligious causes for and influences on conflicts. Even the most holy of the holy wars are usually influenced by nonreligious factors and may even have some nonreligious causes in addition to the religious ones. That is, until the body of theory on general conflict is integrated into this theory, it cannot truly be called comprehensive. Similarly, while it is noted that the various aspects of this theory are interrelated, the exact nature and dynamics of these interrelationships are not clearly defined. In order for the theory to be considered truly dynamic, the exact nature of these relationships needs to be defined more formally in hypotheses that can be tested empirically.

Despite these shortcomings, the theory of religion and conflict described in this chapter is a useful tool for understanding the role of religion in conflict. It also can provide the core for a more comprehensive and dynamic theory. One issue in building such a theory is that different types of conflicts in which religion can become involved have very different dynamics. For instance, the general bodies of theory for international and domestic conflict are very different. Even within domestic conflict theory, politically motivated and ethnically motivated conflicts are covered by distinct bodies of theory. This is not surprising considering that these different types of conflict involve different types of actors and different issues. Accordingly, one cannot simply integrate the theory of religion and conflict described here into conflict theory without specifying which type of conflict theory. That is, because different types of conflict are distinct in their causes and dynamics, one cannot integrate religious factors into all conflict theory at once, rather one must integrate them into each type of conflict separately. In the next chapter, the theory of religion and conflict developed here is integrated into ethnic conflict theory.

Notes

1. Wentz has a broad definition of what constitutes religion, which he calls "religiousness." For him, "religiousness" includes any ritual activity (including watching a football game) that allows one to transcend biological existence and has a broader meaning to the self. Taylor (1998) similarly broadly defines religiosity and likens the ideologies of the

Unibomber and environmentalist radicals to religious movements.

2. The violent tendencies of Christianity, Islam, and Judaism are discussed in more detail in chapter 5.

3. The current ideology of religious Zionism is most influenced by the teachings of Rabbi Avraham Kook as interpreted by his son Rabbi Zvi Yehuda Kook. For a full discussion of Rabbi Avraham Kook's views, see Yaron (1974).

4. For more details on the Jewish Underground, see Segal (1987), Rawking (1985), and Shragai (1995).

5. Ammerman (1994b: 163-167) also argues that the belief in the imminence of the End is an important factor in fundamentalist activism. However she argues that outside factors are also important. These factors include available resources for mobilization and the general political climate.

6. This prayer is inserted into the *Shmoneh Esreh*, a prayer which is recited three times a day on weekdays and four times a day on the Sabbath and holidays as well as into the grace after meals for the entire eight days of *Hannukah*.

7. This monument includes an octagonal stone plaza surrounding the grave, a water tap for visitors who wish to ritually wash their hands after their visit, metal cabinets full of holy books, charity boxes, memorial candles, decorative lighting, and benches *(Ha'Aretz English Edition*, 6/9/98 "The Ticking Tomb Bomb in Kiryat Arba"). In December 1999, this monument was destroyed by the Israeli government under a law prohibiting monuments to terrorists.

8. Italics added for emphasis.

9. This relationship between legitimacy and opposition will be discussed in more detail in the next section.

10. For a more comprehensive discussion on mobilization theory see, among others, Chong (1991), Gurr and Harff (1994), Hannigan (1991), Oberschall (1993), Snow and Rochford (1986), Rule (1988), Tilly (1978) and Webb (1983).

11. See, for example, Appleby (1994: 25), Haynes (1994: 67-70), Lewy (1974: 3), and Lincoln (1985: 272-275).

12. See, for example, Kamrava (1996: 163-165) and Meny (1993: 28-31).

13. See, for example, Drake (1998), Hoffman (1995), and Rapoport (1984, 1989, and 1991a).

14. Lincoln's theory is discussed in more detail in chapter 5.

15. For a discussion of various forms of government support for religious institutions see Durham (1996).

16. Estimates of the number of Algerians killed during the revolution vary, and one million is more or less at the midpoint of these estimates.

17. The items of these laundry lists were taken from Lewy (1974: 539-41, 585-6) and Williamson (1990: 246).

18. This item fits in to none of the categories because it deals with international aspects of conflict, and the theory developed here focuses on intranational conflict.

Chapter 7

The Role of Religion in Ethnoreligious Conflict

Since the end of the Cold War, two of the greatest perceived threats to international security have been religious and ethnic conflict. In fact, many of the conflicts that have made the front pages of the newspapers during the 1990s have been ethnoreligious conflicts, that is, conflicts between ethnic groups who are of different religions. These ethnoreligious conflicts include the civil wars in Afghanistan, Lebanon, and the former Yugoslavian republics, the Palestinian-Israeli conflict, the "troubles" in northern Ireland, the Armenian-Azerbaijani conflict, the Cechen rebellion against Russia, the rebellion in the Kashmir province of India, the East Timorese rebellion against Indonesia, the Tamil rebellion in Sri Lanka, the Tibetan opposition to Chinese rule, the repression of Iran's Bahai minority, and the rebellion by the southerners in the Sudan, to name a few. Many of these conflicts, such as the conflicts in northern Ireland and the former Yugoslavian republics, involve issues that are mostly ethnic in nature, and religion is simply one of the factors that differentiates the ethnic groups involved. In other words, one cannot assume that because two ethnic groups are of different religions that any conflict between them must be inherently religious. However, in some ethnoreligious conflicts, such as the conflicts in Iran and the Sudan, religion is a primary issue.

Be that as it may, all of these conflicts have at least two things in common. First, they have been considered important enough to international stability to receive a considerable amount of diplomatic, journalistic, and academic attention. Second, they are all ethnoreligious conflicts in the sense that they are all conflicts that involve ethnic groups that are distinguished from each other by, among other things, their religions.

Since all of these conflicts involve ethnic groups of different religions, from now on referred to as ethnoreligious groups, there exists a potential for religious involvement in all of these conflicts that does not exist when the ethnic groups involved belong to the same religion. Yet, as noted above and described in more detail in chapter 4, religion is important in a considerable minority of ethnoreligious conflicts, but not important in the majority of them. This begs the question of why this is the case. That is, why is religion an important factor in some ethnoreligious conflicts but not others?

The theory of religion and conflict developed in chapter 6 can provide some insight into this riddle. However, by itself it is not enough. In order to comprehensively and dynamically assess the role of religion in ethnoreligious conflict, this theory of religion and conflict must be integrated into the general body of theory on ethnic conflict. This is so because most ethnoreligious conflicts involve at least some ethnic issues and, in most cases, these issues outweigh the religious considerations. Accordingly, in order to determine the role religion plays in these conflicts, it is necessary to account for their ethnic aspects.

It is important to note that both the model developed in this chapter and the empirical results based upon it deal with ethnoreligious conflict to the exclusion of all other types of religious conflict. Thus the results presented here apply only to this subset of religious conflicts. As noted in chapter 2, ethnoreligious groups are different from other types of religious groups both in the types of demands they make on the state and in the nature of group membership. Accordingly, nothing in this chapter should be taken to apply to anything other than ethnoreligious conflict.

As noted in chapter 1, the reason for this limitation is that the data on religion and conflict is currently limited to ethnoreligious conflict. While it would be preferable to include all types of religious conflict in this study, especially those involving fundamentalist groups, this is not possible due to the nature of the available data. However, given that the study presented here constitutes an analysis of the only cross-sectional data on religion and conflict (of which this author is aware) that goes beyond measuring whether the groups involved are of different religions, it is fair to argue that it can make a considerable contribution to our knowledge of the influence of religion on conflict. Clearly, collecting and analyzing data on other types of religious conflict is an important item on the future research agenda. Nevertheless, it is possible to learn something from this analysis of ethnoreligious conflict that is applicable to other types of religious conflict. Accordingly, a full discussion of the implications of the results presented in this chapter for other types of religious conflict is presented in chapter 8.

The Minorities at Risk Ethnic Conflict Model

Rather than reinvent the wheel by developing a new theory of ethnic conflict, the existing body of theory on religion and conflict is more than adequate to the task of controlling for ethnic factors. The model developed by Ted R. Gurr for the Minorities at Risk project is perhaps the most comprehensive and dynamic extant model of ethnic conflict. It covers all aspects of ethnic conflict and, not only does it relate the various parts of the model to each other, they are designed for and subjected to rigorous empirical testing. That is, the Minorities at Risk model is not only comprehensive and dynamic, it has been statistically tested using a cross-sectional analysis of 268 ethnic minorities worldwide. Of these groups, 105 are ethnoreligious minorities.[1]

Table 7.1: Ethnic Minorities in India

Group	Religiously Different	Relevance of Religion	Grievances over Auton-omy 1994-1995	Political Discrimina-tion 1994-1995
Assamese	No	–	4	1
Bodos	No	–	3	3
Kashmiris	Yes	Marginal	8	8
Mizos	Yes	Marginal	3	1
Moslems	Yes	Significant	0	3
Nagas	Yes	None	3	3
Sikhs	Yes	Significant	4	0
Scheduled Tribes	No	–	1	1
Tripuras	Yes	None	4	3
Max Value	–	–	12	9

Group	Economic Discrimina-tion 1994-1995	Cultural Discrimina-tion 1994-1995	Protest 1995	Rebellion 1995
Assamese	1	1.0	1	4
Bodos	6	2.0	1	5
Kashmiris	7	1.5	6	5
Mizos	0	0.0	0	0
Moslems	6	2.0	6	0
Nagas	0	0.0	0	5
Sikhs	0	0.0	1	2
Scheduled Tribes	3	0.0	6	4
Tripuras	4	0.0	0	5
Max Value	9	10.5	6	7

As implied by the model's name, the Minorities at risk model is designed to evaluate the dynamics of conflicts between ethnic minorities and the dominant groups in the states in which they live. The unit of analysis, that is, the basic unit which is analyzed in this study, is the ethnic minority within a state. This means that ethnic groups like the Kurds who can be found in Turkey, Iran, and Iraq are considered separately for each of these states because the relationship between the Kurds and the state's dominant group is distinctly different in each of these states. Also, one state may have many different ethnic minorities, each of which has a different status within that state. For example, there are nine minority groups within India, the Kashmiris, other Muslims, the Nagas, the Scheduled Tribes, the Sikhs, the Mizos, the Tripuras, the Assamese, and the Bodos.[2] As is demonstrated in table 7.1, each of these groups has its own unique relationship with India's government, with different issues being of different importance to each of the groups. Of these groups, the Scheduled Tribes, Assamese, and Bodos are not religiously differentiated from India's Hindu majority. Of the six ethnoreligious minorities, religion is only a significant issue for the Muslim and Sikh minorities. Autonomy is an issue for all of the groups except the Muslims, but it is a particularly important issue for the Kashmiris. Similarly, while most of the groups suffer from some political discrimination, the Kasmiris experience considerably higher levels. While the Nagas, Sikhs, and Assamese suffer from no or almost no economic discrimination, the other groups experience significant amounts. While the Assamese, Bodos, Kashmiris, and Muslims suffer from some cultural discrimination, the other groups do not. Finally, all of the groups, except the Mizos, engage in varying levels of protest and/or rebellion. In all, while each of these minority groups must deal with the same state, the nature of each group's relationship with the state is unique.

The basic elements of the Minorities at Risk model are shown in figure 7.1. This model describes the causes and dynamics of ethnic conflict, is simple, and posits that there are three basic steps to the ethnic conflict process. First, discrimination against a minority group, causes the group to form grievances over that discrimination. The model specifically deals with economic, political, and cultural discrimination and grievances over these issues. It also looks at grievances over autonomy issues. Unlike other forms of grievances, the most important cause of autonomy grievances is not any form of discrimination but, rather, whether the minority had some form of autonomy in the past (Gurr, 1993a: 76).

The second step, once grievances are formed whatever their original cause, is that they motivate the ethnic minority to mobilize or organize themselves for conflict. This mobilization can take the form of peaceful organizations, which use political protest and other legal means to address the minority's grievances. It can also take the form of violent, rebellious organizations, which use extralegal means to achieve their ends. The key factor that determines whether the minority will form violent or peaceful organizations is democracy. Under democratic governments, most groups can achieve their goals through peaceful means and accordingly usually prefer to do so. Violence is generally seen as a last resort for when all other methods fail (Gurr, 1988, Gurr, 1993a: 137; Gurr, 1996: 69; Gurr and Harff, 1994:

Figure 7.1: Basic Minorities at Risk Model

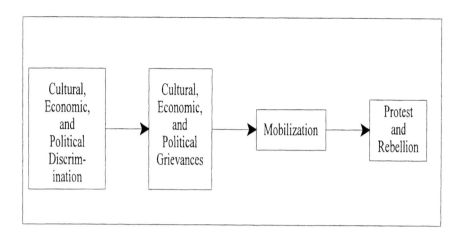

85; Olzak, 1998: 191). Under autocratic governments, the peaceful avenues for addressing grievances are usually cut off. That is, autocracies tend to repress any open political activity against the government, including demands to address ethnic grievances (Tilly, 1978; Gurr and Moore, 1997: 1083-1084; Gurr and Harff, 1994: 85). In these cases, only the violent option is left open. As a general note, demands for autonomy or secession are demands that even most democratic governments balk at granting, so such movements are likely to be violent under any type of government (Gurr, 1993a: 294-300; Gurr and Harff, 1994: 111-114; Kumar, 1997). Also, if a government engages in a high enough level of oppression, it can also reduce the level of violent opposition (Lichbach, 1987). An additional factor that affects a minority's ability to mobilize is the strength of its internal cohesion and group identity. (Gurr and Harff, 1994: 84; Gurr, 1996: 66; Gurr and Moore, 1997: 1083)

These first two steps of the model rely heavily on relative deprivation theory. While in his writings on the Minorities at Risk project, Gurr intentionally avoids the term relative deprivation due to its "intellectual baggage,"[3] these arguments are clearly within the relative deprivation tradition, to which Gurr is a major contributor. All forms of relative deprivation theory posit that any form of group, not necessarily an ethnic minority, which feels deprived relative to some point of comparison, is likely to engage in oppositional or protest activities. Gurr (1970) defines relative deprivation as the discrepancy between "value expectations" and "value capabilities." That is, the frustration is caused by the difference between what you think you deserve and what you expect to get. He describes several sources of rising value expectations including exposure to new modes of life and ideologies; unfavorable comparisons to other groups; value disequilibria– improvement in some types of values leads to the expectation that other types will also improve; and value mobility–the rate and duration of past improvement. Davies (1962), in his J-Curve thesis, believes frustration is created when a long period of economic or social development is followed by "a short period of sharp reversal." Despite this reversal, expectations continue to rise in proportion to the previous growth, thus creating a gap between expectations and reality which, in turn, creates frustration. Olson (1963) posits that frustration results from higher "social disloca- tion" and income inequality due to rapid economic growth. Samuel P. Huntington (1968) maintains that frustration is caused when the rates of economic development are outpaced by the rates of social mobilization. Also, Feierabend and Feierabend (1973) argue that "systemic frustration" occurs due to "specific characteristics of social change." The Minorities at Risk model adds a new nuance to relative depriva- tion theory by essentially arguing that discrimination also causes frustration.[4]

The third and final step is for the mobilized ethnic minority to engage in protest or rebellion. This final step is based on Charles Tilly's mobilization theory. Mobilization theory assumes that collective action is purposefully and rationally oriented toward attaining goals; that collective violence is continuous with other forms of social action; that collective action is not the aggregate of individual actions but is a "juxtaposition of interest and opportunity among contending subsets of populations"; and that collective action is political and bound up in the prevailing power struggles of society (Rule, 1988: 170-171).

Tilly's model for modern collective action contains four major categories of variables: interests, organization, opportunity, and mobilization. Interests are based on both objective group interests based upon social position and the relations of production and what the group itself perceives to be its own interests. Tilly considers the group's collective interests, which are more than the aggregate of individual interests, to be most important. Also, when individual interests do not coincide with those of the group, they increase the costs of collective action. This view of interests is similar to the Marxist point of view, where collective interests are paramount and they are decided by social forces at the group level. The most important determinants for the level of organization, according to Tilly, are "catness" and "netness." Catness is the extent to which a group fits into an ascrip- tive category and has a common identity as such. Netness is the extent to which a group coincides with a "network of people linked to each other, directly or indirectly, by a specific kind of interpersonal bond." Opportunity, according to Tilly, "describes the relationship between interests and the world around it." Opportunity has four major elements: power, repression, facilitation, and opportu- nity/threat, all of which combine to form a complex cost-benefit analysis. Mobiliza- tion is "the process by which a group goes from being a passive collection of individuals to an active participant in public life." It is also "the process by which a group acquires collective control over resources needed for action," with resources being "labor power, goods, weapons, votes, and any number of other things, just so long as they are usable in acting on shared interests." Also, the level of mobilization is the sum of the market value of resources and the probability they will be delivered when called upon (Tilly, 1978: 55, 62-64, 69, 87).

There are also different types of mobilization. Offensive mobilization occurs when groups perceive the opportunity to realize some of their interests. Defensive mobilization occurs when groups mobilize in response to a threat. Finally, preparatory mobilization occurs when groups mobilize in anticipation of future opportunities and threats. This type of mobilization is difficult because it sacrifices present satisfactions for uncertain future gains (Tilly, 1978: 74-75). It is interesting to note that these categories of mobilization parallel the ways religious frameworks can become involved in conflicts. Offensive and preparatory mobilization parallel groups following their rules and standards of behavior and defensive mobilization parallels the defense of a religious framework.

In all, according to Tilly's model, interests, opportunity, and organization all combine to cause mobilization for collective action. Also, opportunities have a direct effect on collective action in addition to their effect on mobilization, and interests also have an effect on opportunities. Thus, these four variables form a complex relationship that helps to explain collective action.[5]

While the core elements of the Minorities at Risk model are simple, in the real world ethnic conflict is influenced by many additional factors. The model accounts for many of them as follows:

- Repressive actions by the dominant group increases the level of group cohesion and identity and decreases minority groups' ability to mobilize.

- Group size and concentration increases a minority group's ability to mobilize.

- Collective disadvantages as well as engagement in communal protest or rebellion increase minority groups' cohesion and identity.

- The level of minority groups' cohesion and identity increases the likelihood of mobilization and the formation of grievances.

- International support for a state increases its ability to engage in repressive control.

- International support for an ethnic minorities increases groups' cohesion and identity.

- The processes of state expansion and economic development increase the level of minority grievances as well as the level of state power.

- The levels of state power and institutional democracy both increase the likelihood that communal action will take the form of protest rather than rebellion.

- The process of democratization, which tends to be destabilizing, increases the likelihood of both communal protest and rebellion.

- The processes of contagion and diffusion, which both postulate that the level of communal protest and rebellion by similar groups elsewhere, increase the likelihood of communal protest and rebellion at home.[6]

Integrating Religion into the Minorities at Risk Model

One of the major drawbacks of the Minorities at Risk Model is that it does not take religious factors into account despite the fact that religion is an important element in many ethnic conflicts, as is demonstrated in chapter 4. Combining the Minorities at Risk model with the theory of religion and conflict developed in chapter 6 rectifies this problem. This merging of models also rectifies two of the shortcomings of this theory of religion and conflict; specifically that it has not been placed into a fully dynamic framework and that it is not comprehensive because it does not include any aspects of general conflict theory.

The first part of the theory of religion and conflict deals with how religion can directly cause a conflict. This can happen either due to a defensive reaction to a challenge to a group's religious framework of belief or due to the imperatives of the rules and standards of behavior of that framework. These aspects of the theory are summed up in the first three propositions of the theory which, as will be recalled are as follows:

- *Proposition 1*: Any challenge to a religious framework is likely to provoke a defensive and often conflictive response from the adherents of that religious framework.

- *Proposition 2*: Group actions influenced by that group's religious frameworks and affecting groups which do not subscribe to the same religious framework are likely to infringe upon those other groups and provoke a conflictive response.

- *Proposition 3*: The rules and standards of behavior included in religious frameworks are often interpreted requiring actions, such as a holy war, which are in and of themselves conflictive in nature.

These propositions can be fit into the Minorities at Risk framework of discrimination causing grievances, leading to mobilization, and finally to protest and rebellion. *Proposition 1* deals with challenges to religious frameworks provoking a defensive reaction. A type of challenge to religious frameworks that is common in ethnoreligious conflicts is religious discrimination. For purposes of clarity it is important to note that this refers to discrimination which is specifically targeted at limiting the religious practices of an ethnic minority, not to political, economic, or cultural discrimination, which is inspired by the majority group's religious beliefs. The focus here is on what kind of activity is actually being restricted, not the motivation for those restrictions. This is because actions can be measured objectively but motivations are a matter for speculation. Be that as it may, the defensive reaction to this religious discrimination, based on the same logic as the Minorities at Risk model, can be described as the formation of grievances which, in turn, lead to mobilization and collective action. This dynamic can be formalized in the following hypotheses:

- *Hypothesis 1*: Religious discrimination, whatever its cause, is likely to result in the formation of religious grievances within the ethnic group suffering from this religious discrimination.

- *Hypothesis 2*: Religious grievances are likely to result in mobilization for protest and rebellion, as well as directly causing protest and rebellion among the ethnic group which has formed these grievances.

Propositions 1, 2, and *3* also encompass a dominant group's motivation to engage in discrimination. Dominant groups may be inspired by the rules and standard of their framework to engage in discrimination. This can include simply declaring their religion the official state religion or it can involve the active persecution of heretical religious minorities. Numerous examples of such behavior exist from biblical times until today. It is also possible for actions taken by an ethnoreligious minority to infringe upon the religious framework of the dominant group, whether or not these actions are inspired or mandated by that ethnic minority's religious framework. Such actions are likely to provoke a conflictive response from the dominant group. Sometimes, the very existence of the minority group can be perceived as a threat to the religious framework of the dominant group, perhaps because the minority religion is considered a heretical offshoot of the dominant group's religion, as is the case with the Bahai in Iran, or perhaps because the minority group is perceived as part of a larger group that poses a historical threat to the dominant group, as is the case with the Hindu Tamil minorities in Buddhist Sri Lanka. The majority group's response in defense of its framework would not necessarily have to be religious discrimination. The response could include any form of repression, including political, social, and economic discrimination. This leads us to the following hypotheses.

- *Hypothesis 3*: Provocative actions by a minority religious ethnic group are likely to provoke a negative reaction from the dominant ethnic group. This negative action can include religious, social, political, and/or economic discrimination as well as other forms of oppression.

The second part of the theory of religion and conflict described in chapter 6 deals with how religion can facilitate or inhibit a conflict regardless of whether it is the cause of that conflict. This can happen through the use of religious legitimacy and religious institutions by religious elites. These aspects of the theory are summed up in the second three propositions of the theory which, as will be recalled, are as follows:

- *Proposition 4*: Any type of grievance among any type of group can lead to the use of religious institutions in the mobilization of that group, thus facilitating conflict, unless the elites in control of the institution have a greater interest in supporting the status quo.

- *Proposition 5*: Religious frameworks can be used to legitimize grievances and mobilization efforts that are not religious in nature.

- *Proposition 6*: Religious frameworks can be used to bolster the legitimacy of governments and other ruling elites and institutions.

It is also argued in chapter 6 that the key factor determining whether religious institutions and legitimacy will support the opposition or the status quo is the interests of the religious elites. These elites will support whatever they deem to be good for their institutions and/or themselves. This dynamic can be formalized in the following hypotheses:

- *Hypothesis 4*: The presence of established religious institutions can facilitate mobilization for protest and rebellion regardless of the more basic causes of that mobilization, unless the elites in control of these institutions have an interest in supporting the status quo.

- *Hypothesis 5*: The use of religious legitimacy can facilitate the growth of economic, political, and social grievances as well as mobilization, regardless of the basic causes of that mobilization, unless the elites who have an influence over the use of religious legitimacy have an interest in supporting the status quo.

There is one further relationship which should be discussed, which is not covered in the set of propositions. As noted earlier, Gurr (1993a and 1993b) discusses the positive relationship that collective economic, political, and social discrimination and disadvantages have with group cohesion and identity. For similar reasons, group cohesion and identity should also have such a relationship with religious discrimination and disadvantages. This leads to the following hypothesis:

- *Hypothesis 6*: The presence of religious discrimination and disadvantages is likely to cause an increase in the levels of group identity and cohesion among the group which suffers from these disadvantages and discrimination.

The model defined by these hypotheses, combined with the Minorities at Risk model, constitutes a model that is considerably more comprehensive and dynamic than previous models of ethnoreligious conflict. It covers most ways religion can become involved in conflict as well as most other factors that are important in ethnic conflict. It also relates the various parts of the theory to each other in a dynamic framework which is pictured in figure 7.2.

Figure 7.2: Religious Conflict Between Dominant and Minority Religious Groups

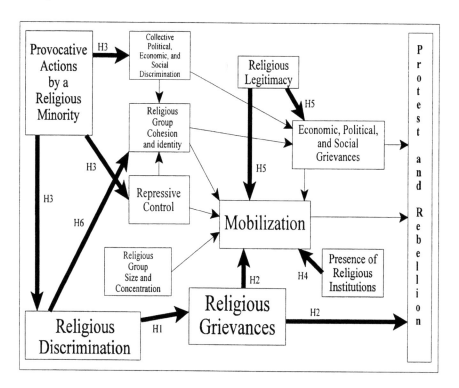

Fleshing Out the Model

This model is a theoretical model that is intended to aid in the understanding of ethnoreligious conflict. Like all theoretical models of its sort, it is based on certain assumptions, the most important of which is that all other things are equal.

However, when dealing with ethnic conflict, all other things are generally not equal. The process of ethnic conflict, even when not taking religion into account, is generally very complicated. The Minorities at Risk model described above, not including the religious factors, includes 27 distinct variables, many of which were collected yearly or biyearly. These variables are used to test, depending on how one counts, as many as 40 distinct relationships. That is, the Minorities at Risk model defines a process of ethnic conflict that includes as many as 40 subprocesses involving 27 distinct factors. As complicated as this seems, it is fair to say that each of the 268 examples of ethnic conflict contained in the Minorities at Risk dataset involve local factors that are unique and not accounted for in the 27 variables and 40 subprocesses included in the model. Given this, a fuller discussion of each of these hypotheses and the ethnic factors that influence them is in order.

The following analysis is based on an analysis of the Minorities at Risk data as well as additional data collected by the author on the religious aspects of ethnic conflict. The variables used are described fully in appendix A and a list of the groups included in the study is provided in appendix B. The statistical analysis presented here has been deliberately kept as simple as possible. This is because this book is meant for as broad an audience as possible and there is an old adage that, for every scientific equation included in a book, the readership is cut in half. Unfortunately, this also applies to statistical techniques like correlations and multiple regressions. For this reason the analysis here is limited to averages presented in bar charts and cross-tabulations. More sophisticated statistical analyses of this data are presented elsewhere.[7]

Hypothesis 1: Religious Discrimination and Religious Grievances

Hypothesis 1 states that *Religious discrimination, whatever its cause, is likely to result in the formation of religious grievances within the ethnic group suffering from this religious discrimination.* This hypothesis is, perhaps, the most straightforward of the hypotheses. It mirrors the hypotheses in the general Minorities at Risk model that predict that political, economic, and cultural discrimination will cause ethnic minorities to form grievances over this discrimination. As shown in table 7.2, as religious discrimination gets higher, so does religious grievances. To reiterate, religious discrimination and religious grievances refer specifically to restrictions on religious activities and grievances expressed over these restrictions. In fact, there is only one case where religious discrimination occurs in which no religious grievances are expressed. This case, the Nagas in India, represents one in which the primary issue is not religion but separatism.

The Naga people are of Tibeto-Burman extraction and inhabit the northeast hill areas between the Ganges-Brahmaputra basin of Bengal and the Irrawaddy basin of Burma. Although they are a mostly Christian people (about 90 percent) living in a Hindu-dominated state, religion is not the major issue between them and the central government. The Nagas were, more or less, isolated until British colonial rule was forced upon them. As is the case with other northeastern Indian tribes, the Nagas resent Indian control of their territory, regarding it as a continuation of British colonialism, and are pushing for self-determination. Given this, it is clear that this sole exception to the rule of religious discrimination causing religious grievances can be explained by the fact that the low-level religious discrimination present against the minority is overshadowed by a considerably more urgent desire for self-determination.

Table 7.2: Religious Discrimination and Religious Grievances

		Religious Discrimination 1994-1995		
		None (0)	Low (1-3)	High (4+)
Religious Grievances 1994-1995	None (0)	34	1	0
	Low (1-3)	14	32	7
	High (4+)	2	4	11

Table 7.2 also shows that there are sixteen groups which express religious grievances in the 1994-1995 period despite the fact that there is no religious discrimination against them at that time. Of these groups, eleven of them are in the former Soviet Union. A closer examination of the causes for the religious grievances expressed by the minorities in the former USSR, shown in table 7.3, shows that in seven of these cases, the grievances are due to resentment over religious discrimination in the past. In an additional case, the Russian minority in Kyrgyzistan, the grievances represent fears of future discrimination. In the other three cases, the religious grievances are part of a larger set of grievances over other social and cultural issues. Thus, it is clear that the general concept of religious discrimination causing grievances over that discrimination also applies in these cases, and the fault is not with the theory but with the variables that are used to test it.

In sum, the case of the Nagas in India and the cases in the former Soviet Union illustrate several nuances relevant to how religious grievances are formed. First, as is the case with the Nagas in India, other issues can overshadow religious discrimination to the extent that it is ignored due to these more pressing issues. Second, religious grievances can continue to be felt and expressed long after the discrimination that caused them disappears. Third, fears that religious discrimination will occur are enough to cause religious grievances. Finally, even in the absence of religious discrimination, when other forms of cultural and social discrimination exist, religious grievances may be expressed along with the cultural and social grievances formed over that discrimination.[8]

Table 7.3: Minority Groups in the Former Communist Block Suffering from No Religious Discrimination but Expressing Religious Grievances

Country	Group	Relig. Griev. 1994-95	Explanation
Azerbaijan	Lezghins	1	Fears of assimilation.
Kyrgyzstan	Russians	3	Fears of future discrimination.
Russia	Buryat	4	Past discrimination: want help to re-build religious infrastructure (schools & places of worship).
	Chechens	2	Past discrimination.
	Ingushes	2	Past discrimination.
	Karachays	2	Past discrimination.
	Lezghins	1	Past discrimination.
	Tatars	3	Past discrimination.
	Tuvinians	4	Past discrimination: want help to re-build religious infrastructure (schools & places of worship).
Tajikistan	Russians	3	Reaction to societal changes.
Turkmenistan	Russians	3	Reaction to societal changes

Hypothesis 2: Religious Grievances, Protest and Rebellion

Hypothesis 2 states that *religious grievances are likely to result in the mobilization for protest and rebellion as well as directly causing protest and rebellion among the ethnic group which has formed these grievances.* While this hypothesis predicts a simple positive relationship between religious grievances and various forms of ethnic conflict, in actuality, this relationship is considerably more complicated.

Perhaps the most perplexing and counterintuitive result of this study is the relationship between religious grievances and protest. Two forms of religious grievances are addressed here, passive religious grievances and active religious grievances, otherwise known as religious demands. Passive religious grievances, are those religious grievances expressed in response to religious discrimination. For example, the Shi'i minority in Iraq suffer restrictions on their places of worship, their religious schools, and access to their clergy. The grievances they express in reaction to this discrimination are passive religious grievances. Active religious grievances, on the other hand, are not a reaction to discrimination but an active demand for religious rights and privileges. Such demands can include the recognition of the group's religion as one of the official state religions, demands for some other privileged status for the religions, or even demands that some aspect of the religion be imposed upon the entire state, including the majority group.

Figure 7.3: Passive Religious Grievances in 1994-1995 and Protest in 1995

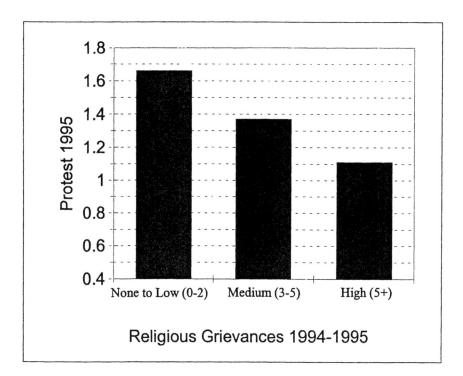

As shown in figure 7.3, as passive religious grievances increase, the average level of protest among ethnoreligious minorities decreases. This means that the more ethnoreligious minorities get upset over religious discrimination, the less the protest. This is the exact opposite of the relationship predicted in *Hypothesis 2.*

There are several possible explanations for this dynamic. The first can be found in Gurr's (1993a: 144-146, 1993b) original analysis of the Minorities at Risk data. He found that minorities in democratic societies are far more likely to engage in protest rather than rebellion. This is because democratic societies usually allow protest as a legitimate means for a group to address its grievances. In less democratic societies, protest tends to be repressed, leaving rebellion as the only remaining option for addressing grievances. Tilly (1978) and Lichbach (1987) make similar arguments. Also, autocratic states are the states that are most likely to engage in all forms of discrimination. Thus, it is precisely in those countries in which peaceful protests are most likely to occur that religious discrimination, and thus, the formation of religious grievances, is least likely. This could account for the negative relationship between protest and religious grievances. However, as the sample cases in table 7.4 illustrate, this explanation is not confirmed by the data.[9] The Ogani in Nigeria and the Zapotecs in Mexico, who live in nondemocratic states, engage in high levels of protest despite expressing no religious grievances, yet the Muslims in Greece and the Hindus in Pakistan, who live in relatively democratic states and express high levels of religious grievances, engage in relatively low levels of protest.

Table 7.4: Examples of the Relationship Between Religious Grievances, Protest, and Democracy

Group	Religious Grievances 1994-1995	Protest 1995	Democracy 1994	Political Dis-crimination 1994-1995
Ogani in Nigeria	0	6	0	4
Zapotecs in Mexico	0	4	1	4
Moslems in France	2	4	8	7
Moslems in Greece	8	1	10	2
Hindus in Pakistan	9	0	8	6
Copts in Egypt	8	1	0	6
Maximum Value	24	6	10	9

Group	Religious Dis-crimination 1994-1995	Religious Legitimacy 1994-1995	Religious Relevance, 1990s
Ogani in Nigeria	0.0	0	0
Zapotecs in Mexico	0.0	0	0
Moslems in France	0.5	0	1
Moslems in Greece	2.0	2	2
Hindus in Pakistan	1.5	3	4
Copts in Egypt	3.5	3	4
Maximum Value	9.0	4	5

A second possible explanation is to focus not on a government's level of democracy, but rather to focus on the level of repression in which a government engages. It is reasonable to argue that governments engaging in high levels of religious discrimination are precisely the governments that are most likely to engage in other forms of repression. The more repressive a government, the more difficult it is to engage in protest activities. Thus, high levels of religious grievances, which are highly correlated with religious discrimination, should be correlated with lower levels of protest. In fact, Jaggers and Gurr (1995) argue that variables that measure democracy, or the lack of it, are really indirect measures of the amount of repression in which a government engages.[10] This means that, according to them, this explanation is, in fact, another version of the first. As is the case with the first explanation, this one is also at odds with the data as illustrated in table 7.4. All of the groups in the table suffer from high levels of political discrimination, so it is fair to say they all live under repressive governments. Despite this, those groups that express high levels of religious grievances engage in lower levels of protest and those that express no such grievances engage in higher levels of protest.

A third possible explanation for the low levels of protest at high levels of religious grievances, is that religious discrimination, and as a result religious grievances over them, is most likely to occur in societies where such behavior is considered acceptable. That is, in some societies, religion has a history of involvement in politics and conflict and in such societies, a certain level of religious discrimination is considered a normal part of life. Accordingly, while there may be some grievances over religious discrimination in such societies, these grievances would be less likely to surface in the form of protest. Why protest against what is considered to be a normal part of one's daily existence? However, in societies where there is no such history of legitimacy of religious involvement in politics and conflict, religious grievances should contribute to protest activity. The data, as illustrated in the sample cases in table 7.4, supports this argument. As religious legitimacy goes up, so do religious discrimination, relevance of religion to the conflict, and religious grievances.

The Copts in Egypt and Afro-Arab Muslims in France provide good examples of this phenomenon. The Copts are a Christian sect in Egypt who, in addition to considerable political and economic discrimination, are also subject to considerable religious discrimination, both official and unofficial. The government restricts Christian broadcasting, public speech, holiday celebrations and the number of Coptic institutions. In fact, many Coptic hospitals, schools, and church lands have been confiscated. To make matters worse, the government strictly enforces an 1856 law making it illegal to build or repair a church without presidential approval, which is not given very often. All of this is in addition to harassment by Islamic militants which includes the spreading of false rumors, extortion, and violence up to and including murder. This violence often occurs with the tacit approval of local officials. The group Gama'a al-Islamiya is believed to be responsible for much of this violence, but it is only one of the numerous militant Islamic organizations. That is not to mention the violence perpetrated by individuals.

Despite all of this, the Copts have engaged in relatively low levels of protest and no rebellion. One explanation for this is the historical legitimacy of religious discrimination against them. Historically, under Muslim rule, the Christian Copts have been alternately treated with tolerance or repressed. As Dhimmi or "peoples of the Book," Copts are a tolerated religion under Islamic law. However, Islamic law can be interpreted in different ways to produce different levels of tolerance, varying from considerable to none. In any case, Dhimmi, under Islamic law, are always second-class citizens. Also, the involvement of religion in politics has a high level of legitimacy in Egypt.[11]

Figure 7.4: Active Religious Grievances in 1994-1995 and Protest in 1995

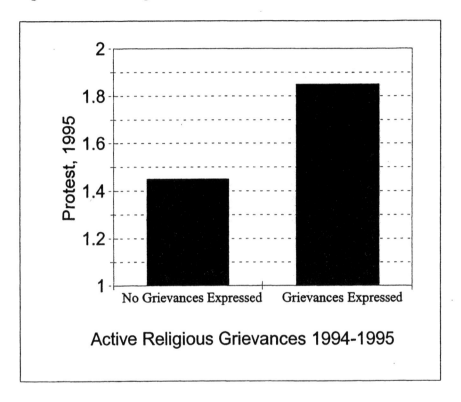

On the other hand, in France, the involvement of religion in politics has a low level of legitimacy. Accordingly it is not surprising that relatively minor levels of religious discrimination provoke more protest there than the considerable levels of religious discrimination endured by the Copts in Egypt. Muslim girls in France have been on several occasions denied the right to wear traditional Muslim head scarves while attending public schools. This has sparked a considerable amount of protest and the occasional public demonstration. However, it should be noted that the primary grievances of most North African Muslims in France are economic and political. In any case, these two examples provide support for the argument that where religious discrimination is historically a normal part of society, it is more likely to be tolerated by the victims of that discrimination.[12]

However, a more rigorous analysis of the data,[13] shows that while these three factors, religious legitimacy, repression, and democracy, all affect the level of protest, they still do not account for the negative relationship between religious grievances and protest. That is, even when accounting for other factors, as religious grievances increase, the level of protest tends to decrease.

A fourth possible explanation is that the positive correlation between religious grievances and protest predicted in *Hypothesis 2* exists only with respect to active religious grievances. Thus far, the discussion has focused on passive religious grievances, that is, complaints about religious discrimination. Active religious grievances, which are active demands for additional religious rights, as opposed to demands for an end to religious restrictions, should have a qualitatively different relationship to protest. Any group expressing demands for more religious rights is by definition willing to openly petition a government for more rights and is, accordingly, probably more disposed to protest than other groups. Such a group probably also lives in an environment where it is possible to express such complaints. In other words, if a group is able to express the type of demands measured by the religious demands variable, it is very likely that they live in an environment where the levels of autocracy and repression are not sufficiently high to prevent them from engaging in protest and that they are willing to do so. The results in figure 7.4 confirm that this is the case. On average, those ethnoreligious groups which express active religious grievances engage in higher levels of protest

Thus far, the discussion has focused on the relationship between religious grievances and protest, but *Hypothesis 2* also predicts that as religious grievances increase, so does rebellion. As is the case with protest, the actual relationship between religious grievances and rebellion is more complicated than the simple relationship predicted in *Hypothesis 2*.

Table 7.5: Grievances over Autonomy and Rebellion

		Rebellion in 1995		
		None (0)	Low (1-3)	High (4+)
Grievances over Autonomy 1994-1995	None (0)	36	2	0
	Low (1-3)	29	3	5
	High (4+)	15	4	13

The key to understanding the relationship between religious grievances and rebellion among ethnoreligious minorities is that the desire for separatism must be taken into account. Gurr (1993a and 1993b), in his analysis of the Minorities at Risk data found that grievances over autonomy were the single most important predictor of rebellion during the 1980s. That is, ethnic minorities are unlikely to rebel unless they want some form of autonomy or independence. As shown in table 7.5, this is also the case for ethnoreligious minorities in the 1990s. Only 2 out of 105 ethnoreligious minorities engage in any rebellion without making any demands for autonomy. Both of these groups, the Maronite Christians in Lebanon and the Muslims in Greece, engage in the lowest level of rebellion measured in the data, "political banditry or sporadic terrorism," in 1995. The rebellion by the Maronites reflects the aftermath of Lebanon's civil war and the rebellion by the Muslims in Greece reflects a struggle to protect their culture and for political inclusion.

Figure 7.5: The Level of Rebellion Controlling for Religious Grievances and Grievances over Autonomy in 1994-1995

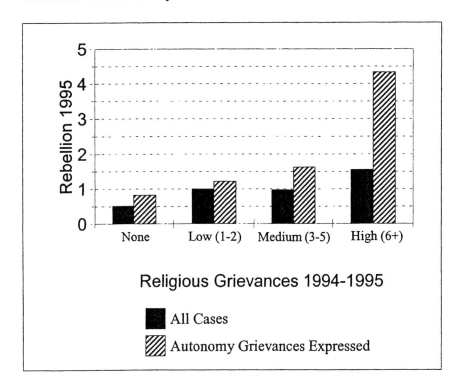

In all, the evidence provides mixed support for *Hypothesis 2,* which predicts that *religious grievances are likely to result in the mobilization for protest and rebellion as well as directly causing protest and rebellion among the ethnic group which has formed these grievances.* The evidence also uncovers some interesting and counterintuitive results. While active religious grievances cause the level of protest to increase, as predicted by *Hypothesis 2,* passive religious grievances contradict this hypothesis and cause the level of protest to drop. Religious grievances, as expected, cause the level of ethnoreligious rebellion to increase, but only in cases where the group is predisposed to rebel because they have a desire for some form of autonomy or independence.

These results, taken in their entirety, hint at another explanation for the perplexing relationship between religious grievances and protest: the emotional nature of religious grievances. As argued in chapters 2 and 6, religions provide their adherents with frameworks for understanding the world, and these frameworks, in many ways, constitute an important element of the reality of those adherents. Thus, religious grievances are based on something that is more fundamental than most other types of grievances. Such a challenge can be considered so fundamental and so important that protest is considered a wholly inadequate response. That is, when religious grievances are high protest cannot begin to address them and more drastic action, such as rebellion, is required. Active religious grievances, on the other hand, are simply a political agenda. If protest is capable of achieving that agenda's goals, there is no reason to forgo its use.

Thus, perhaps the difference between passive and active religious grievances among ethnoreligious minorities is the difference between defending a religious framework and following that framework's rules and standards of behavior. Passive religious grievances reflect the need to defend the religion against the challenge posed by religious discrimination. This challenge is a fundamental one that may require a response beyond simple protest. Active religious grievances represent the rules and standards of behavior for creating an environment wherein the religion can thrive. Any available means, including protest, which are likely to succeed at this are likely to be used.[14]

Hypothesis 3: Reactions to Provocations

Hypothesis 3 states that *provocative actions by a minority religious ethnic group are likely to provoke a negative reaction from the dominant ethnic group. This negative action can include religious, social, political, and/or economic discrimination as well as other forms of oppression.* While the previous hypotheses test how ethnoreligious minorities behave, mostly in reaction to discrimination by dominant groups, this hypothesis tests how dominant groups react to provocations by ethnoreligious minorities. As will be recalled, provocative actions by an ethnoreligious minority, like making active demands for more religious rights, are likely to challenge the religious frameworks of the dominant group, thus provoking a defensive reaction by that dominant group. It is posited here that this defensive reaction can take the form of various forms of discrimination including religious, economic, political, and cultural discrimination.

There is considerable evidence for a link between religious demands (active religious grievances) expressed by ethnoreligious minorities and discrimination against them. As shown in figure 7.6, every type of discrimination tested here rises markedly when religious demands are expressed. Religious discrimination nearly quadruples, cultural discrimination nearly triples, political discrimination nearly doubles, and economic discrimination increases by almost 40 percent.

Figure 7.6: Religious Demands and Discrimination in 1994-1995

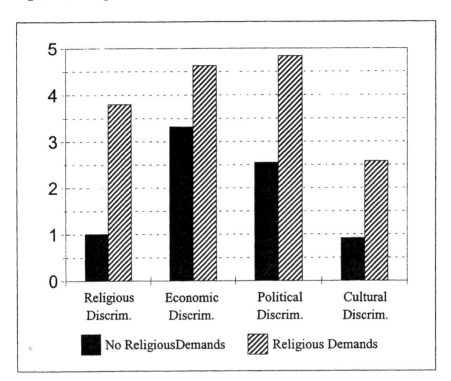

However, there is an alternate explanation for these results that must be considered. The Minorities at Risk model predicts that discrimination against an ethnic minority causes them to form grievances (*Hypothesis 1*). Religious demands are a form of grievance. Thus, it is logical to argue that the direction of the relationship between religious demands and discrimination is the opposite of what is described here. That is, religious demands do not cause discrimination, rather, discrimination causes religious demands.

While this argument is logical, it is not supported by the data. First, while it is logical that religious discrimination causes religious grievances, the argument that cultural, economic, and political discrimination cause religious grievances is considerably weaker. Second, those groups that make the highest levels of religious demands express relatively low levels of religious grievances. The three groups which made the highest religious demands in 1994-1995 are the Arabs in Israel, the Palestinians in the West Bank and Gaza, and the Shi'i in Lebanon.[15] The first two of these groups express low levels of religious grievances.[16] These grievances are based on "diffuse grievances" over religious issues. This category was only used if no other more specific categories were relevant. The third group, the Shi'i in Lebanon, express no religious grievances at all. In addition, the Arabs and Palestinians suffer from the lowest level of religious discrimination that can be reflected in the data used here.[17] This low-level discrimination reflects the fact that there is some religious discrimination and prejudice against the Arabs and Palestinians by Israeli society, but the government has explicit policies to protect and improve their freedom of religion. The Shi'i in Lebanon suffer from no religious discrimination. Thus, precisely in the cases where the highest religious demands are made, religious discrimination and grievances are relatively low or nonexistent.

This supports the argument made earlier that, while passive religious grievances reflect a defensive reaction to discrimination, religious demands reflect a completely separate process of ethnoreligious groups following the rules and standards of behavior of their religions in dealing with creating an environment more congenial to the practice of their religion. The defensive reaction associated with religious demands is not by the ethnoreligious minorities but by ethnoreligious majorities. These majority groups often see the demands made by ethnoreligious minorities as a challenge to their framework and respond with all forms of discrimination against the offending minority. In the cases described above, all three minorities suffer from high levels of economic discrimination and all but the Shi'i in Lebanon suffer from high levels of political discrimination.[18,19]

Hypothesis 4: Religious Institutions and Mobilization

Hypothesis 4 states that *the presence of established religious institutions can facilitate mobilization for protest and rebellion regardless of the more basic causes of that mobilization unless the elites in control of these institutions have an interest in supporting the status quo.* While this hypothesis is straightforward, it leaves open the question of when elites are likely to be satisfied with the status quo and when they feel their interests are best served by challenging or opposing it. One factor that is likely to affect elite interests is whether the religion or its institutions are threatened. On a spiritual level, such a threat would constitute a challenge to any religious elite's framework of belief, leading them to use all of their resources, including religious institutions, to fight that threat. On a more mundane level, a threat to a religious institution is also a threat to the power base of the elites who control it. It is reasonable to assume that they would want to defend their power base.

There is considerable evidence that the presence of religious institutions influences mobilization and that this influence is affected by whether the religion or its institutions are perceived to be at risk. There are two types of mobilization addressed here: peaceful mobilization and mobilization for rebellion. The former deals with nonviolent and legal institutions whose goals are to pursue group interests using mostly legal and peaceful methods like lobbying, running candidates for political office, and peaceful protest. The latter involves illegal organizations that use systematic violence to achieve their goals. This can include terrorism, guerilla warfare, and other forms of organized violence. The religious institutions variable measures the level of formal organization of the ethnoreligious minority's religious institutions.

Figure 7.7: Peaceful Mobilization in the 1990s, Controlling for Religious Institutions and Religious Grievances in 1994-1995

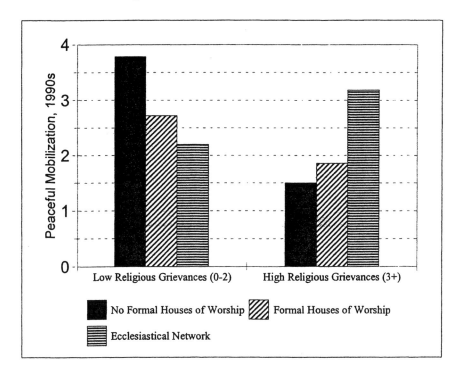

The relationship between religious institutions and peaceful mobilization is shown in figure 7.7. Perceived challenge to the religion is represented by religious grievances. This is a particularly good measure of elite perceptions because this variable was constructed based on grievances expressed by group leaders. The evidence clearly shows that when perceived risk to the religion, as measured by religious grievances, is low, the more organized the religious institutions, the less likely is peaceful mobilization. However, when the religion is perceived to be at risk, institutional organization tends to facilitate peaceful mobilization. This supports the supposition that religious elites use religious institutions to support the status quo when the religion is not at risk and use them to oppose the status quo when the religion is perceived to be at risk.

Figure 7.8: Mobilization for Rebellion in the 1990s, Controlling for Religious Institutions and Grievances over Autonomy in 1995-1995

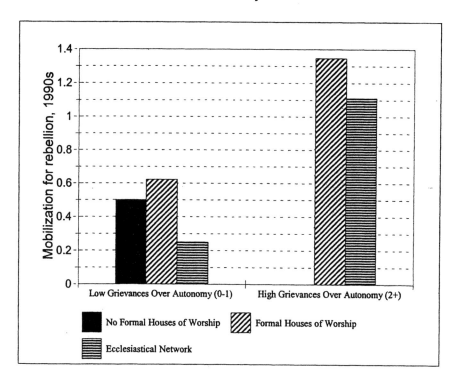

The relationship between religious institutions and mobilization for rebellion does not seem to be affected by religious grievances. As shown in figure 7.8, the variable that most influences this relationship is grievances over autonomy. On average, mobilization for rebellion is considerably higher when grievances over autonomy are higher. This is not surprising considering the findings in *Hypothesis 2* that almost no rebellion occurred among ethnoreligious minorities unless they expressed grievances over autonomy. When grievances over autonomy are low, mobilization for rebellion is higher when there is no ecclesiastical network and drops when there is one. When grievances over autonomy are high, mobilization is also at its highest when there are formal houses of worship but no overarching ecclesiastical network. There are no cases where autonomy grievances are high and there are no formal houses of worship. Thus, we see a general drop in mobilization for rebellion when grievances over autonomy are low and a general rise when these grievances are high.

It is interesting to note that regardless of grievances over autonomy, mobilization for rebellion is highest when there are formal houses of worship but no ecclesiastical network. This implies that mobilization for rebellion tends to be at its highest in cases where there are formal houses of worship, but the existence of an ecclesiastical network somehow moderates this tendency. This trend is logical in terms of elite interests. When there are many formal houses of worship but no real ecclesiastical network, the leader of each house of worship is more or less autonomous. Thus, if there are many houses of worship, it is likely that the leaders of at least some of them will be willing to support a rebellion. When these leaders are autonomous, the only thing to stop them is their calculations of the costs and benefits of supporting a rebellion. However, if there is an ecclesiastical network to which they must answer, aiding in rebellion becomes more difficult if that overarching authority disapproves.

While the following cases are not ethnic, they provide an excellent example of this dynamic. The Catholic Church provides, perhaps, the ultimate example of an ecclesiastical network. All clergy members as well as all adherents of the religion are, at least in theory and to a great extent in practice, responsible to that network and ultimately to the Pope who is considered to be God's representative on earth. In Latin America, an interpretation of Catholic theology, known as liberation theology, has become popular among many Catholics. This theology, which is a mixture of traditional Catholic theology and Marxist doctrine, legitimizes the struggle of Latin America's poor against what they believe is the economic oppression of their governments. The leaders of this movement are mostly grassroots priests and lay persons. However, the upper levels of the Catholic hierarchy oppose liberation theology. Thus, while liberation theology, as advocated by many low-level Catholic elites, has an impact on Latin American politics, it is limited by the more conservative interests of high level Catholic elites (Pottenger, 1989; Berryman 1987). On the other hand, the Catholic church in Poland supported, within limits, the Solidarity movement that opposed the Communist government of that country in the 1980s. While it is not clear that the central Church actively supported the activities of its Polish branch, neither did it actively oppose these activities. However, even in this case, many argue that the involvement of the Catholic Church contributed to the Solidarity movement's nonviolence (Piekalkiewiez, 1991; Weigel, 1992: 180-181).

A more ethnic example of this trend is the opposition to Chinese rule in Tibet. While this often violent opposition has been recently led by young Buddhist priests, the opposition of the Dalai Lama to the use of violence has probably moderated the violence of this opposition. (Kolas, 1996)

While the above results pertain to mobilization for rebellion, the direct relationship between religious institutions and rebellion are less complicated. As shown in figure 7.9, when grievances over autonomy are low, religious institutions discourage rebellion. When grievances over autonomy are high, they encourage it.

As is the case for mobilization for rebellion, when grievances over autonomy are high, rebellion in general rises. Also, as shown in figure 7.10, religious grievances do cause both mobilization for rebellion and rebellion to increase. However, religious grievances do not affect the involvement of religious institutions in either mobilization for rebellion or rebellion.

Figure 7.9: Rebellion in 1995, Controlling for Religious Institutions and Grievances over Autonomy in 1995-1995

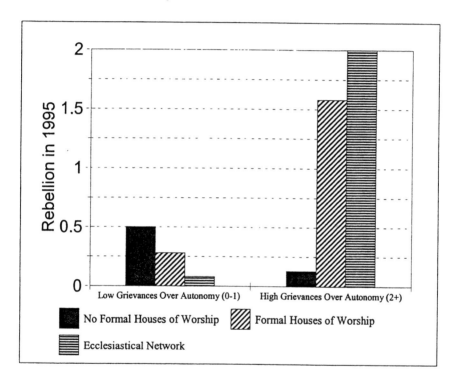

It is posited here that it is elite interests that determine the involvement of religious institutions in mobilization for protest and rebellion. The results show that while threats to religious institutions, as measured by religious grievances, define elite interests with regard to aiding protest, they do not do so for rebellion. Rather, it is grievances over autonomy that determines their involvement in rebellion. This implies that while threats to religious institutions are important to religious elites, they can be overridden by issues of self-determination. It is documented in the discussion of *Hypothesis 2* that rebellion among ethnoreligious minorities rarely occurs unless issues of self-determination are at stake. Thus, reactions to threats to religious institutions, in cases where self-determination is not an issue, are only expressed through protest. In these cases, when the religion is at risk, religious institutions tend to facilitate the process of organizing for protest, but when the religion is not at risk, they tend to inhibit this process. However, when self determination is an issue and rebellion becomes a factor, religious issues are overshadowed by the desire for self determination.

Figure 7.10: Mobilization for Rebellion in the 1990s and Rebellion in 1995, Controlling For Religious Grievances in 1994-1995

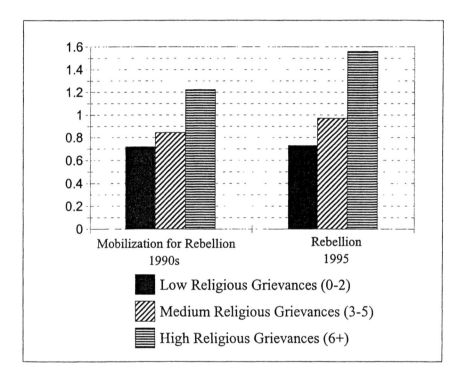

For example, in India, the issue of autonomy appears to be more important than religion in determining rebellion among Muslim groups. The Sunni Muslims live in most of India, have formal houses of worship, and express grievances over religious issues[20] but none over autonomy issues. They engaged in large protests, numbering more than 100,000 protestors in 1995, but no rebellion. However, the Shi'i Muslims living in the Kashmir province of India have similar formal houses of worship and express less grievances over religious issues, but express high grievances over autonomy issues, some wanting autonomy or independence and others wanting to unify with Pakistan. In 1995, they engaged in levels of protest similar to those of the Sunni Muslims in India,[21] but also engaged in guerilla warfare and terrorism against the Indian government.

Another interesting implication is that despite the findings in *Hypothesis 2* that passive religious grievances cause lower levels of protest, there are some circumstances where they can facilitate protest. At high levels of passive religious grievances, religious elites and institutions facilitate mobilization for protest. However, it should be noted that the average level of mobilization for protest remains lower when passive religious grievances are high.[22]

Figure 7.11: Nonreligious Grievances in 1994-1995, Controlling for Religious Legitimacy in 1994-1995 and Religious Relevance in the 1990s

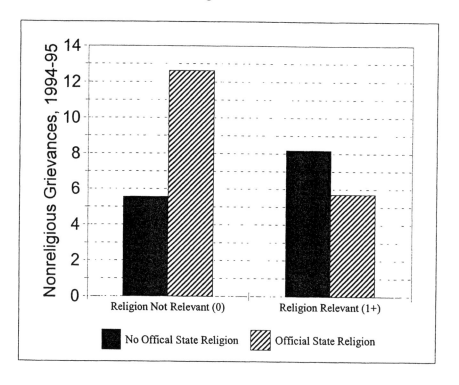

Hypothesis 5: Religious Legitimacy, Grievances, and Mobilization

Hypothesis 5 states that *the use of religious legitimacy can facilitate the growth of economic, political, and social grievances as well as mobilization, regardless of the basic causes of that mobilization, unless the elites who have an influence over the use of religious legitimacy have an interest in supporting the status quo.* Like *Hypothesis 4*, this hypothesis leaves open the question of when religious elites have an interest in supporting the status quo and when they have an interest in opposing it. Also like *Hypothesis 4*, it is posited here that elite interests are defined, at least in part, by whether the religion is at risk.

As shown in figure 7.11, religious legitimacy appears to facilitate nonreligious grievances when religion is not relevant to the conflict, but inhibits them when religion is relevant. However, as shown in figure 7.12, religious legitimacy appears to facilitate religious grievances in all cases. That is, religious legitimacy is only likely to facilitate nonreligious grievances when the conflict in question has nothing to do with religion. When religion becomes important, it causes a focus on religious issues.

Figure 7.12: Religious Grievances in 1994-1995, Controlling for Religious Legitimacy in 1994-1995

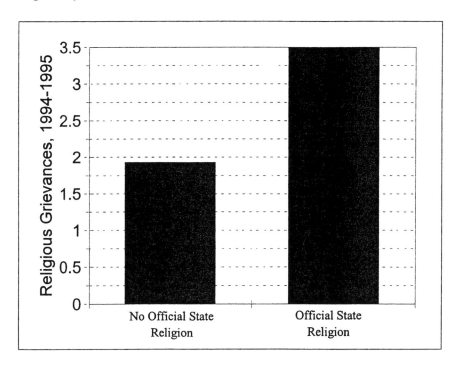

In terms of elite interests, this is a plausible scenario. Religious elites and institutions can benefit from lending their legitimacy to secular causes. It puts them and their institutions in the spotlight and can help to increase the number and commitment of their active supporters. Many fundamentalist movements have successfully used this strategy. Islamic fundamentalists all over the world are particularly known for doing so. This includes the early stages of the Islamic opposition in Algeria, as discussed in chapter 6, as well as ethnic-based Islamic movements like Hamas, which is the primary Islamic fundamentalist movement among the Palestinians in the West Bank and Gaza. However, when religion becomes an important issue, secular issues become overshadowed by it. That is, when religion itself is an issue, using nonreligious issues as a tool to increase one's flock becomes less important than defending the foundation upon which that flock stands. Accordingly, other issues are deemphasized in favor of a focus on defending the religion itself. An example of this phenomenon are the Bahai in Iran, who suffer from high levels of political and economic discrimination as well as religious discrimination.[23] Despite this, they express few grievances over political and economic issues and very high grievances over religious issues.[24]

Figure 7.13: Mobilization for Protest in the 1990s, Controlling for Religious Relevance in the 1990s and Religious Legitimacy in 1994-1995

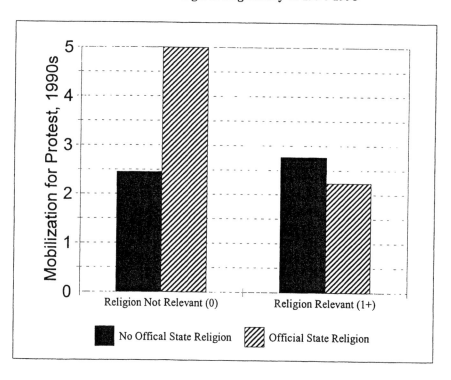

The relationship between religious legitimacy and peaceful mobilization, shown in figure 7.13, is similar to the relationship between religious legitimacy and nonreligious grievances. When religion is not an issue, religious legitimacy appears to facilitate peaceful mobilization; when it is an issue, it appears to inhibit peaceful mobilization. This is the exact opposite of the relationship between religious institutions and peaceful mobilization shown in figure 7.7. Elite interests ought to, as they do through religious institutions, encourage mobilization in defense of the religion when it is at risk.

Figure 7.14: Mobilization for Rebellion in the 1990s, Controlling for Grievances over Autonomy and Religious Legitimacy in 1994-1995

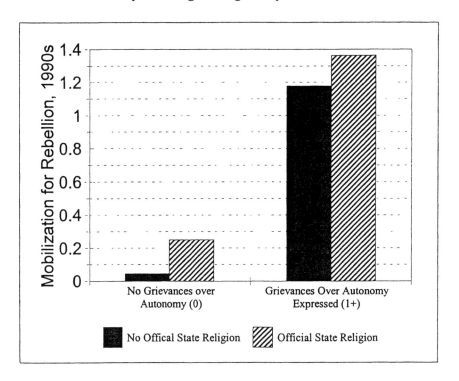

One explanation for what appears to be the opposite influences of religious institutions and legitimacy on peaceful mobilization is the relationship between religious legitimacy and nonreligious grievances. As noted earlier, Gurr (1993a and 1993b) and Gurr and Moore (1997) have established that some of the most important contributing factors to mobilization are all forms of grievances. Thus, as grievances rise, so does peaceful mobilization. It has also been established here that when religion is not relevant to the conflict, religious legitimacy greatly increases the level of nonreligious grievances; when religion is not relevant, religious legitimacy causes a decrease in nonreligious grievances. Accordingly, that religious legitimacy causes peaceful mobilization to rise when religion is not relevant and to drop when religion is relevant is due to the influence of religious legitimacy on nonreligious grievances. That is, when religion is not relevant, religious legitimacy causes nonreligious grievances to rise which, in turn, causes a rise in peaceful mobilization. When religion is relevant, religious legitimacy causes nonreligious grievances to drop which, in turn, causes a similar drop in peaceful mobilization. Thus, the relationship between religious legitimacy and peaceful mobilization is an indirect relationship that involves nonreligious grievances as a mediating variable.

Figure 7.15: Group Cohesion in 1994-1995, Controlling for Religious Discrimination in 1994-1995

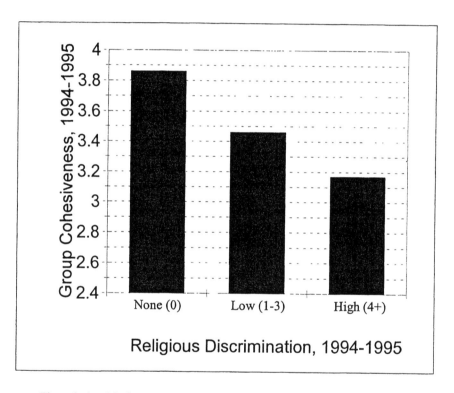

The relationship between religious legitimacy and mobilization for rebellion is more straightforward. The relevance of religious issues to the conflict does not seem to significantly affect the relationship between these two factors. As shown in figure 7.14, the most important mediating factor is grievances over autonomy. When grievances over autonomy are present, the level of mobilization for rebellion is considerably higher. This is consistent with earlier results. More importantly, religious legitimacy appears to cause a slight rise in mobilization for rebellion regardless of whether religion is a relevant issue.[25]

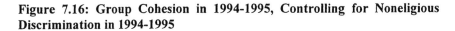

Figure 7.16: Group Cohesion in 1994-1995, Controlling for Noneligious Discrimination in 1994-1995

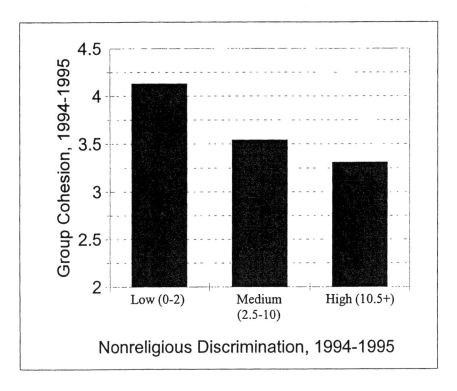

Hypothesis 6: Religious Discrimination and Group Cohesion

Hypothesis 6 states that *the presence of religious discrimination and disadvantages is likely to cause an increase in the levels of group identity and cohesion among the group which suffers from these disadvantages and discrimination.* This prediction is based on findings by Gurr (1993a and 1993b) that other types of discrimination add to group cohesion and identity. However, as shown in figure 7.15, the exact opposite is the case with religious discrimination, which appears to cause a drop in group cohesion. An examination of the relationship between all nonreligious discrimination and group cohesion, shown in figure 7.16, shows that this drop also occurs for these types of discrimination. Thus, for ethnoreligious minorities, all types of discrimination appear to detract from, rather than add to, group cohesion and identity.

This result, that all types of discrimination, religious and nonreligious, reduce, rather than increase, the level of group cohesion among ethnoreligious minorities runs counter to Gurr's (1993a and 1993b) findings. Discrimination does not cause ethnoreligious minorities to rally around the flag; rather it causes dissension within the group. One possible reason for this is that, in most cases (81 out of 105), the ethnoreligious minority in question suffers from more than one type of discrimination. Perhaps the dissension occurs due to disagreements over which type of discrimination must be addressed first. In other words, if an ethnoreligious minority has only one issue to deal with, it is easier to rally the group to a single cause. However, when there are multiple issues to be addressed, there may be agreement over rallying to a cause, but there will probably be disagreement over exactly which cause around which to rally.

Figure 7.17: Group Cohesion in 1994-1995, Controlling for the Number of Types of Discrimination in 1994-1995

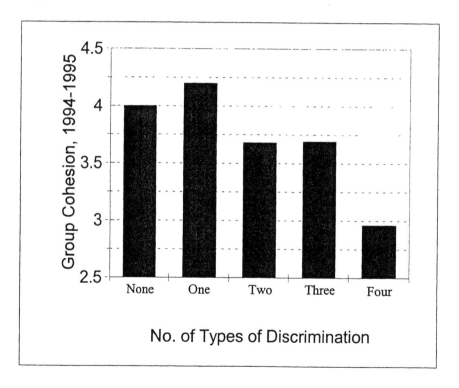

Figure 7.17 provides some evidence for this supposition. When there is only one type of discrimination against ethnoreligious minorities, the level of group cohesion rises, but when there is more than one type of discrimination, group cohesion drops. Figure 7.18 shows that this is true with regard to religious discrimi-

nation specifically. When all other types of discrimination are low, the presence of religious discrimination adds slightly to group cohesion, but when nonreligious discrimination is high, the presence of religious discrimination detracts slightly from group cohesion. While the evidence in these two figures is by no means definitive, it does provide some support for the supposition that when ethnoreligious minorities must deal with multiple issues, disagreement over which issue should be given priority can detract from group unity.

Figure 7-18: Group Cohesion in 1995-1995, Controlling for Religious Discrimination in 1994-1995 and Nonreligious Discrimination in 1994-1995

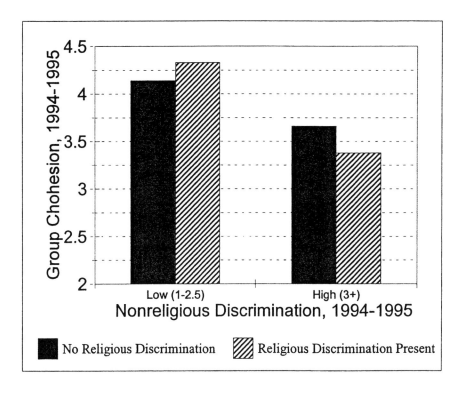

Conclusion

Overall, the basic model of discrimination causing grievances, causing mobilization for protest and rebellion, as well as protest and rebellion, holds true for ethnoreligious conflict. However, the analysis provided here reveals that this process has many nuances and is affected by outside factors.

The relationship between religious discrimination and grievances expressed over that discrimination is straightforward. As expected, religious discrimination against an ethnic minority does challenge that minority's religious framework and causes it to form grievances. In fact, even fears of future discrimination or resentment over past discrimination can activate this defensive reaction. The analysis also provides some insight into the causes of religious and other types of discrimination. Demands by religious minorities for more religious rights can challenge the religious framework of the dominant group, causing them to react in defense of their religious framework by discriminating against and repressing that minority. This discrimination can be religious discrimination as well as economic, political, and/or cultural. It is also likely that the rules and standards of behavior of the dominant group often inspire religious discrimination, but this proposition is difficult to test empirically.

The defense of religious frameworks also requires action. For ethnoreligious minorities this action takes the form of protest and/or rebellion. Although there is clearly a relationship between religious grievances and these activities, this relationship is complicated by other factors. While religious grievances are clearly one of the causes of rebellion, they are overshadowed by grievances over autonomy. An ethnoreligious minority is unlikely to rebel unless it is actively seeking some form of autonomy or independence. Once a minority is seeking some form of autonomy or independence, religious grievances can significantly increase the likelihood of rebellion.

The relationship between religious grievances and protest is more complicated. While active religious grievances, that is, demands for more religious rights independent of any religious discrimination, cause a rise in protest, passive religious grievances, which are a reaction to religious discrimination, cause a drop in protest. This counterintuitive relationship between passive religious grievances and protest holds true even when controlling for democracy, repression, and religious legitimacy. One likely explanation for this is that the difference between passive and active religious grievances is the difference between defending religious frameworks and following the rules and standards of behavior contained in these frameworks. Passive religious grievances are complaints due to religious discrimination. Such discrimination is clearly a form of challenge to a religious framework and, accordingly, passive religious grievances represent an element of the defense of that framework. It is argued here that religion is such an emotional issue that it is beyond simple protest and requires more drastic actions, like rebellion. Active religious grievances, however, are goals that a religious minority wishes to attain because they believe their religious rules and standards of behavior mandate them to aspire to these goals. Any means which can achieve these ends, including protest, are acceptable.

Another possible explanation is that all statistical studies are limited by the quality of their data. This concept is discussed in more detail in the next chapter. What is important here is that it is possible that religious grievances are statistically associated with lower protest because religious discrimination, which causes religious grievances, is likely to occur in repressive autocratic societies where religious discrimination is legitimate. In such societies, protest is at the very least discouraged by the government and is unlikely to have any positive result. The fact that this did not show up in the analysis can be due to the limitations of the democracy and repression variables used here. There is considerable disagreement as to how to define democracy, above and beyond the difficulties of measuring it.[26] The same is true to a lesser extent for repression. Thus, it is possible that the lower levels of protest when passive religious grievances are high is due to these factors and the variables used here are simply inadequate to the task of revealing this relationship

Another factor that influences the process of ethnoreligious conflict is the interests of religious elites as they exercise them through their control of religious institutions and religious legitimacy. They influence the grievance formation process through the use of religious legitimacy. When religion is not an issue in the conflict, religious legitimacy facilitates the formation of grievances over nonreligious issues. This is a good way for religious elites to co-opt issues, thereby increasing their influence in society. However, when religious rights are in jeopardy, emphasizing other issues at the expense of religious ones increases the risk that the religious issues, which religious elites most likely consider more important, will be ignored. Accordingly, when religious issues are at stake, religious legitimacy is used to deemphasize grievances over all other issues. Regardless of what other issues are elements of a conflict, religious legitimacy always facilitates the expression of religious grievances.

Religious elites also influence the process of mobilization, or organizing for political activities. When religious issues are at stake, religious elites use religious institutions to facilitate peaceful mobilization. That is, religious institutions are used to aid in peaceful protest and opposition movements when religion is an important issue in a conflict. However, when religion is not an issue, religious elites prefer not to risk or burden their institutions and discourage this mobilization. Paradoxically, religious legitimacy has the opposite affect. When religious issues are not at stake, religious legitimacy facilitates peaceful mobilization, but when religious issues are at stake religious legitimacy inhibits it. This is probably because religious legitimacy facilitates or inhibits nonreligious grievances under the exact same circumstances. Thus, because nonreligious grievances are a contributor to peaceful mobilization, religious legitimacy indirectly causes or inhibits this mobilization, depending on the circumstances, through facilitating these grievances.

This begs the question of why religious elites would encourage nonreligious grievances, but at the same time discourage peaceful mobilization. This behavior is logical if it is assumed that the facilitation of nonreligious grievances is intended as a means to increase the power and influence of religious elites. If they are able to affect the grievance formation process, they become powers to be reckoned with in society, because they become the representatives of the disaffected masses. As long as this disaffection is expressed within the context of the religious institutions, which are controlled by the religious elites, the power of these elites increases. If separate organizations to pursue group goals are formed, this creates or gives more power to alternative elites. Accordingly the religious elites oppose this. However, when the religion itself as at stake, defending it becomes more important and any effective means to do so is used. Also, if the issues of the conflict are religious, it is more likely that the religious elites will control, or at least influence, any separate organizations that are created to pursue group objectives.

Like religious grievances, the influence of religious elites over mobilization for rebellion and rebellion itself is overshadowed by the influence of autonomy issues. Mobilization for rebellion and rebellion are mostly motivated by a desire for self-determination, and the influence of religious elites is marginal. Religious legitimacy is associated with higher levels of mobilization for rebellion, but this influence is slight. Religious institutions are most likely to facilitate mobilization for rebellion when there are formal houses of worship that are not affiliated with an authoritative ecclesiastical network. This is probably because when there are many religious leaders, there are generally a few who desire to promote rebellion. When these leaders do not have to answer to any institutional authority, they can do as they please. However, if they have higher-ups they must answer to, other than their deity, those higher officials are likely to be more conservative and discourage the grass-roots leadership from inciting rebellion. As is the case with religious legitimacy, this influence is marginal, especially when compared to the influence of autonomy issues.

Given all of this, it is clear that religion can significantly influence ethnoreligious conflict. However, as discussed in chapter 4, religion is important only in a large minority of ethnoreligious conflicts. Of the 105 ethnoreligious conflicts studied here religion is not relevant in 28 of them and only marginally relevant in another 38. Thus religion is not a significant issue in 62.9 percent of ethnoreligious conflicts. An examination of the frequencies of some of the major religion variables for the 1994-1995 period provides similar results. fifty , or 47.6 percent, of the 105 ethnoreligious minorities experience no religious discrimination. Thirty-five, exactly one third, of them express no passive religious grievances. Eighty-five, or 81 percent express no active religious grievances. fifteen, or 15.4 percent have no formal houses of worship. Finally, thirty, or 28.6 percent, live in states where the use of religion in politics has no legitimacy at all.

Despite this, the evidence provided here shows that religion is a factor that can not be discounted when studying causes of ethnoreligious conflict. Even if it is not a factor in all cases, when it is a factor, it clearly influences the dynamics of the conflict as well as the levels of protest and rebellion. Furthermore, when all of the above variables are examined at once, only seven, or 6.7 percent, of these groups express no passive or active religious grievances, experience no religious discrimination, have no formal houses of worship, and live in a state where religion has no legitimacy in political discourse. Thus, while religion is not always the most important issue, it is fair to say that religion has at least some minor influence on some aspect of the dynamics of the vast majority of ethnoreligious conflicts.

The model developed and tested in this chapter focuses on the role of religion in *ethnic* conflict. However, the principles on which the model is based can be applied to the involvement of religion in any type of conflict, as well as to the involvement of nonreligious ideologies in such conflicts. Due to the narrow focus of this model, many of the findings may apply only to the case of a religious ethnic minority in conflict with a dominant group within a state, while other findings may be more general in their application. The general application of these findings is examined in the next chapter.

Notes

1. For a more detailed discussion of the differences between ethnoreligious minorities and other ethnic groups in the Minorities at Risk study, see chapter 4.

2. For more details on each of these groups see the Minorities at Risk website at http://www.bsos.umd.edu/cidcm/inscr/mar

3. This was related to me in a personal conversation with Gurr.

4. For a further discussion and criticism of relative deprivation theory see Rule (1988). His summary of the major criticisms of relative deprivation (RD) theory include: RD is a theory that deals with individual motivations yet it is applied to group behavior; it could be forms of frustration other than RD that cause violence; the violence caused by RD may not be directed at the government; RD assumes that conditions leading to rebellion are enduring and therefore easy to measure despite the possibility that other factors, which are more transient, are the actual causes of the violence; many studies use circular reasoning, and violent action is taken as proof that someone was dissatisfied with something; in general, RD theory formulations do not explain both the presence and the absence of violence consistently; RD is not specific enough regarding which individuals feel and act on RD and which particular needs are most relevant; and other explanations, such as the rational action model, provide a better explanation for collective action. He adds that for RD to explain series of violent events it must meet three conditions. First, "that the participants share a single standard of justice, appropriateness, equity, minimal acceptability or the like." Second, that the action must ensue from the experience of RD. Third, that the participants in the action are distinguished from nonparticipants by virtue of their experiencing RD.

Lichbach (1989) argues that another problem with RD is that RD theorists cannot agree on the type of relationship RD has with political dissent. He notes that researchers have found positive, positive curvilinear, negative, U-shaped, and inverted U-shaped relationships as well as the absence of any relationship at all. He notes that these differences can be explained by different definitions, indicators, and data but does not come to a conclusion about the nature of the relationship.

5. For a more comprehensive discussion on mobilization theory see, among others, Chong (1991), Gurr and Harff (1994), Hannigan (1991), Oberschall (1993), Snow and Rochford (1986), Rule (1988), Tilly (1978), and Webb (1983). Rule (1988) has several criticisms of mobilization theory. First, Tilly's assertion that participants in collective action are representative of the groups for whom they act and are not generally from the "scum of the earth," as many theorists suggest, is not always the case. Second, the assertions that civil

violence is the outgrowth of other forms of political action, and that their objectives reflect the long term collective. Third, Tilly's assertion that collective action is more likely to occur when the stakes (opportunities and threats) are high and when groups have sufficient resources and participation needs further examination. There needs to be more empirical work on the "negative cases" where such conditions existed and collective action did not occur. Fourth, individuals can be members of more than one group, thus confusing the situation even further.

6. For a more detailed discussion of the Minorities at Risk model, see Gurr (1993a and 1993b), Gurr and Harff (1994), and Gurr and Moore (1997).

7. More sophisticated analyses are provides in Fox (1997, 1999a, 1999b, 2000a, 200b, 2000c. and 2001).

8. For a more sophisticated analysis of this relationship see Fox (2000c).

9. The cases presented in table 7.4 are representative of a more rigorous analysis of the data presented in Fox (2001). This method of providing sample cases is used here in order to enhance ease of understanding.

10. Poe, Tate, and Keith (1999) make a similar argument.

11. This description is based on the Minorities at Risk report on the Copts in Egypt, written by Jonathan Fox. The report is available at HTTP://www.bsos.umd.edu/cidcm/inscr/ mar

12. This description is based on the Minorities at Risk report on the Muslims in France. The report is available at HTTP://www.bsos.umd.edu/cidcm/inscr/mar

13. See Fox (2000c).

14. For a more rigorous statistical analysis of *Hypothesis 2* see Fox (2000c).

15. Religious demands in 1994-1995 are coded as 3 or higher for these groups.

16. Religious grievances in 1994-1995 are coded as 2 for both groups.

17. Religious discrimination in 1994-1995 (rdisal95) is coded as 1 for both of these groups.

18. Economic discrimination in 1994-1995 (alled94) against the Palestinians, Arabs, and Shi'i is 9, 7, and 5 respectively out of a possible 9 and political discrimination (allpd94) against them is 7,6, and 0 respectively, also out of a possible 9. Only the Arabs in Israel suffered from any cultural discrimination in 1994-1995 and this level of discrimination (1) is relatively low.

19. For a more sophisticated analysis of the causes of discrimination against ethnoreligious minorities, see Fox (2000a).

20. Religious grievances expressed by the Muslims in India in 1994-1995 is coded as 5.

21.Religious grievances expressed by the Kashmir Muslims in India in 1994-1995 is coded as 2, grievances over autonomy in the same period is coded as 8, and protest in 1995 is coded as 6.

22. For a more rigorous statistical analysis of *Hypothesis 4* see Fox (1999a).

23. Economic, Political, and Religious discrimination in 1994-1995 against the Bahai in Iran are coded as 7, 8, and 8 respectively, all out of a possible 9.

24. Grievances over economic and political issues for the Bahai in Iran are coded as 1.5 and 2, respectively, out of a possible 15. Religious grievances are coded as 18 out of a possible 24.

25. For a more rigorous statistical analysis of *Hypothesis 5* see Fox (1999b).

26. For a discussion of how to empirically measure democracy see Gurr and Jaggers (1995).

Chapter 8

Some Implications and Clarifications

The theory presented here is intended as a framework to better understand the role religion plays in conflict. It provides a comprehensive and dynamic framework for understanding religious conflicts in general and ethnoreligious conflicts specifically. The method to achieve this was to develop a set of general principles that define the role religion plays in conflict, use them to build a more formal model for ethnoreligious conflict, and finally, to flesh out that model by testing it with empirical data.

While this process has helped to provide a perspective on religious and ethnoreligious conflict that does not yet exist in the literature, it has several shortcomings and implications that must be addressed. First, the empirical part of this study focuses on ethnoreligious conflict. How, if at all, do the findings here apply to other types of religious conflicts? Second, do the findings of this study apply to secular ideologies, such as nationalism? Third, there are several shortcomings of this type of analysis that must be taken into account. Fourth, how can this information be used to prevent or at least mitigate the detrimental affects of religious conflict?

Religious Involvement in Ethnic vs. Nonethnic Conflict

While the formal model developed and tested in the previous chapter focuses on ethnic conflict, the general principles upon which it is based apply to a wider range of religious conflicts. However, there are many aspects of ethnoreligious conflict that are ethnic rather than religious. This means that there is a qualitative difference between ethnoreligious conflicts and religious conflicts that do not also involve ethnicity. Thus, many of the findings from this study apply only to ethnoreligious conflicts. It is, therefore, essential to sort out which aspects of the findings apply

185

only to ethnoreligious conflicts and which apply on a more general level.

It is clear that religion plays a role in politics and in conflicts that have nothing to do with ethnic issues or groups. For example, many Middle Eastern governments are challenged by widespread militant Islamic movements, and the "religious right" in the United States has been politically active in its advocation of religious values in American society. Both of these movements have been described as fundamentalist and neither of them are ethnically distinct from the governments which they are seeking to influence or challenge. These challengers differ from the governments they challenge mainly in the intensity of their religious beliefs and the role they believe religion should play in government, politics, and society.

The behavior of both of these movements, as well as others around the world, including most fundamentalist movements, however, can be understood through applying the general principles developed here that define the role of religion and conflict. That is, they behave according to the four social functions of religion discussed in chapters 2 and 6. Both are motivated, at least in part, by the challenge that they believe is posed to their religious frameworks by modern secular society (social function of religion #1). Both are acting to impose their interpretation of the rules and standards of their religion on the rest of society (social function of religion #2). Both make use of religious institutions in order to organize and otherwise further their cause (social function of religion #3). Also, elements of both use religious legitimacy to justify violent actions (social function of religion #4). In the case of Islamic movements in the Middle East, this includes violent rebellion against the state, and in the United States, elements of the religious right support often violent protests against abortion, which on occasion have led to murder. While both of these movements are fundamentalist movements, and this discussion applies especially to fundamentalists, it also applies to other types of nonethnic-based religious movements

This study provides empirical evidence that religion can be relevant in ethnic conflict. This implies that it can be relevant to other types of conflict, including conflicts between secular and religious elements of the same ethnic group and especially including conflicts between fundamentalists and nonfundamentalists. However, the model and data used here focus on ethnic conflict. Accordingly, while the general principles behind the model are probably true of nonethnic religious conflict, many specific aspects of the model are not.

Hypothesis 1 states that *religious discrimination, whatever its cause, is likely to result in the formation of religious grievances within the ethnic group suffering from this religious discrimination.* While it is argued here that this is essentially true of all types of religious conflict, the types of discrimination involved in ethnic conflict and in conflict between secular and religious elements in a society differ. In the case of ethnic conflict, the discrimination is by a majority group, which belongs to one religion, against a minority group which belongs to another. This produces grievances that are mostly a reaction to this discrimination. In the case of secular vs. religious elements in a society, such targeted discrimination is unlikely to occur. In fact, there is no minority religion against which to discriminate because everyone involved is generally of the same religion. The dispute between these groups is about the role that religion should play in society. While some regimes are officially secular and discourage all religious observances, the prime example of this being the late Communist governments, most such regimes tend not to prevent their citizens from privately practicing their religions. Thus, the religious challengers to secular governments generally tend to express less passive religious grievances based on religious discriminations than do ethnic religious minorities. They, rather, tend to make active demands that religious ideology be used to guide society and/or as a basis for government. They sometimes go as far as advocating the current government be replaced with a religious one. Thus, in such cases, the government's espousal of secular values, or at least values that are not sufficiently religious, motivates religious demands by the religious element of society. While this dynamic is similar to that of religious discrimination against an ethnic minority causing grievances, it is qualitatively different.

This difference becomes apparent when analyzing the application of *Hypothesis 2*, which states that *religious grievances are likely to result in the mobilization for protest and rebellion as well as directly causing protest and rebellion among the ethnic group which has formed these grievances* and *Hypothesis 3* which states that *provocative actions by a minority religious ethnic group are likely to provoke a negative reaction from the dominant ethnic group. This negative action can include religious, social, political, and/or economic discrimination as well as other forms of oppression.* The findings for these hypotheses show that, while the passive religious grievances described in *Hypothesis 2* detract from the level of protest by ethnoreligious minorities, the active religious grievances described in *Hypothesis 3*, such as active demands that religious ideology be used to guide society and/or as a basis for government, directly contribute to protest activities. This distinction between passive religious grievances and religious demands is crucial. Most ethnic religious minorities are less likely to engage in protest over religious issues because they are far more likely to express passive religious grievances than active religious demands.[1] However, religious elements of secular societies tend to have little cause to express passive religious grievances and, if they are politically active, tend to focus on active demands. In fact, most conflicts between secular and religious elements of society are defined by such demands. This implies that religious elements of secular societies are likely to engage in higher levels of protest.

For example, the desire among many in the religious right in the United States to make abortion illegal is an active demand rather than a grievance over religious discrimination. In fact, this group, arguably suffers from no overt discrimination other than the consequences of some of their members engaging in violent and illegal actions. The demands made by these groups tend to be active demands to implement or codify their religious beliefs in the public sphere. A ban on abortion, prayer in public schools, and various demands regarding education, such as a ban on sex education and the teaching of evolution, are but some examples of such demands.

The dynamics of religion and rebellion found in this study and discussed in

Hypothesis 2 are probably also unique to ethnic conflict. The results show that issues surrounding autonomy and separatism, rather than religious issues, are the primary cause of ethnic rebellion. In fact, such rebellions rarely occur in the absence of such issues. Passive religious grievances can, however, contribute to ethnic rebellion by acting as a catalyst. That is, when autonomy and/or separatism is already an issue, religious issues make ethnic rebellion more likely.

These results are, most likely, unique to ethnic conflict for two reasons. First, the passive religious grievances that contribute to rebellion by ethnic minorities are less common among religious elements of secular societies. Second, this relationship is only strong when the ethnic minority expresses grievances over autonomy. However, demands for autonomy are rarely expressed by religious elements of secular societies. This is because politically active religious elements of secular societies generally do not want to exit society; rather they want to change it. When they engage in rebellion, it is not to secede from a state, but rather to replace its government. Thus, the issue of autonomy should be irrelevant to most such conflicts.

Two of the key factors in determining whether religious elements in a secular society will engage in protest or rebellion are repression and democracy. Democracies generally permit freedom of religion, thus creating an environment in which minority religions are comparatively free from restrictions. This environment also allows, and often encourages, religious movements to pursue their social agenda in a peaceful manner. Not surprisingly, in more democratic and less repressive societies, most groups, including religious ones, with political agendas take advantage of this environment and use protest and other peaceful forms of political expression to pursue their agenda. However, rebellion, or other nonpeaceful forms of political expression, do occur in democratic settings when peaceful methods failed to achieve the group's goals or it is believed that such methods would be useless. Thus the general rule is, in democratic settings, when peaceful methods are believed to have a chance of succeeding, they are usually used and violence only occurs when these methods were unsuccessful.

However, in autocratic and repressive societies, these forms of peaceful political activity are generally not possible and rebellion is the only avenue for pursuing a political agenda. Thus, when a group engages in rebellion or political violence it is usually because peaceful political expression is not possible or has been unsuccessful in attaining that group's goals.[2] This general rule does not apply to cases of where violence is, for some reason, ideologically required by a religion regardless of the political setting:, for example messianic movements, as discussed in chapter 6, or the Thugs in ancient India.[3]

Thus, when, the religious elements of a secular society engage in violence or rebellion it is seldom because they seek autonomy. Rather, it is because protest is not possible or has not successfully addressed their demands. Also, when religious violence occurs in democratic societies, it is generally because more peaceful tactics failed or are believed to be ineffective. An excellent example of this dynamic is the pro-life movement in the United States. At first, the movement focused on legal protest activity in order to stop abortions. Only when it became clear that this strategy was not working did the radical elements of the movement begin to engage in illegal and more violent techniques.[4] Another example of this dynamic is the Islamic rebellion in Algeria which is discussed in more detail in chapter 6.

Hypotheses 2 and *3* are both variations of the argument that if one group provokes a second group, the second group is likely to reply in kind. While this argument is obviously applicable to conflicts between religious and secular elements in societies, it is generally not central to such conflicts. The religious elements in such conflict are usually differentiated from the secular elements only in the strength of their religious beliefs. In most cases, they are not singled out for discrimination or repression unless their activities challenge the state government. Thus, the religious right in the United States which, except perhaps on its extreme fringes, does not challenge the right of the U.S. government to rule, does not suffer from any overt discrimination directed specifically against it, other than the legal consequences of the illegal actions taken by some of its members. This is not considered discrimination, because actions like violent protest, murder, and bombings are equally illegal for all residents of the United States. Overt discrimination occurs when a specific group is singled out and suffers from restrictions that do not apply to other groups. However, the Islamic militant challenge to the right and ability of Egypt's government to rule has provoked a violent and repressive response.

Hypothesis 4, which states that *the presence of established religious institutions can facilitate mobilization for protest and rebellion regardless of the more basic causes of that mobilization unless the elites in control of these institutions have an interest in supporting the status quo* describes the relationship between religious institutions and mobilization for protest and rebellion. The general rule seems to be that these institutions support protest only when their leaders perceive that there is a threat to the religion or its institutions. They also have a slight influence over rebellion, but this influence is overshadowed by the influence of the desire for autonomy or independence. However, the role of religious institutions in conflicts between secular and religious elements of society is more complicated because these elements usually belong to the same religion. Thus, unlike religious minorities, who have their own separate religious institutions, the religious and secular elements of a homogeneous society may often share religious institutions. These institutions may support one of the elements in the conflict or be divided, with both progovernment and antigovernment elements, as well as some elements somewhere in between. For instance, most Middle Eastern countries have a traditional institutionalized set of Islamic religious institutions that are supported by the state and tend to support the government. Yet many such countries, including Egypt, Algeria, Tunisia, and Saudi Arabia are being challenged by militant Islamic elements which act through official or informal religious institutions. Thus, in such conflicts, both sides of the conflict may be supported by parts of the same set of religious institutions. With regard to the influence of religious institutions on rebellion, there is the added factor that, as noted earlier, secular-religious conflicts generally do not involve autonomy issues.

Hypotheses 5, which states that states that *the use of religious legitimacy can facilitate the growth of economic, political, and social grievances as well as mobilization, regardless of the basic causes of that mobilization, unless the elites who have an influence over the use of religious legitimacy have an interest in supporting the status quo* is derived from the fourth social function of religion, which is that *religion has the ability to legitimize actions and institutions*. The findings presented here show that the type of action legitimized depends upon the relevance of religion to the conflict. When religion is not relevant, religious legitimacy facilitates the expression of economic, political, and social grievances; but, when it is relevant, the expression of these types of grievances is lessened, whereas the expression of religious grievances is advanced. However, conflicts between religious and secular elements of society hinge precisely on the fact that religion is relevant to the conflict. Based on this, only religious grievances should be facilitated.

There is some support in the literature for the argument that religious legitimacy can transform secular grievances into a religious conflict. Juergensmeyer (1993: 23-24) argues that the failure of governments led by secular elements, which he calls secular nationalists, to provide political freedom, economic prosperity, and social justice is one of the factors that enhances the legitimacy of religious ideologies as an alternative ideological basis for government. Appleby (1994: 23) argues that "while all opposition or protest movements tend to swell in numbers under conditions of severe economic crisis and social displacement, fundamentalist movements appear to be particularly successful in exploiting widespread social discontent." In fact, according to Appleby (1994: 40) such movements thrive when the masses are dislocated by rapid and uneven modernization, there are haphazard changes in economic and cultural patterns, and education and social welfare systems fail. This shows a pattern where the religious elements in society echo political, social, and economic grievances present in society, and in the process, transform these secular-based grievances into demands for a more religious society. Given this, it is not surprising that the functionalist school of thought argues that economic, political, and social imperatives are the true forces behind religious involvement in society. However, while religious movements do make use of such secular grievances, it is clear that religious movements exist independently of them and are far more than mere tools of economic, social, and political imperatives.[5] The Islamic rebellion in Algeria, discussed in more detail in chapter 6, provides an excellent example of a movement that transformed secular-based discontent into a religious opposition movement.

In all, the specific dynamics of conflicts between secular and religious elements of society are different from those of conflicts between religious ethnic minorities and dominant groups. However, the basic principles of religion and conflict defined by the four social functions of religion apply in both cases. In both cases, adherents of religious frameworks often respond to perceived challenges in those frameworks and often behave in a conflictive manner in accordance with their interpretation of the rules and standards of behavior that are part of those frameworks. Also, religious institutions and legitimacy can facilitate or inhibit both types of conflict, depending on the interests of religious elites.

Secular Ideologies and Nationalism

As will be recalled, the four social functions of religion are derived in chapter 2 from definitions of both religion and ideology. Accordingly, it is reasonable to argue that secular ideologies can perform the same social functions as religion and, accordingly, contribute to conflict in a similar manner.[6]

Ideologies can clearly provide a meaningful framework for understanding the world (social function #1). They also can provide rules and standards of behavior that link individual actions and goals to this meaningful framework (social function #2). For example, both Communist ideology and the social democratic school of classical liberal ideology fulfill these two social functions. However, being very different from each other these ideologies often explain the same situation differently and advocate different actions to deal with social situations.

An example is provided by the wretched conditions in which the working classes lived during the Industrial Revolution. Classical Marxist ideology explained this immiseration as a result of a dialectical historical process of class conflict. At this stage, the capitalist class exploits the working class. The solution to this problem, according to Marx, is that when the working class gains class consciousness, it will overthrow the capitalists and establish a dictatorship of the proletariat that will help to create the perfect Communist society. An adherent of the social democratic school of classical liberal ideology would look at this situation differently. While capitalism is a good thing, the wretched condition of the masses is the result of a particular form of capitalism, *laissez-faire* capitalism. The solution to this problem is not to get rid of capitalists, but to fix capitalism. This can be done through regulation of industry, unions, and income redistribution policies, like progressive taxation, welfare, and social security, in order to assure that workers are not exploited. Thus, both of these ideologies fill the social functions of explaining the world to their adherents and providing means to deal with it, but do so in very different manners.

Ideologies often become associated with institutions (social function #3). Such institutions include unions, political parties, and often the government apparatus itself. Marxist-Leninist ideology was particularly associated with Communist parties as well as the government apparatus in Communist states.

Ideologies also have the ability to legitimize actions and institutions (social function #4). Communist governments have used Marxist-Leninist ideology to legitimize themselves as the true representatives of the workers. The fall of the former Soviet and Eastern European Communist governments indicates that this claim of legitimacy had its limits. However, all forms of classical liberal ideology are excellent sources of legitimacy for democratic governments. That many non-democratic states put on the facade of democracy says much about the strength of this source of legitimacy.

Given that ideologies perform the same social functions as religion, it is not hard to argue that they can similarly contribute to conflict. However, the specifics of these contributions may differ from the model developed here. This is so because ideologies are qualitatively different from religions. Religious frameworks are based on the belief in a divine or supernatural authority which has communicated rules and standards of behavior that are generally not open to question by mortal man. Secular ideologies are based on the belief in a set of principles that are mostly human in origin. It is difficult to argue with divine edicts, assuming that one believes in the validity of the source of those edicts, but human ideas are, on the average, more open to question. This is not to say that there have not been those who believed in an ideology as strongly as the most zealous of the religious zealots or that religious doctrines have never been questioned. Rather, it is argued here that religious frameworks tend to inspire stronger, deeper, and more intractable belief than ideologies. Accordingly, the four social functions of religions and ideologies probably, on average, contribute less to conflict with respect to ideologies than with respect to religions.

Currently, the one possible exception to this is nationalism. Nationalism is basically the combination of ethnic or national identity with the belief that the nation should have some form self-determination, usually realized through statehood or autonomy within a state.[7] Thus, nationalism is a framework that defines the world as one made up of many nations, each of which should have their own state. It has been used by political elites to justify rebellion, war, and "ethnic cleansing." A powerful indicator that nationalism and religion are unique in their ability to inspire violence is a finding by Rapoport (1984: 659) that, until the advent of nationalism in the nineteenth century, religion was the only justification for terrorism. For these reasons, and others, many believe that nationalism and the concept of self-determination are major dangers in today's international politics.[8]

Thus, many contend that the ideological frameworks associated with nationalism are contributing to violent conflict worldwide, especially in the former Soviet block. Nationalist ideologies call for the nation to be united with the state (social function #1). As a result, many nationalities which have no state have taken up arms in order to attain one, and many nations which control states have engaged in discrimination or worse against other nationalities living within their state (social function #2). This has resulted in the creation of nationalist parties and revolutionary movements that seek to facilitate these actions (social function #3). Finally, many scholars argue that modern nationalism is the creation, or at least the tool, of elites. These elites use the legitimacy of national symbols and myths to create nationalist ideologies that are used to legitimize the rule of those elites (social function #4).[9]

The events of the past fifteen years in the former Soviet bloc are strong evidence that nationalism is capable of contributing to conflict on a par with religious beliefs. What nationalism and religion seem to have in common is that both are often an integral part of many individuals' and groups' core identities. That this is true of religion needs no further demonstration.[10] That this is true of nationalism is implicit in what constitutes a nationality. While common traits like ethnicity, shared historical experience, myths, symbols, religious beliefs, region of residence, and language contribute to defining a nationality, they are not its essence. The essence of nationality is the shared perception that whatever traits define the group set them apart as a unique national entity.[11] Thus, the strength of nationalism is dependent upon the extent to which membership in a national group is a core element of the identity of the national group members. Accordingly, it is likely that a data analysis similar to the one performed here, if applied to national groups, would produce similar results.

The power of nationalism is attested to in this study. In many instances, the issue of autonomy, which is a very nationalist issue, overshadows religion as an issue in ethnoreligious conflict. Ethnoreligious rebellions rarely occur unless autonomy is an issue. Autonomy also overshadows the influence of religious institutions and legitimacy on mobilization for rebellion. However, it is telling that rebellion reaches its highest levels when the issues of autonomy and religion are combined in the same conflict. In fact, all of the ethnoreligious minorities in this study that engage in large-scale guerilla activity or protracted civil war, the highest levels of rebellion measured here, express grievances over both religious and autonomy issues. This includes the Sri Lankan Tamils in Sri Lanka, the Chechens in Russia, the Armenians in Azerbaijan, and the Southerners in the Sudan.

Problems with Large-N Studies

The study presented here is a large-n study. This means that similar information from many cases is used to create variables that can be studies using statistical methodology. There are several unavoidable problems with all large-n studies. In order to put the findings presented here in their proper context, these problems must be addressed.

The first two such problems are interrelated. The first is whether the variables you use are measuring what you think they are measuring. The second is whether variables are selected based on what is easiest to measure, as opposed to what actually should be measured. That is, are certain factors ignored because they are difficult or impossible to measure empirically? This problem is illustrated by a famous parable where a man sees another man on his hands and knees, apparently searching for something near a lamppost and a dialogue ensues:

First man: What are you doing?
Second man: I lost my glasses and have been searching for them here under this lamppost for several hours.
First man: Why it is taking so long to find the glasses?

Second man: Probably because I lost them over there in the dark.
First man: Then why are you looking for them over here?
Second man: Because it's light over here and dark over there.

The moral of the parable is that looking in the light doesn't help if your answer lies in the dark. Both of these problems deal with the issue of whether the study truly reflects the reality it is attempting to explain.

For example, when this study measures passive religious grievances, the intent is to capture the collective feeling of an ethnoreligious minority on religious discrimination against them, but what is really being measured? The religious grievances variable actually measures grievances that are publically expressed by group leaders. While the grievances group leaders express most probably reflect how the group as a whole feels, the two are not the same thing. There are many reasons why group leaders may avoid expressing grievances that exist. Expressing grievances under repressive regimes may be hazardous to one's health. Perhaps some leaders feel more can be accomplished through private channels than public ones. Perhaps some leaders even personally benefit from the deprived situation of their group and have no desire to change it. On the other side of the coin, group leaders may choose to exaggerate or even fabricate group grievances. Doing so can help to rally the group around their leadership, increasing the power and influence of this leadership. It can also provide publicity to a publicity-hungry demagogue.

Nevertheless, the passive religious grievance variable used here, as well as most of the other grievance variables, are based on public expressions of grievances by group leaders, because this is what can be measured. Even if the resources to poll all 105 of the ethnoreligious minorities in this study were available, polling data has its own set of problems, and many of the minorities in question live in autocratic states that would prevent such polling; are engaged in violent conflicts, making such polling dangerous to the pollers; and/or simply live in remote regions where access is limited. Furthermore, such extensive polling would be extremely expensive. This is not to mention that, in the most perfect of worlds, this study would have measured not what people say, but what they are really thinking. Unfortunately, no method for doing this exists or is likely to exist in the near future. Thus, the public statements of group leaders are probably the best available measure of passive religious grievances available, even if they do not measure exactly what optimally should have been measured.

Similar problems with other variables in this study include:

- All of the nonreligious grievance variables, including those over auton-omy, economic, political, and cultural issues, are similarly based on the public expression of grievances by group leaders.

- The democracy variable measures only institutional democracy. This means that it focuses on issues like the competitiveness of political participation, the competitiveness of executive recruitment, the openness of executive recruitment, and the constraints on the chief executive. However, it does not address the human rights aspect of democracy because such information is not systematically available in many of the cases.[12]

- The religious legitimacy variable is intended to measure the legitimacy of the use of religion in political discourse. Legitimacy issues are notoriously hard to measure. The indicator used here measures whether the state has an official religion. While this does crudely reflect the legitimacy of religion in political discourse, it is by no means an exact measure.[13]

- The mobilization variables measure the number of organizations that represent a group and the amount of support for those organizations. While this does reflect mobilization, it does not account for other factors, like the enthusiasm of this support and the material and financial resources available to the organizations.

- The religious institutions variable measures the formal level of organiza-tion of religious institutions. That is, whether they are unaffiliated lay-led prayer meetings or an international ecclesiastical network such as the Catholic Church. A preferable measure would have also included atten-dance figures, but there are not available in many of the cases.[14]

Despite these problems, all of the variables reflect what they are intended to measure even if they are not perfect measures. Using indirect and imperfect measures when no better ones are available is a time honored practice in the social sciences. However, it is important to be aware that they are being used and that the nature of the variables used in a study, by definition, color its results. For more details on these variables see appendix B.

A third, and related, problem is that when collecting information on a large number of cases both the quantity and quality of the information varies from case to case. For instance, there is no shortage of information on a well-publicized case like the Palestinians in the West Bank and Gaza, but information is often limited on less publicized groups living in the remote regions of the Third World. Similarly, better information is generally available in democracies with a free and independent media than in autocracies, which often try to limit the information available to outsiders. As a result, coding some variables for groups in remote regions and living under autocracies is often guesswork based on poor information. Over time, however, the international media has been penetrating even the most repressive autocracies and has been gaining access to even the remotest of regions. Thus, the information available to researchers in the 1990s has generally been better that it has been in the past. There is no reason to expect this trend will not continue.

A fourth problem with large-n studies is that they focus on general trends. By their nature, these studies focus on factors that are present in a large number of the cases. While this methodology is excellent at presenting an overall picture, many unique local factors are not accounted for. It is a cliche that all politics are local. The failure to account for the local nuances which undoubtably affect each and every case in this study is a serious shortcoming. On the other hand, looking at an issue on a higher level of analysis has the ability to uncover trends that are extremely unlikely to be found when looking at the problem case by case. A good example from this study is the finding that passive religious grievances cause a decline in peaceful protest. It is fair to say that it is very unlikely that this counterintuitive finding would have occurred in any type of study other than a large-n study.

Thus, this weakness of large-n studies is counterbalanced by a weakness in more traditional comparative studies. That is, while large-n studies often miss nuances unique to individual cases, comparative studies often miss larger trends that may be counter-intuitive. Given this, using a combined comparative and large-n approach should produce better results than either approach used individually. Those using large-n approaches usually base their theories on the wisdom gained from the comparative approach, as is the case with this study. Less common are comparative studies which use the findings of large-n studies in order to better understand individual cases. Doing so should improve the quality of comparative studies which, in turn, would provide better foundations for a new generation of theories that can be tested in a large-n format. Thus, by building upon each other, the two approaches have the potential to produce a level of understanding of social phenomena that neither could achieve alone.

A final shortcoming is that the model of religion and ethnic conflict described here, like all such general models, makes the classic assumption of "all other things being equal." However, in the real world, all other things are generally not equal. Because of this, this model can describe the general paths along which ethnoreligious conflict is likely to occur, but not the specifics and not with total accuracy. That is, this model can note that a particular ethnoreligious minority is presently living under conditions that make it likely to engage in protest or rebellion, but it cannot predict the exact location and time of a protest or a terrorist bombing. Rather, it can only predict that such incidents are likely to occur within the next few years.

Even this is based on the assumption that conditions do not change and no other factor that is not contained in the model intervenes to affect the conflict process. Gurr and Moore (1997: 1088-1101) provide examples of cases where the general Minorities at Risk model predicted rebellion in the early 1990s, but did not occur. Minorities like the Indigenous Highlanders in Equador, the Palestinians in Jordan, the Turks in Bulgaria, the Aboriginals in Taiwan, and the Berbers in Morocco, gained concessions on at least some of their demands. Minorities like the Indian Tamils in Sri Lanka and the Blacks in Brazil chose to work within the system to attain their goals. Also, groups like the Ahmadis in Pakistan, the Tibetans in China, the Shi'i in Saudi Arabia, and the Vietnamese in Cambodia were repressed to the extent that rebellion was probably not a viable option.

Early Warning

The study presented here is, among other things, part of the literature on early warning. The immediate objectives of early warning research are to identify what information can be used to predict conflict and to create frameworks for evaluating this information. The long term-goal is to provide this information to policymakers who are in a position to use it to prevent the predicted conflicts from occurring or at least to mitigate some of their detrimental effects (Gurr and Harff, 1994b: 1-3).

The model presented here is what Gurr and Harff (1994b: 4-5) call a correlation model. Such models show whether causal connections between factors are universal or specific only to a few cases and are able to identify the relative importance of each causal connection. However, they are limited in that causal relations may change over time and such models do not identify points at which policy changes or intervention are most likely to affect a conflict's outcome. In short, such models can identify what is likely to cause a conflict but are weak in providing specific solutions.

This is true of the model of ethnoreligious conflict presented here. For example, the model predicts that the combination of grievances over religious and autonomy issues greatly increase the likelihood of violent rebellion. However, it does not provide much in the way of advice on how to prevent this from happening, or any specifics on how to address those grievances. However, even this limited information can be valuable to policymakers. Foreknowledge, even if it is limited and based only on probabilities, can increase the effectiveness of policymakers by giving them time to prepare for a situation and form a basic understanding of its causes. It can also provide the basis for a more detailed and in-depth analysis. Thus, the risk assessments provided by a correlational analysis like this study can effectively identify potential trouble spots, thereby allowing policymakers to focus their attention on places where it is most needed. This helps to ensure that potential conflicts that need the most attention are granted such attention and that scarce resources are not wasted on places where the actual conflict potential is low.

There are several other types of early warning models. First, sequential models, which track a single conflict over time, controlling for international background conditions, internal background conditions, and other intervening conditions, as well as "accelerators" which worsen conditions if the necessary background conditions for conflict exist. These models are good at tracking specific conflicts over time and can assess the effects of specific events on conflict. However, these models require a large amount of resources to collect information on a single case and require a large number of cases to test (Gurr and Harff, 1994b: 5). The most recent development in this field is the development of artificial intelligence software, which can read electronic news feeds, such as Reuters, and extract the necessary information for this type of analysis. However, the application of this process is at the time of this writing still problematic.[15]

Second, response models try to identify the points at which interventions can make a difference. These models are also referred to as "good enough" models. Third, conjectural models specify possible conflict scenarios and check to see if they happen (Gur and Harff, 1994b: 5-6). This approach is used by some branches of the U.S. military.[16]

It should be noted that early warning is a double-edged sword. The same information that identifies where conflicts are likely to occur, and thus helps to prevent them, can also be used to inflame conflicts. A better understanding of the causes of conflicts, ethic, religious, or otherwise, can potentially be used by those who wish to cause or exacerbate a conflict. As is the case with swords or any other type of weapon or information, the use to which the information gleaned from early warning studies depends on the hand that wields it.[17]

Conclusion

It is argued here that belief systems, whether religious or ideological, can become an integral element of the conflict process. This large-n cross-sectional study provides a considerable body of empirical evidence that this is true in the case of religion and ethnic conflict. It also provides a strong inference that religious and ideological beliefs can affect many other types of conflict in a similar manner. Despite the fact that much of the scholarly work in this field has focused on the debate over whether religion is relevant to conflict[18] and on case studies,[19] it is surprising that this is the first study of its kind.

While this study provides a good beginning for the database analysis of religion and conflict, much has yet to be done. The results create at least as many questions as they answer. The negative correlation between the expression of passive religious grievances and protest is one of the most perplexing such questions, but by no means the only one. Also, this study focuses on the specific case of religious ethnic minorities in conflict with states controlled by dominant ethnic groups. No large-n cross-sectional analysis has been performed on any other type of religious conflict, including the active religiously based or influenced opposition movements and/or interest groups in many states worldwide. While the model for religion and conflict developed here can be applied to these cases, neither it nor any other model has been so applied using a large number of cases.

Based on the results presented here, large-n cross-sectional studies built on a strong theoretical foundation can significantly add to our understanding of the relationship between religion and society, politics, and conflict. While much of the current comparative literature, which focuses on case studies, is informative and insightful, it often is lacking in generalizable theoretical content. This, and the reliance on a single method of research, limits our potential understanding of an integral aspect of modern society. It is time for the behavioralist approach to be more widely applied to the study of religion and conflict, not to replace the comparative approach, but to enhance it. The theory developed here is based on the work of scholars using the comparative approach. It is fair to say that the analysis presented here can provide comparative scholars with insights they would not otherwise have had, thus allowing them to improve their comparative analysis. This improved comparative analysis, in turn, should help improve future large-n studies. Thus, the combined use of the comparative and the behavioralist methods of studying religion and conflict is likely to produce better results than either approach would be likely to produce by itself.

Notes

1. While 70 out of 105 of the religiously differentiated groups in this study expressed passive religious grievances in 1994-1995, only 20 expressed active religious demands during the same period.

2. See, for example, Gurr (1970, 1993a, and 1993b) for an analysis of this argument with regard to general ethnic conflict.

3. For more details on the Thugs in India, see Rapoport (1984)

4. For details see Ginsburg (1991), especially pp. 561-563.

5. For details on the functionalist school of thought and the arguments against it, see chapter 4.

6. Juergensmeyer (1993: 13-19) makes the argument that in Third World countries, Western ideologies based on the notion of the nation-state, which he calls secular nationalism, have taken the place of religion in many societies. Smart (1983: 27) argues that secular nationalism has many of the characteristics of a religion including doctrine, myth, ethics, ritual, experience, and social organization.

7. There is little agreement among scholars as to the definition of nationalism. An example of this is Comaroff and Stern's edited volume *Perspectives on Nationalism and War* (1995), a multidisciplinary work whose contributors differ considerably in how they define nationalism, as well as in their explanations of its causes.

8. For example, see Hobsbawm (1990) and Tilly (1993).

9. For an example of this perspective, known in the literature as constructionalism or functionalism, see Anderson (1983). The other major explanation for the origin of nationalism in the literature is the primordial perspective, which sees nationalism as the result of primordial identities that have always existed. For a more comprehensive discussion and comparison of these two schools of thought, see Connor (1972 and 1994). For some attempts at alternative explanations see Comaroff and Stern (1995).

10. For details see the discussions of religious frameworks in chapters 2 and 6.

11. Gurr (1993a: 3) makes this point with respect to communal groups arguing that "the key to identifying communal groups is not the presence of a particular trait or combination of traits, but rather a shared perception that the defining traits, whatever they are, set the group apart." Horowitz (1985: 39) argues that "it is, in the end, ascriptive affinity and disparity, and not some particular inventory of cultural attributes, that found the group." Also see Montville (1990) and Hannum (1990).

12. For more details see Jaggers and Gurr (1995: 472).

13. For a more comprehensive discussion of the religious legitimacy variable, see Fox (1999b).

14. For a more comprehensive discussion of the religious institutions variable, see Fox (1999a).

15. For an example of such a study see Bond (1998).

16. This was communicated to the author by a military analyst who asked to remain anonymous. Other branches of the U.S. military have hired former research assistants from the Minorities at Risk project, presumably to implement more sophisticated correlational and sequential analyses.

17. For more details on the early warning literature, see Davies and Gurr (1998) and Harff and Gurr (1998).

18. See chapters 3 and 4 for details.

19. See chapter 5 for details.

Appendix A

Groups Included in the Dataset

This analysis is limited to cases contained in the Minorities at Risk dataset. However, not all cases of ethnic conflict involve religion. For this reason, only those cases in which religion is or can potentially become involved are included in this study. It is important to include all such groups even if, in fact, religion is not at all a factor in the conflict. This is because when one asks when, how, and why religion becomes significant in a conflict, one is implicitly asking when, how, and why it does not. Thus, all cases with a potential for religious differences to affect the conflict should be considered.

It is assumed here that in any case where the minority group is of a religion different from the majority group, religion can potentially become involved in the conflict. There are 105 such cases included in Phase 3 of Minorities at Risk. Operationally, if more than 80 percent of an ethnic minority are members of a religion different from the dominant group, that ethnic minority is included in this study.

While this criteria seems simple to execute, there are several complications. The most important is that many religions have within them different denominations or sects which have historically engaged in conflict with each other. It is basically a judgment call to decide which sects are to be considered operationally different religions and which are not. In this study, the Sunni and Shi'i sects of Islam are operationally defined as separate religious groupings. Among Christian groups, only cases where the majority and minority are Catholic and Protestant are included. Different Protestant denominations are operationally defined as the same religion and, accordingly, conflicts between ethnic groups belonging to different Protestant denominations are not included. Also, Orthodox Christianity is not treated as analytically distinct from either Catholic or Protestant Christianity.

A similar complication can be found among many indigenous groups, mostly in Third World countries. Many such groups have nominally adopted the religion of the dominant group but still adhere to indigenous animist or shamanist practices and beliefs. This is, to some extent, the case with most indigenous groups in Latin America and many in Africa and Asia. These indigenous minorities are only included in this study if their animist or shamanist practices are considered to be sufficiently different from the religious practices of the dominant group to constitute a distinct set of religious practices. Often this is a close judgment call which is open to dispute.

As noted above, 105 out of the 268 groups in the Minorities at Risk dataset meet the above criteria and are included in this study. Below is a full listing of all of the ethnic groups included in the Minorities at Risk Phase 3 dataset. Those cases that are included in this study are marked. Also listed are the religions of all 268 of the ethnic minorities included in the Minorities at Risk dataset, as well as those of the dominant ethnic groups in the states in question.

The religious affiliations provided below represent the religious affiliations of the majority (at least 80 percent to 90 percent) of the group in question. More general terms (i.e. Christian instead of Catholic) are used in some cases for one or both of two reasons: (1) information on many groups is limited, requiring the use of more general categories; (2) the group may belong to several sects of the same religion.

Table A.1: Groups in the Dataset

Country	Group	Relig. Min.	Minority Religion	Majority Religion
Western Democracies				
Australia	Aborigines		Christian	Christian
Britain (UK)	Afro-Caribbeans		Prot. (Anglican)	Prot. (Anglican)
	Asians		Hindu and Chr.	Prot. (Anglican)
	Catholics of N. Ireland	√	Catholic	Prot. (Anglican)
	Scots	√	Cath. and Prot.	Prot. (Anglican)
Canada	French Canadians	√	Catholic	Protestant
	Quebecois	√	Catholic	Protestant
	Native Peoples		Christian	Protestant
France	Basques		Catholic	Catholic
	Corsicans		Catholic	Catholic
	Afro-Arabs	√	Islam (Sunni)	Catholic
	Roma		Christian[1]	Catholic
Germany	Turks	√	Islam (Sunni)	Prot. (Lutheran)
Greece	Muslims (Turks)	√	Islam (Sunni)	Greek Orthodox

Continued on next page

Table A.1—Continued

Country	Group	Relig. Min.	Minority Religion	Majority Religion
Greece	Roma	√	Chr. and some Muslim [1]	Greek Orthodox
Italy	South Tyroleans		Catholic	Catholic
	Sardinians		Catholic	Catholic
	Roma		Christian[1]	Catholic
Japan	Koreans		Mixed	Mixed
New Zealand	Maoris		Christian and traditional beliefs	Christian
Nordic (Scandanavian Countries)	Sami		Protestant	Prot. (Lutheran)
Spain	Basques		Catholic	Catholic
	Catalans		Catholic	Catholic
	Roma		Christian[1]	Catholic
Switzerland	Jurassiens	√	Catholic	Protestant
	Foreign Workers		Christian	Christian
USA	African-Americans		Christian	Protestant
	Hispanics		Christian	Protestant
	Native Americans		Protestant	Protestant
	Hawaiians		Protestant	Protestant

Ex-Soviet Bloc Countries

Country	Group	Relig. Min.	Minority Religion	Majority Religion
Albania	Greeks	√	Orthodox	Islam (Sunni)
Azerbaijan	Armenians	√	Chr (Armenian Apostic)	Islam (Shi'i)
	Lezghins	√	Islam (Sunni)	Islam (Shi'i)
	Russians	√	Orthodox	Islam (Shi'i)
Belarus	Russians		Orthodox	Orthodox
	Poles		Catholic	Orthodox
Bosnia	Serbs		Orthodox	no government[2]
	Croats		Catholic	no government[2]
	Muslims		Islam (Sunni)	no government[2]
Bulgaria	Turks	√	Islam (Sunni)	Orthodox
	Roma		Chr. (60%) and Islam (40%)[1]	Orthodox
Croatia	Roma		Christian and Islam[1]	Catholic

Continued on next page

Table A.1—Continued

Country	Group	Relig. Min.	Minority Religion	Majority Religion
Croatia	Serbs		Orthodox	Catholic
Czech Rep.	Slovaks		Orthodox	Orthodox
	Roma		Christian[1]	Orthodox
Estonia	Russians		Orthodox	Prot. (Lutheran)
Georgia	Abkhazians	√	Sunni Islam and Orthodox minority	Orthodox
	Adzhars	√	Islam (Sunni)	Orthodox
	Ossetians		Orthodox	Orthodox
	Russians		Orthodox	Orthodox
Hungary	Roma		Christian[1]	Lutheran
Kazakhstan	Russians	√	Orthodox	Islam (Sunni)
	Germans	√	Prot. (Lutheran)	Islam (Sunni)
Kyrgyzstan	Russians	√	Orthodox	Islam (Sunni)
	Uzbeks		Islam (Sunni)	Islam (Sunni)
Latvia	Russians		Orthodox	Prot. (Lutheran)
Lithuania	Poles		Catholic	Orthodox
	Russians		Orthodox	Orthodox
Macedonia	Albanians	√	Islam (Sunni)	Orthodox
	Serbs		Orthodox	Orthodox
	Roma		Christian[1]	Orthodox
Moldovia	Gagauz		Christian	Orthodox
	Russians/Slavs		Orthodox	Orthodox
Romania	Hungarians		Christian (Calvinist, Catholic, and Lutheran)	Orthodox
	Roma		Christian[1]	Orthodox
Russia	Avars	√	Islam (Sunni)	Orthodox
	Buryat	√	Buddhist	Orthodox
	Chechens	√	Islam (Sunni)	Orthodox
	Ingushes	√	Islam (Sunni)	Orthodox
	Karachays	√	Islam (Sunni)	Orthodox
	Kumyks	√	Islam (Sunni)	Orthodox
	South Ossetians		Orthodox, minority Islam (Sunni)	Orthodox
	Lezghins	√	Islam (Sunni)	Orthodox
	Tatars	√	Islam (Sunni)	Orthodox

Continued on next page

Table A.1—Continued

Country	Group	Relig. Min.	Minority Religion	Majority Religion
Russia	Yakuta		Othodox	Orthodox
	Tuvinians	√	Buddhist	Orthodox
	Roma		Christian[1]	Orthodox
Slovakia	Hungarians		Catholic	Orthodox
	Roma		Christian[1]	Orthodox
Tajikistan	Russians	√	Orthodox	Islam (Sunni)
Turkmenistan	Russians	√	Orthodox	Islam (Sunni)
Ukraine	Russians		Orthodox	Orthodox
	Crimean Russians		Orthodox	Orthodox
	Crimean Tatars	√	Islam (Sunni)	Orthodox
Uzbekistan	Russians	√	Orthodox	Islam (Sunni)
Yugoslavia (Serbia and	Albanians (of Kosovo)	√	Islam (Sunni)	Orthodox
Monte-	Hungarians		Catholic	Orthodox
negro)	Sandzak	√	Islam	Orthodox
	Roma		Christian[1]	Orthodox
	Croatians		Catholic	Orthodox

Asia

Country	Group	Relig. Min.	Minority Religion	Majority Religion
Afghanistan	Hazaras		Islam (Shi'i)	no government[2]
	Pashtuns		Islam (Sunni)	no government[2]
	Tajiks		Islam (Sunni)	no government[2]
	Uzbeks		Islam (Sunni)	no government[2]
Bangladesh	Chittagong Hill People		Buddhist and Islam (Shi'i)	Islam (Shi'i)
	Hindus	√	Hindu	Islam (Shi'i)
	Biharis		Islam (Shi'i)	Islam (Shi'i)
Bhutan	Lhotshampas	√	Hindu	Buddhist and Animist
Myanmar (Burma)	Rohingya Muslims (Arakanese)	√	Islam (Sunni)	Buddhist
	Zomis (Chins)	√	Mostly Christian but some Animist	Buddhist
	Kachins	√	Anim. and Chr.	Buddhist
	Karen		Budd., Animist, And Chr.	Buddhist

Continued on next page

Table A.1—Continued

Country	Group	Relig. Min.	Minority Religion	Majority Religion
Myanmar	Mons		Buddhist	Buddhist
(Burma)	Shans		Buddhist	Buddhist
China	Hui (Muslims)	√	Islam (Sunni)	Secular
	Tibetans	√	Buddhist	Secular
	Turkmen (of Xiaja-ng-Kazak and Uighur)	√	Islam	Secular
India	Kashmiris	√	Islam (Shi'i)	Hindu
	Muslims	√	Islam (Sunni)	Hindu
	Nagas	√	Christian	Hindu
	Scheduled Tribes		Hindu	Hindu
	Sikhs	√	Sikh	Hindu
	Mizos	√	Chr. and Anim.	Hindu
	Tripuras	√	Chr. and Buddhist	Hindu
	Assamese		Hindu with Muslim minority	Hindu
	Bodos		Hindu	Hindu
Indonesia	Chinese	√	Buddhist	Islam (Sunni)
	East Timorese	√	Catholic	Islam (Sunni)
	Papuans	√	Chr. and Anim.	Islam (Sunni)
	Aceh		Islam (Sunni)	Islam (Sunni)
Kampuche (Cambodia)	Vietnamese		Buddhist	Buddhist
South Korea	HoNamese (in Cholla Province)		Mixed Animist, Buddhist, and Chr.	Mixed Animist, Buddhist, and Chr.
Laos	Hmong	√	Animist	Buddhist
Malaysia	Chinese	√	Buddhist	Islam (Sunni)
	Dayaks (Sarwak)	√	Chr. and Anim.	Islam (Sunni)
	Indians	√	Hindu (80%)	Islam (Sunni)
	Kadazans (Sabah)	√	Cath. and Anim.	Islam (Sunni)
Papua New Guinea	Bougainvilleans		Christian	Christian
Pakistan	Ahmadis	√	Ahmadi Islam	Islam (Sunni)
	Baluchis		Islam (Sunni)	Islam (Sunni)
	Hindus	√	Hindu	Islam (Sunni)
	Pashtuns (Pathans)		Islam (Sunni)	Islam (Sunni)

Continued on next page

Table A.1—Continued

Country	Group	Relig. Min.	Minority Religion	Majority Religion
Pakistan	Sindhis		Islam (Sunni)	Islam (Sunni)
	Mohajirs		Islam (Sunni)	Islam (Sunni)
Phillippines	Cordilleras (Igorots)		Christian	Christian
Singapore	Moros (Muslims)	√	Islam	Christian
	Malays	√	Islam	Buddhist and other traditions
Sri Lanka	Indian Tamils	√	Hindu	Buddhist
	Sri Lankan Tamils	√	Hindu	Buddhist
Taiwan	Aboriginals		Christian	Chr. and Buddh.
	Mainlanders		Mixed	Chr. and Buddh.
	Taiwanese		Mixed	Chr. and Buddh.
Thailand	Chinese		Buddhist	Buddhist
	Malay-Muslims	√	Islam (Sunni)	Buddhist
	Northern Hill Tribes	√	Chr. and Anim.	Buddhist
Vietnam	Chinese		Buddhist	Buddh. and sec.
	Montagnards	√	Chr. and Anim.	Buddh. and sec.

North Africa and the Middle East

Country	Group	Relig. Min.	Minority Religion	Majority Religion
Algeria	Berbers		Islam (Sunni)	Islam (Sunni)
Egypt	Copts	√	Christian	Islam (Sunni)
Iran	Azerbaijanis		Islam (Shi'i)	Islam (Shi'i)
	Bahais	√	Ba'Hai	Islam (Shi'i)
	Bakhtiari		Islam (Shi'i)	Islam (Shi'i)
	Baluchis	√	Islam (Sunni)	Islam (Shi'i)
	Kurds		Mixed Sunni and Shi'i Islam	Islam (Shi'i)
	Turkomans	√	Islam (Sunni)	Islam (Shi'i)
	Arabs		Mixed Sunni and Shi'i Islam	Islam (Shi'i)
	Christians	√	Christian	Islam (Shi'i)
Iraq	Kurds		Islam (Sunni)	Islam (Sunni)
	Shi'is	√	Islam (Shi'i)	Islam (Sunni)
	Sunnis		Dominant group	Islam (Sunni)
Israel	Israeli Arabs	√	Islam (Sunni)	Jewish
	Palestinians	√	Islam (Sunni)	Jewish

Continued on next page

Table A.1—Continued

Country	Group	Relig. Min.	Minority Religion	Majority Religion
Jordan	Palestinians		Islam (Sunni)	Islam (Sunni)
Lebanon	Druze	√	Druze	Christian
	Maronite Christians	√	Christian	Christian
	Palestinians	√	Islam (Sunni)	Christian
Lebanon	Shi'i Muslims	√	Islam (Shi'i)	Christian
	Sunni Muslims	√	Islam (Sunni)	Christian
Morocco	Berbers		Islam (Sunni)	Islam (Sunni)
	Saharawis		Islam (Sunni)	Islam (Sunni)
Saudi Arabia	Shi'i	√	Islam (Shi'i)	Islam (Sunni)
Syria	Alawis		Dominant group	Islam (Sunni)
Turkey	Kurds		Islam (Sunni)	Islam (Sunni)

Sub-Saharan Africa

Country	Group	Relig. Min.	Minority Religion	Majority Religion
Angola	Bakongo		Chr. and Anim.	Chr. and Anim.
	Ovimbudu		Chr. and Anim.	Chr. and Anim.
	Cabinda		Chr. and Anim.	Chr. and Anim.
Botswana	San (bushmen)	√	Animist	Christian
Burundi	Hutu		Catholic	Catholic
	Tutsi		Catholic	Catholic
Cameroon	Kirdi	√	Animist	Islam (Sunni)
	Westerners		Mixed	Islam (Sunni)
	Bamileke	√	Animist	Islam (Sunni)
Chad	Southerners	√	Chr. and Anim.	Islam (Sunni)
Djibouti	Afars		Islam (Sunni)	Islam (Sunni)
Eritrea	Afars		Islam (Sunni)	Islam (Sunni) and Christian
Ethiopia	Afars	√	Islam (Sunni)	Chr. (Coptic)
	Oromo		Islam, Ani., and Chr. (Coptic)	Chr. (Coptic)
	Somalis	√	Islam (Sunni)	Chr. (Coptic)
	Tigreans		Christian	Chr. (Coptic)
	Amhara		Christian	Chr. (Coptic)
Ghana	Ashanti		Christian	Christian
	Ewe		Christian	Christian
	Mossi, Dagomba	√	Islam	Christian
Guinea	Fulani (Fulbe)		Islam	Islam
	Malinke		Islam	Islam

Continued on next page

Table A.1—Continued

Country	Group	Relig. Min.	Minority Religion	Majority Religion
Guinea	Susu		Islam	Islam
Kenya	Kikuyu		Mostly Chr.	Mostly Chr.
	Luo		Mixed	Mostly Chr.
	Maasai	√	Animist	Mostly Chr.
	Kalenjins		Dominant group	Mostly Chr.
	Luhya		Mostly Chr.	Mostly Chr.
	Kisii		Mostly Chr.	Mostly Chr.
Madagascar/ Malagasy	Merina		Mixed Chr. and Animist	Mixed Chr. and Animist
Mali	Tuareg		Islam (Sunni)	Islam (Sunni)
	Mande		Islam (Sunni)	Islam (Sunni)
Mauritania	Kewri		Islam (Sunni)	Islam (Sunni)
Nambia	Black Moors		Islam (Sunni)	Islam (Sunni)
	Europeans		Christian	Christian
	San	√	Animist	Christian
Niger	Basters		Christian	Christian
Nigeria	Tuareg		Islam (Sunni)	Islam (Sunni)
	Ibo	√	Christian	Islam
	Ogni	√	Chr. and Anim.	Islam
	Yoruba		Islam Chr. and Animist	Islam
Rwanda	Tutsi		Cath. and Prot.	Cath. and Prot.
	Hutu		Cath. and Prot.	Cath. and Prot
Senegal	Casmance Region (Diola & others)	√	Catholic	Islam (Sunni)
Sierra Leone	Creoles		Animist, Chr., and Islam.	Animist, Chr., and Islam.
	Limba		Dominant group	Animist, Chr., and Islam.
	Mende		Animist, Chr., and Islam.	Animist, Chr., and Islam.
	Temne		Animist, Chr., and Islam.	Animist, Chr., and Islam.
South Africa	Asians	√	Hind. and Islam	Christian
	Coloreds		Christian	Christian
	Europeans		Christian	Christian
	Xhosa		Christian	Christian
	Zulus		Christian	Christian
Sudan	South Sudanese	√	Chr. and Anim.	Islam (Sunni)
Togo	Ewe		Chr. and Anim.	Animist

Continued on next page

Table A.1—Continued

Country	Group	Relig. Min.	Minority Religion	Majority Religion
Togo	Kabre		Dominant group	Animist
Uganda	Acholi		Christian	Christian
	Baganda		Christian	Christian
Zaire	Luba		Christian	Christian
	Lunda, Yeke		Christian	Christian
	Banyarwandans		Christian	Christian
	Nagbundi		Christian	Christian
Zambia	Bembe		Christian	Christian
	Lozi (Barotse)		Christian	Christian
Zimbabwe	Europeans		Christian	Christian
	Ndbele		Christian	Christian

Latin America and the Caribbean

Country	Group	Relig. Min.	Minority Religion	Majority Religion
Argentina	Native Peoples	√	Mixed Shamanist and Catholic[3]	Catholic
Bolivia	Native Highland Peoples	√	Mixed Shamanist and Catholic[3]	Catholic
	Native Lowland Peoples	√	Mixed Shamanist and Catholic[3]	Catholic
Brazil	Afro-Brazilians		Catholic	Catholic
	Amazonian Indians		Catholic	Catholic
Chile	Native Peoples	√	Shamanist	Christian
Colombia	Afro-Americans		Catholic	Catholic
	Native Peoples		Catholic	Catholic
Costa Rica	Antillean Blacks	√	Prot. (Anglican)	Catholic
Domin. Rep.	Afro-Americans		Catholic	Catholic
Ecuador	Afro-Americans		Catholic	Catholic
	Native Highlanders		Catholic	Catholic
	Native Lowlanders	√	Mixed Shamanist and Catholic[3]	Catholic
El Salvador	Native Peoples		Catholic	Catholic
Guatemala	Native (Maya)		Catholic	Catholic

Continued on next page

Table A.1—Continued

Country	Group	Relig. Min.	Minority Religion	Majority Religion
Honduras	Black Caribs		Catholic	Catholic
	Native Peoples		Catholic	Catholic
Mexico	Mayans		Catholic	Catholic
	Zapotista	√	Mixed Shamanist and Catholic[3]	Catholic
	Other Native Peoples Native		Catholic	Catholic
Nicaragua	(Miskitos)	√	Protestant	Catholic
Panama	Afro-Caribbeans	√	Protestant	Catholic
	Native Peoples		Catholic	Catholic
	Chinese	√	Confucianism and Buddhist	Catholic
Paraguay	Native Peoples	√	Mixed Shamanist and Catholic[3]	Catholic
Peru	Afro-Americans		Catholic	Catholic
	Native, Highland		Catholic	Catholic
	Native, Lowland		Catholic	Catholic
Venezuela	Afro-Americans		Catholic	Catholic
	Native Peoples	√	Mixed Shamanist and Catholic[3]	Catholic

Notes

1. Information on the religious affiliation of the Roma is difficult to obtain. For this reason the most general category is used unless better information is available. For instance Christian may be used instead of Catholic. Also, while this may represent the religious affiliation of the majority of the Roma in the country in question, it cannot be assumed that all Roma in that country are affiliated with that religion.

2. No single government is in control of the state. A state of civil war exists. Since the model presented here deals with the relationship between minorities and the state, none of these groups is included in this study.

3. Most native peoples in South America tend to mix their Shamanist beliefs with the Christianity brought to them by missionaries. Such groups are included in this study if the Shamanist element of the group's religious practices us sufficiently strong to result in a set of religious practices that is significantly different from that of the dominant group.

Appendix B

Dataset and Variable Descriptions

The Minorities at Risk Project

Much of the data used in this study are taken from the Minorities at Risk Phase 3 dataset. These data are supplemented by data collected specifically for this study. However, while the use of the Phase 3 dataset makes this study possible, it also complicates and places some restrictions on this study.

The Minorities at Risk dataset contains data on 268 politically significant ethnic minorities worldwide. The unit of analysis is the ethnopolitical minority within a specific state. The groups included in the dataset meet one or more of the following criteria: they are subject to discrimination at present; they are disadvantaged because of the results of past discrimination; and/or the group (in whole or in part) supports one or more political organizations that advocate greater group rights, privileges, or autonomy. They also must constitute at least 1 percent of the population of the state in which they reside or number at least 100,000 in that state. Of these 268 groups, 105 are religiously distinct and, therefore, included in this study.[1]

This dataset focuses on the relationship between the minority group and the state. For this reason, many ethnic groups are coded as a separate group in each state in which they meet the above criteria. For instance, ethnic Russians are included in the dataset several times because they meet the above criteria in Azerbaijan, Kazakhstan, Kyrgyzstan, Tajikistan, Turkmenistan, and Uzbekistan as well as in several other of the former Soviet republics.[2]

The Minorities at Risk dataset contains several types of information on ethnopolitical minorities including general background data; the level of discrimination against the group; the level of group grievances; the level of group organization and mobilization; the amount of protest and rebellion in which the ethnic minority engages; and international factors that can influence an ethnic conflict. Some of

213

these variables are coded for every five-year period between 1945 and 1989; most are coded yearly or every other year between 1990 and 1995. This study focuses on the data from 1990 to 1995 because the codings are more detailed and accurate. These variables are mostly judgmental ordinal variables coded based on strictly defined criteria.

The nature of the dataset has several implications for this study. First, this study is limited to the same unit of analysis as the Minorities at Risk dataset, the ethnic minority within a state controlled by a coherent government. This eliminates from the study all cases of religious conflict within the same ethnic group, especially conflicts between secular and religious elements within a state. For example, while this study does look at the Christian Coptic minority in Egypt, it does not include any evaluation of the Islamic militant challenge to Egypt's government. This is because the Copts are a religiously distinct ethnic minority in Egypt, but the Islamic militants are members of Egypt's ethnic majority. That is, these militants constitute a contemporary political movement in Egypt but are not a distinct social entity that persists over time. While it is clear that cases such as the Islamic militants in Egypt are worthy of study, the nature of the available data places such cases beyond the scope of this study.

Second, because the data focus on the relationship between a dominant ethnic group that, more or less, controls a state's government and an ethnic minority, there must be a working state government for a group to be included in this study. That is, if a country is in a state of anarchy, where there is effectively no state government and the country's ethnic groups are in a state of total war, there is no relationship between a state government and an ethnic minority to be measured. Thus, even though they are worthy of study, minority groups in states like Bosnia and Afghanistan, where there were effectively no governments during the 1990 to 1995 period, are not considered here.

Third, in order for the information on religion to be as compatible with the Minorities at Risk dataset as possible, it is best collected in a similar manner. That is, the religion variables were modeled after the ethnicity variables used by the Minorities at Risk project. While this can potentially complicate the data collection process, in this case it did not. However, it does influence the structure of the religion variables.

Fourth, that the unit of analysis is the ethnic minority greatly complicates the analysis. That is not to say that the issue of religion and conflict is not complicated in and of itself. The model developed here is not particularly simple, and many real-world factors can complicate the dynamics predicted in this model. These include but are by no means limited to the type of government involved and economic conditions within the state. However, ethnic conflicts can be complicated by all of these factors as well as many others. These include, but are by no means limited to, discrimination directed against the ethnic minority, a desire for autonomy by the ethnic minority, linguistic and cultural differences between the ethnic minority and the dominant group, and the level of ethnic conflict among similar groups elsewhere, otherwise known as contagion or diffusion. This means many more independent factors can complicate the predicted relationships and, accordingly, must be taken into account.

Variables

All variables in the datasets described here are judgmentally coded variables or composite indicators constructed from judgmental variables. That is, coders familiar with the cases covered in these datasets coded the variables based upon their assessment of the facts of the case and the criteria provided for the coding of the variables. The criteria used by the coders are specified below.

Religion Variables

All of the religion variables, unless otherwise, noted are coded separately for 1990-1991, 1992-1993, and 1994-1995. Labels for variables coded for 1990-1991 end in 91, those coded for 1992-1993 end in 93, and those coded for 1994-1995 end in 95.

Religious Discrimination Variables
There are three religious discrimination variables used here. The first (RELDSC91, 93, and 95) codes the severity of religious discrimination on a judgmental scale of negative-one to four using the following categories:

0. None.
1. Substantial religious discrimination in society due to general prejudice in society. Explicit public policies protect and/or improve the position of the group's ability to practice its religion.
2. Substantial religious discrimination in society due to general prejudice in society. Public policies are neutral, or if positive inadequate to offset discriminatory practices.
3. Public policies of formal restrictions on religious observance. Religious activities are somewhat restricted by public policy. This includes religions that are tolerated but given a formal second class status. (Example: Christian sects in many Muslim states.)
4. Public policies of formal restrictions on religious observance. Religious activity is sharply restricted or banned. (Example: Ba'Hais in Iran.)

The second religious discrimination variable (RDIS91, 93, and 95) is a composite indicator of the scope of discrimination which combines several coded variables. These variables each measure restrictions on a specific type of religious activity based either upon deliberate public policy or prevalent social practice. Each

of these variables is measured using the following scale: 2 = the activity is prohibited or sharply restricted for most or all group members; 1 = the activity is slightly
restricted for most or all group members or sharply restricted for some of them;
0 = not significantly restricted for any. The following types of restrictions are so
coded:

- Restrictions on public observance of religious services, festivals, and/or
  holidays.
- Restrictions on building, repairing, and/or maintaining places of worship.
- Forced observance of religious laws of other group.
- Restrictions on formal religious organizations.
- Restrictions on the running of religious schools and/or religious education
  in general.
- Restrictions on the observance of religious laws concerning personal
  status, including marriage and divorce.
- Restrictions on the ordination of and/or access to clergy.
- Restrictions on other types of observance of religious law. (Specify.)

The coded values for the eight variables were added and the sum was divided by
two to create a set of indicators (one for each biennium) with values that range from
0 to 8.

The third religious discrimination variable (RDISAL91, 93, and 95) was
created by combining the severity and scope variables using the following table:

Table B.1: Coding Guidelines for Religious Discrimination (RDISAL)

RDISAL91, 93, and 95 Pattern		RDIS91, RDIS93, and RDIS95					
		0	0.5-1.0	1.5-3.0	3.5-5.0	5.5-7.0	7.0-8.0
RELDSC91,	0	0	1	2	3	4	5
RELDSC93,	1	1	2	3	4	5	6
and	2	2	3	4	5	6	7
RELDSC95	3	3	4	5	6	7	8
	4	4	5	6	7	8	9

Religious Grievances Variables

There is only one set of religious grievances variable, RELGRVX91, 93, and
95, indexed in a similar manner to RELDIS91, 93, and 95. The component
variables were coded on the following scale, based on statements and actions by
group leaders, members, and outside observers: 3 =issue important for most of the
group; 2 = issue is significant but its relative importance cannot be judged; 1 =

issue is of lesser importance, or of major concern to only one faction of the group; 0 = issue is not judged to be of any significant importance. The following type of religious grievances are so coded:

- Diffuse religious grievances, explicit objectives not clear. (Only code if more specific category below can not be coded.)
- Greater right to observe festivals, holidays, and/or other forms of public observance.
- Greater right to build, repair, and/or maintain places of worship.
- Freedom from imposition of religious laws of other group.
- Right to maintain formal religious organizations.
- Right to maintain religious schools and/or teach religion.
- Right to observe religious laws concerning personal status, including marriage and divorce.
- Right to ordain and/or have access to clergy.
- Right to observe other religious practices. (Specify).

The total scores of these variables are added to create a composite variable ranging from 0 to 24.

Religious Demands by a Religious Minority

Religious demands are defined as the demand for religious rights and/or privileges. This variable differs from religious grievances, which are complaints against religious discrimination. Thus, religious grievances are reactive, whereas religious demands are active demands for more rights and privileges. According to the model, religious demands by a minority group can provoke both religious and nonreligious discrimination against that group.

Religious demands (RPROV91, 93, and 95) were coded using this scale:

0. None.
1. The group is demanding more religious rights.
2. The group is seeking a privileged status for their religion which offends the religious convictions of the dominant group.
3. The group is seeking to impose some aspects of its religious ideology on the dominant group.
4. The group is seeking a form of ideological hegemony for its framework which will affect some of the dominant group.
5. The group is seeking a form of ideological hegemony for its framework which will affect most or all of the dominant group.

The Presence of Religious Institutions

This variable measures the level of formal organization and centralization of the religious institutions of an ethnic minority. According to the model, the presence of religious institutions can facilitate mobilization for protest and rebellion. The presence of religious institutions (RELINST) was coded only once during the 1990 to 1995 period using the following scale:

0. No religious institutions exist.
1. Informal institutions exist. (I.e. lay-person led prayer meetings.)
2. A formally ordained clergy exists but there are no established houses of worship.
3. Formal houses of worship exist but they are not organized under a formal unified ecclesiastical structure. (I.e. mosques in most Muslim states.)
4. Formal houses of worship organized under a formal unified ecclesiastical structure. (I.e. the Catholic Church)

Religious Legitimacy

Religious legitimacy is defined here as the extent to which it is legitimate to invoke religion in political discourse. According to the model, religious legitimacy can facilitate the articulation of nonreligious grievances as well as the mobilization for protest and rebellion.

Religious legitimacy (RLEG91, 93 and 95) is a composite indicator based upon codings for four factors. The presence of each of these factors is posited to indicate indirectly that it is legitimate to invoke religion in political discourse. These component variables were coded as follows: 1 = The factor is present; 0 = The factor is not present. The factors so coded are as follows:

- A history of religious involvement in politics and/or conflict.
- Religious leaders are actively using religious rhetoric to mobilize the population.
- Religion is offered as the solution to nonreligious economic, political, and/or social problems.
- The presence of an official religion in the state's constitution, laws, or de-facto public policy.

The sum of these codings creates a religious legitimacy indicator ranging from 0 to 4.

Relevance of Religion to the Conflict

There are two indicators used here to measure the relevance of religion to the conflict. The first (RRELEVANT) measures the importance of religious issues as compared to other issues in the conflict. It was coded only once for the entire 1990 to 1995 period using these categories.

0. None.
1. Marginal relevance. Issues are basically of a nonreligious nature but religion is being used to legitimize those issues and/or mobilize the group.
2. Religious issues are significant but are less important than other non-

religious issues.
3. Religion is one of several significant issues which are of roughly equal importance.
4. Religion is the primary issue of the conflict but there are other significant issues involved.
5. Religion is the only issue relevant to the conflict.

The second indicator of the relevance of religion to the conflict (RELALLX91, 93, and 95) is a composite one created from RDISAL, RGRV, and RLEG. Each was transformed to a scale of 0 to 10 and the three were added to form a composite indicator ranging from 0 to 30.

Religion Type
The religions of the groups involved in the conflict are used as a control variable, to test the contention that different religious traditions may affect the behavior of their adherents in different ways. This may be true of the religions of both the minority and dominant groups involved in the conflict. Accordingly, the religion of both is used as a control variable. Religions are divided into three categories: Christian, Islam, and other. These general categories are used because they contain a sufficient number of cases for statistical analysis.

General Ethnic Conflict Variables

The general ethnic conflict variables in this study are taken from the Minorities at Risk Phase 3 dataset. These variables are also judgmental variables coded in a similar manner to the religion variables. Also, like the religion variables they are coded unless otherwise noted for the 1990-1991, 1992-1993, and 1994-1995 periods. However, unlike the religion variables, the names of the variables for these three periods end in 90, 92, and 94 respectively.

Protest
Protest is coded on the following Guttman scale for each year from 1990 to 1995:

0. None reported
1. Verbal opposition (public letters, petitions, posters, publications, agitation, etc.). Code requests by a minority-controlled regional group for independence here.
2. Scattered acts of symbolic resistance (e.g. sit-ins, blockage of traffic, sabotage, symbolic destruction of property).
3. Political organizing activity on a substantial scale. (Code mobilization for autonomy and/or secession by a minority-controlled regional government

here.)

4. A few demonstrations, rallies, strikes, and/or riots, total participation less than 10,000.
5. Demonstrations, rallies, strikes, and/or riots, total participation estimated between 10,000 and 100,000.
6. Demonstrations, rallies, strikes, and/or riots, total participation over 100,000.

Rebellion

Rebellion is coded on the following Guttman scale each year from 1990 to 1995:

0. None.
1. Political banditry, sporadic terrorism.
2. Campaigns of terrorism.
3. Local rebellions: armed attempts to seize power in a locale. If they prove to be the opening round in what becomes a protracted guerrilla or civil war during the year being coded, code the latter rather than local rebellion. Code declarations of independence by a minority-controlled regional government here.
4. Small-scale guerrilla activity. (Small-scale guerrilla activity has all these three traits: fewer than 1000 armed fighters; sporadic armed attacks [less than 6 reported per year]; and attacks in a small part of the area occupied by the group, or in one or two other locales.)
5. Intermediate-scale guerrilla activity. (Intermediate-scale guerrilla activity has one or two of the defining traits of large-scale activity and one or two of the defining traits of small-scale activity.)
6. Large-scale guerrilla activity. (Large-scale guerrilla activity has all these traits: more than 1000 armed fighters; frequent armed attacks [more than 6 reported per year]; and attacks affecting large part of the area occupied by group.)
7. Protracted civil war, fought by rebel military with base areas.

Mobilization for Protest and Rebellion

There are three indicators each for mobilization for protest and rebellion. The indicators are identical except that the protest mobilization variables measure open (legal) political organizations and the mobilization for rebellion variables measure militant (illegal) organizations. The first pair of variables OPORG9 (protest) and MILORG9 (rebellion) are tallies of the number of communal organizations during the 1990s:

0. None reported.
1. One.
2. Two.

3.   Three or more.

The second pair of variables, OPSCOP9 (protest) and MILSCOP9 (rebellion) are estimates of the scope of support for those organizations during the 1990s on the following scale:

0.   No political movements recorded.
1.   Limited: No political movement is supported by more than a tenth of the minority. If movements are identified by name but information is not sufficient to code scope of support for any of them, also code here.
2.   Medium: The largest political movement is supported by a quarter to half of the minority.
3.   Large: The largest political movement is supported by more than half of the minority.

The third pair of variables, OPMOB9 (protest) and MILMOB9 (rebellion) are composite variables created from the above variables as follows:

$$OPMOB9 = OPORG9 \times OPSCOP9$$
$$MILMOB9 = MILORG9 \times MILSCOP9$$

Political Discrimination

Political discrimination is defined as restrictions on a minority's access to political power and its ability to participate in the political process. The Minorities at Risk dataset contains three political discrimination indicators. Only the third is used in this study, but since it is a composite indicator based on the first two, all three are described. The first political discrimination variable (POLDIS90, 92, and 94) is measured using a Guttman scale, which codes the most severe of the categories described below which affect the group in question:

0.   None
1.   Substantial underrepresentation in political office and/or participation due to historical neglect or restrictions. Explicit public policies are designed to protect or improve the group's political status.
2.   Substantial underrepresentation due to historical neglect or restrictions. No social practice of deliberate exclusion. No formal exclusion. No evidence of protective or remedial public policies.
3.   Substantial underrepresentation due to prevailing social practice by dominant groups. Formal public policies toward the group are neutral or, if positive, inadequate to offset discriminatory practices.
4.   Public policies (formal exclusion and/or recurring repression) substantially restrict the group's political participation by comparison with other groups. (Note: Discount repression during group rebellions. What is decisive is patterned repression when the group is not openly resisting

state authority.)

The second political discrimination indicator (POLRES90, 92, and 94) is a composite variable created from a checklist of specific aspects of the group's political status and participation that are selectively and deliberately restricted by public policy. The scope of each type of restriction is coded on the following scale: 2 = the activity is prohibited or sharply restricted for most or all group members; 1 = the activity is slightly restricted for most or all group members or sharply restricted for some of them; 0 = not significantly restricted for any. The following activities are so coded:

- Restrictions on freedom of expression
- Restrictions on free movement, place of residence
- Restrictions on rights in judicial proceedings
- Restrictions on political organization
- Restrictions on voting
- Restrictions on recruitment to police, military
- Restrictions on access to civil service
- Restrictions on attainment of high office
- Other

The codings are summed and divided by two, creating an indicator ranging from 0 to 9.

These two indicators are combined to form the third political discrimination indicator (ALLPD90, 92, and 94) which is used in this study. ALLPD is generated using this table:

Table B.2: Coding Guidelines for Political Discrimination (ALLPD)

POLDIS pattern	POLRES Scores				
	0 - 0.5	1 - 2.5	3 - 5.0	5.5 - 7	7.5 - 9
1. Policies to improve status	1	2	3	4	5
2. No policies	2	3	4	5	7
3. Neutral policies	3	4	6	7	8
4. Restrictive policies	5	6	7	8	9

Economic Discrimination

Economic discrimination is defined as restrictions on a minority's ability to participate in normal economic activities. The Minorities at Risk dataset contains three economic discrimination indicators. Only the third is used, but since it is a composite indicator based on the first two, all three are described. The first economic discrimination variable (ECDIS90, 92, and 94) is measured using a Guttman scale, which codes the most severe of the categories described below which affect the group in question:

0. None
1. The group is economically advantaged. Public policies are designed to improve the relative economic position of other groups.
2. Significant poverty and underrepresentation in desirable occupations due to historical marginality, neglect, or restrictions. Public policies are designed to improve the group's material well-being.
3. Significant poverty and underrepresentation due to historical marginality, neglect, or restrictions. No social practice of deliberate exclusion. Few or no public policies aim at improving the group's material well-being.
4. Significant poverty and underrepresentation due to prevailing social practice by dominant groups. Formal public policies toward the group are neutral or, if positive, inadequate to offset active and widespread discrimination.
5. Public policies (formal exclusion and/or recurring repression) substantially restrict the group's economic opportunities by contrast with other groups.

The second economic discrimination indicator (ECPOV90, 92, and 94) measures the level of poverty of the minority group in question from 0 (none) to 3 (very poor). The third economic discrimination variable (ALLED90, 92, 94) combines these two indicators based on the following table:

Table B.3: Coding Guidelines for Economic Discrimination (ALLED)

ECDIS Pattern	ECPOV Category			
	None	Slight	Substant.	Very
1. Policies to improve status	0	1	2	3
2. No Policies	1	3	4	5
3. Neutral Policies	2	4	6	8
4. Restrictive Policies	3	5	7	9

Cultural Restrictions

Cultural restrictions are defined as restrictions on a minority's ability to engage in the group's cultural practices. The cultural restrictions indicator (CULRES91, 92, and 94) measures the restrictions that are placed on the pursuit or expression of the group's cultural interests. However, according to the Minorities at Risk coding manual,

> public restrictions that apply to all citizens because they are necessary for the common good, e.g. requirements that families have only one child, or that all children be vaccinated, are not restrictions even if they violate the cultural norms of the communal group being coded. Lack of public support for group cultural activities is not a restriction unless public support is provided to similar activities by other groups.

The indicators that are combined to form the cultural discrimination variable are coded on the following scale: 3 = the activity is prohibited or sharply restricted by public policy; 2 = the activity is somewhat restricted by public policy; 1 = the activity is restricted by widespread but informal social practice, (e.g., by discrimination against people who follow group customs or use the group's language); 0 = no significant restrictions on the activity. The following restrictions are so coded:

- Restrictions on observance of group religion
- Restrictions on speaking and publishing in group's language or dialect
- Restrictions on instruction in group's language
- Restrictions on celebration of group holidays, ceremonies, cultural events
- Restrictions on dress, appearance, behavior
- Restrictions on marriage, family life
- Restrictions on organizations that promote the group's cultural interests

The codings are summed and divided by two, creating an indicator ranging from 0 to 10.5.

Nonreligious Grievance Variables

Non-religious grievances are defined here as complaints openly expressed by group representatives over the political, economic, or cultural status of the group. All of the grievance variables are measured using composite indicators coded separately for 1990-1991, 1992-1993, and 1994-1995. Each of the categories of grievance was coded on the following scale, based on statements and actions by group leaders, members, and outside observers: 3 = issue important for most of the group; 2 = issue is significant but its relative importance cannot be judged; 1 = issue is of lesser importance, or of major concern to only one faction of the group; 0 = issue is not judged to be of any significant importance. The following types of political grievances are so coded:

- Diffuse political grievances, explicit objectives not clear (code only if more specific categories, below, cannot be coded).
- Greater political rights in own community or region (own leaders, assembly, legal system, end to military rule, etc.).
- Greater participation in politics and decision-making at the central state level.
- Equal civil rights and status.
- Change in unpopular local officials or policies.
- Other.

The highest possible value of the composite indicator is 15. The following types of economic grievances are so coded.

- Diffuse economic grievances, explicit objectives not clear (code only if more specific categories, below, cannot be coded).
- Greater share of public funds, services.
- Greater economic opportunities (better education, access to higher status occupations, resources).
- Improved working conditions, better wages, protective regulations (if sought specifically for group members).
- Protection of land, jobs, resources being used for the advantage of other groups.
- Other.

The highest possible value of the composite indicator is 15. The following types of cultural grievances are so coded:

- Freedom of religious belief and practice.
- Promotion of group culture and lifeways.
- Right to teach and publish in own language.
- Right to use own language in dealings with other groups, including government.
- Protection from threats and attacks by other communal groups.

The highest possible value of the composite indicator is 15.

Group Cohesiveness

Group cohesiveness is defined as the level of unity and identification within the group. Group Cohesiveness (COHESX90, 92, and 94) is coded on the following scale:

0. Category. No evidence of significant collective identity among those who share the defining traits.
1. Mosaic. Multiple local or cross-cutting identities are found within the

group, based on shared traits, but there is little evidence of a broader sense of identity.

2. Dispersed group. Some shared values and objectives define a group that is geographically dispersed, (e.g., between separate urban or rural areas, or distributed among several countries).
3. Factionalized group. There are multiple and competing identities within the group (lines of division may be clan-based, territorial, religious, political, etc.).
4. Weak identity group. Some values and objectives are held in common but are of limited or secondary importance for most members most of the time.
5. Strong identity group. Highly important values and objectives are shared by most members.

Control Variables

The following control variables are thought to potentially affect the relationship between religion and ethnic conflict and, accordingly, are used in some analyses.

Democracy and Autocracy

The levels of democracy and autocracy of governments affect the level and type of conflict that occur in a state. Democracies tend to be more tolerant of protest and accordingly rebellion is relatively uncommon in democracies. Autocracies tend to repress protest and thus rebellion is often the only option for a minority group to express its grievances. The level of a government's democracy in 1994 (NDEM94) is measured on a scale of 0 to 10, with 0 being the least democratic and 10 being the most democratic. The level of a government's autocracy in 1994 (NAUT94) is measured on a scale of 0 to 10, with 0 being the least autocratic and 10 being the most autocratic.[3]

Grievances Over Autonomy

Grievances over autonomy are one of the most important factors in determining whether or not a group will engage in rebellion. Since rebellion is one of the dependent variables in this study, grievances over autonomy thus must be taken into account. Grievances over autonomy (AUTGR90, 92, and 94) are measured using a composite indicator. Each of the following components are coded using the same scale as other types of nonreligious grievances:

- General concern, explicit objectives not clear (code only if more specific categories below cannot be coded).
- Union with kindred groups elsewhere.
- Political independence.
- Regional autonomy with widespread powers.

- Regional autonomy with limited powers.

The highest possible value of this indicator is 12

Data Collection and Reliability

The religion variables were all coded by the author of this study. In order to test coding reliability, 26 of the 105 cases were recoded by coders for the Minorities at Risk project. All coders were graduate assistants who did the primary Minorities at Risk data coding for the groups for which they recoded the backup data.[4] A full listing of the cases coded for the reliability test is provided in *Table B.4. Table B.5* shows the correlations between the primary and backup codings. The correlations are all satisfactorily high, especially considering the judgmental and soft nature of the variables in question.[5] The rest of the data, as already noted, is taken from the Minorities at Risk Phase 3 dataset.

Table B.4: Reliability Test Cases

Region	Country	Group	Region	Country	Group
Frmr Com.	Georgia	Abkhazians	Africa	Ghana	Mossi
Frmr Com.	Georgia	Adzhars	Africa	Kenya	Maasai
Frmr Com.	Russia	Buryat	Africa	Nambia	San
Frmr Com.	Russia	Chechens	Africa	Nigeria	Ibo
Frmr Com.	Russia	Tuvinians	Africa	Nigeria	Ogoni
Asia	China	Tibetans	Africa	Senegal	Casamance
Asia	China	Turkmen	Africa	S. Africa	Asians
Asia	India	Muslims	L. America	Argentina	Indigenous
Asia	India	Sikhs	L. America	Bolivia	Indig. High
Asia	Pakistan	Ahmadis	L. America	Bolivia	Indig. Low
Asia	Pakistan	Hindus	L. America	Chile	Indigenous
Africa	Botswana	San Bushmen	L. America	Mexico	Zapotecs
Africa	Chad	Southerners	L. America	Niceragua	Miskitos

Table B.5: Correlations Between Primary and Backup Codings for Religion Variables[6]

	Rel. Disc. (RDIS)			Rel. Disc. (RELDSC)		
	1990-91	1992-93	1994-95	1990-91	1992-93	1994-95
Corr.	.8945	.8928	.8683	.8831	.9228	.9097

Continued on next page

Table B.5 Continued

	Rel. Grievances (RGRV)			Rel. Legitimacy (RLEG)		
	1990-91	1992-93	1994-95	1990-91	1992-93	1994-95
Corr.	.6090	.6550	.6638	.7368	.7239	.7332

	Rel. Demands (RPROV)			Institutions (RELINST)	Relevance (RRELEVNT)
	1990-91	1992-93	1994-95		
Corr.	.8353	.8353	.8383	.8762	.8762

Notes

1. The definition of a religiously distinct ethnic minority as well as the methodology used here for case selection are discussed in appendix A.

2. They are also coded in the Minorities at Risk Phase 3 dataset in Belarus, Estonia, Georgia, Latvia, Moldova, and Ukraine. However, in these states ethnic Russians are not religiously distinct minorities and are, accordingly, not considered in this study.

3. For a discussion of how these scales were constructed see Jaggers and Gurr (1995).

4. Cases in the former Soviet bloc were coded by Michael Dravis (n = 5). Asian cases were coded by Deepa Kholsa (n = 6). Sub-Saharan African cases were coded by Anne Pitsch (n = 9). Latin American cases were coded by Pamela Burke (n = 6).

5. The correlations for religious grievances are a little low, but the significance of these correlations is very strong. Also, religious grievances are probably the softest and most difficult to code of the religion variables.

6. All correlations in this table have a significance (p-value) of .001 or lower in two-tailed correlations.

Bibliography

Ajami, Faoud, "The Summoning" *Foreign Affairs* 72 (4), 1993, 2-9.

Allen, Douglas ed., *Religion and Political Conflict in South Asia*, London: Greenwood, 1992.

Almond, Gabriel, "Introduction: A Functional Approach to Comparative Politics" in Almond and James C. Coleman eds., *The Politics of the Developing Areas*, Princeton: Princeton University Press, 1960.

Alston, Jon P., Charles W. Peek, and C. Ray Wingrove, "Religiosity and Black Militancy: A Reappraisal" *Journal for the Scientific Study of Religion* 11, 1972, 252-261.

Ammerman, Nancy T., "The Dynamics of Christian Fundamentalism: An Introduction" in Martin E. Marty and R. Scott Appleby eds., *Accounting for Fundamentalisms: The Dynamic Character of Movements*, Chicago: University of Chicago Press, 1994a, 13-17.

———, "Accounting for Christian Fundamentalisms: Social Dynamics and Rhetorical Strategies" in Martin E. Marty and R. Scott Appleby eds., *Accounting for Fundamentalisms: The Dynamic Character of Movements*, Chicago: University of Chicago Press, 1994b, 149-170

Anderson, Benadict, *Imagined Communities: Reflections on the Origins and Spread of Nationalism*, London: Verso, 1983.

Anderson, Gordon L. and Mortan A. Kaplan, *Morality and Religion in Liberal Democratic Societies*, New York: Paragon, 1992.

Anderson, Lisa, "Religion and the State in Libya: The Politics of Identity" *Annals of the American Association of Political and Social Science* 483, 1986, 61-72

Anwar, Said Tariq, "Civilizations Versus Civilizations in a New Multipolar World" *Journal of Marketing*, 62 (2), 1998, 125-128.

Appleby, R. Scott, *The Ambivalence of the Sacred: Religion, Violence, and Reconciliation*, New York: Rowman & Littlefield, 2000.

————, "Religion and Global Affairs: Religious 'Militants for Peace'" *SAIS Review* Summer-Fall, 1998, 38-44.

————, *Religious Fundamentalisms and Global Conflict*, New York: Foreign Policy Association Headline Series #301, 1994.

Apter, David ed., *Ideology and Discontent*, New York: Free Press, 1964

————, *The Politics of Modernization*, Chicago: University of Chicago Press, 1965.

Ariyaratne, A. T., "Living with Religion in the Midst of Violence" *Bulletin of Peace Proposals* 21 (3), 1990, 281-285.

Arjomand, Said Amir ed., *The Political Dimensions of Religion*, New York: State University Press of New York, 1993.

Assefa, Hizkias, "Religion in the Sudan: Exacerbating Conflict or Facilitating Reconciliation?" *Bulletin of Peace Proposals* 21 (3), 1990, 255-262.

Badal, Raphael K., "Religion and Conflict in the Sudan: A Perspective" *Bulletin of Peace Proposals* 21 (3), 1990, 263-272.

Balandier, Georgrs, "An Anthropology of Violence and War" *International Social Science Journal* 1986, 499-511.

Banton, Michael ed., *Anthropological Approaches to the Study of Religion*, London: Tavistock Publications, 1966.

Barber, Benjamin R., "Fantasy of Fear" *Harvard International Review* 20 (1), Winter 1997/1998, 66-71.

Barnhart, Joe, "The Incurably Religious Animal" in Emile Sahliyeh ed., *Religious Resurgence and Politics in the Contemporary World*, New York: State University of New York Press, 1990, 27-32.

Barth, Fredrik ed., *Ethnic Groups and Bounderies: The Social Organization of Culteral Difference*, Boston: Little, Brown and Co., 1969.

Bartley, Robert L., "The Case for Optimism" *Foreign Affairs* 72 (4), 1993, 15-18.

Bax, Mart, Peter Kloos, and Adrianus Koster, *Faith and Polity: Essays in Religion and Politics*, Amsterdam: VU University Press, 1992.

Beckford, James A., "The Sociology of Religion: 1945-1989" *Social Compass* 37 (1), 1990, 45-64.

————, "The Insulation and Isolation of the Sociology of Religion" *Sociological Analysis* 46 (4), 1985, 347-354.

————, "The Restoration of 'Power' to the Sociology of Religion" *Sociological Analysis* 44 (1), 1983, 11-32.

Beedham, Brian, "The New Geopolitics: A Fading Hell" *The Economist* Jul 31, 1999, s10.

Bell, D., "Religion in the Sixties" *Social Research* 38, 1971, 447-497.

Bellah, Robert N., "Christianity and Symbolic Realism" *Journal for the Scientific Study of Religion* 9, 1970, 89-96.

Berger, P.L., *The Sacred Canopy*, Garden City, N.J.: Doubleday, 1969.

Berryman, Phillip, *Liberation Theology*, Philadelphia: Temple University 1987.

————, *The Religious Roots of Rebellion: Christians in Central American Revolutions*, New York: Orbis, 1984.

Beyer, Peter, "Secularization from the Perspective of Globalization: A Response to Dobbelaere" *Sociology of Religion* 60 (3), 1999, 289-301.

————, *Religion and Globalization*, London: Sage, 1994.

Billings, Dwight B., "Religion and Political Legitimation" *Annual Review of Sociology* 20, 1994, 173-201.

Billings, Dwight B., and Shaunna L. Scott "Religion as Opposition: A Gramscian Analysis" *American Journal of Sociology* 96 (1), July 1990, 1-31.

Bienen, Henry, "Religion Legitimacy and Conflict in Nigeria" *Annals of the American Association of Political and Social Science* 483, 1986, 50-60.

Binyan, Liu, "Civilization Grafting" *Foreign Affairs* 72 (4), 1993, 19-21.

Bolce, Louis and Gerald De Maio, "The Anti-Christian Fundamentalist Factor in Contemporary Politics" *Public Opinion Quarterly* 63, 1999, 508-542.

Bond, Doug, "Timely Conflict Risk Assessments and the PANDA Project" in John L. Davies and Ted R. Gurr eds., *Preventive Measures: Building risk Assessments and Crisis Early Warning Systems*, Boulder, Colo.: Rowman & Littlefield, 1998, 110-122.

Brecher, Michael, "International Studies in the Twentieth Century and Beyond: Flawed Dichotomies, Synthesis, Cumulation" *International Studies Quarterly* 43 (2), 1999, 213-264.

Brecher, Michael and Jonathan Wilkenfeld, *Crisis, Conflict and Inatability*, New York: Pergamon, 1989

Brown, David, "Ethnic Revival: Perspectives on State and Society" *Third World Quarterly* 11 (4), 1989, 1-17.

Campbell, Robert A. and James E. Curtis, "Religious Involvement Across Societies: Analysis for Alternative Measures in National Surveys" *Journal for the Scientific Study of Religion* 33 (3), 1994, 215-229.

Cardoso, F.H. and E. Faletto, *Dependency and Development in Latin America*, Berkeley: University of California Press, 1978.

Carment, David and Patrick James, "Escalation of Ethnic Conflict" *International Politics* 35, 1998, 65-82.

————, "The International Politics of Ethnic Conflict: New Perspectives on Theory and Policy" *Global Society* 11 (2), 1997a, 205-232.

————, eds, *Wars in the Midst of Peace*, Pittsburgh: University of Pittsburgh Press, 1997b.

————, Two-Level Games and Third-Party Intervention: Evidence from Ethnic Conflict in the Balkans and South Asia" *Canadian Journal of Political Science* 29 (3), 1996, 521-554.

Chaliand, Gerard ed., Translated by Tony Berrett, *Minority Peoples in the Age of Nation-States*, London: Pluto Press, 1989.

Chaves, Mark, "On the Rational Choice Approach to Religion" *Journal for the Scientific Study of Religion* 34 (1), 1995, 98-104.

Chong, Dennis, *Collective Action and Civil Rights*, Chicago: University of Chicago Press, 1991.

Cockcroft, James D. ed., *Dependence and Underdevelopment*, New York: Anchor

Books, 1972.

Cole, Juan R. I. and Nikki R. Keddie, *Shi'sm and Social Protest*, New Haven: Yale, 1986.

Coleman, James S., "Commentary: Social Institutions and Social Theory" *American Sociological Review* 55, 1990, 333-339.

Comaroff, John L. and Paul C. Stern eds., *Perspectives on Nationalism and War*, Luxenbourg, Australia: Gordon and Breach, 1995.

Connor, Walker, *Ethnonationalism: The Quest for Understanding*, Princeton: Princeton University Press, 1994.

————, "Nation Building or Nation Destroying?" *World Politics* 26, 1972, 319-355.

Cox, Harvey, *The Secular City: Seculariztion and Urbanization in Theological Perspective*, London: SCM Press, 1965.

Crenshaw, Martha, "Political Violence in Algeria" *Terrorism and Political Violence* 6 (3), 1994, 261-281.

Dabashi, Hamid, *Theology of Discontent,* New York: New York University Press, 1993.

Davies, James C., "Toward a Theory of Revolution" *American Sociological Review* 27, 1962, 5-19.

Davies, John L. and Ted R. Gurr eds., *Preventive Measures: Building risk Assessments and Crisis Early Warning Systems*, Boulder, Colo.: Rowman & Littlefield, 1998.

Davis, Charles, *Religion and the Making of Society*, Cambridge: Cambridge University Press, 1994.

Deane, Herbert A., *The Political and Social Ideas of St. Augustine*, New York: Columbia University Press, 1963.

Deeb, Mary J., "Militant Islam and the Politics of Redemption" *Annals, American Acadamey of Political and Social Sciences* 524, 1992, 52-65.

Demerath, N.J. III, "Rational Paradigms, A-Rational Religion, and the Debate over Secularization" *Journal for the Scientific Study of Religion* 34 (1), 1995, 105-112.

Deutsch, Karl W., "On Nationalism, World Regions, and the Nature of the West" in Per Torsvik ed., *Mobilization, Center-Periphery Structures, and Nation Building*, Oslo: Universitesforlaget, 1981, 51-93.

————, "The Limits of Common Sense" in Nelson Polsby ed., *Politics and Social Life*, Boston: Houghton Mifflin, 1963, 51-57.

————, *Nationalism and Social Communication*, Cambridge, Mass.: MIT Press, 1953.

Dinstein, Yoram, "Freedom of Religion and the Protection of Religious Minorities" *Israel Yearbook on Human Rights* 20, 1991, 155-179.

Dobbelaere, Karel, "Towards an Integrated Perspective of the Processes Related to the Descriptive Concept of Secularization" *Sociology of Religion* 60 (3), 1999, 229-247.

————, "Secularization Theories and Sociological Paradigms: A Reformulation of the Private-Public Dichotomy and the Problem of Societal Integration" *Sociological Analysis* 1985, 46 (4), 377-87.

Dodson, Michael, "The Politics of Religion in Revolutionary Nicaragua" *Annals of the American Association of Political and Social Science* 483, 1986, 36-49.

Don-Yehiyah, Eliezer, "The Book and the Sword: The Nationalist Yeshivot and Political Radicalism in Israel" in Martin E. Marty and R. Scott Appleby eds, *Accounting for Fundamentalisms: The Dynamic Character of Movements*, Chicago: University of Chicago Press, 1994, 264-302.

———, "The Negation of Galut in Religious Zionism" *Modern Judaism* May 1992, 129-155.

Drake, C. J. M., "The Role of Ideology in Terrorists' Target Selection" *Terrorism and Political Violence* 10 (2), 1998, 53-85.

Durham, W. Cole Jr., "Perspectives on Religious Liberty: A Comparative Framework" in John D. van der Vyver and John Witte Jr., eds, *Religious Human Rights in Global Perspective: Legal Perspectives*, Boston: Martinus Njhoff, 1996, 1-44.

Durkheim, Emile, "Concerning the Definition of Religious Phenomena" in W. S. F. Pickering, ed, *Durkheim on Religion: A Selection of Readings with Bibliographies*, London: Routledge, 1975, 74-99.

———, The *Elementary Forms of Religious Life*, translated by Joseph Ward Swain, London: George Allen and Unwin, 1964.

Eisenstadt, S. N., "The Reconstruction of Religious Arenas in the Framework of 'Multiple Modernities'" *Millennium* 29 (3), 2000, 591-611.

Ellison, Christopher G., "Rational Choice Explanations of Individual Religious Behavior: Notes on the Problem of Social Embeddedness" *Journal for the Scientific Study of Religion* 34 (1), 1995, 89-97.

Ellison, Christopher G., John P. Bartkowski, and Kristin L. Anderson, "Are There Religious Variations in Domestic Violence" *Journal of Family Issues* 20 (1), 1999, 87-113.

Entelis, John P., *Algeria: The Revolution Institutionalized*, Boulder, Colo.: Westview, 1986.

Enyat, Hamid, *Modern Islamic Political Thought*, Austin: University of Texas, 1982

Esposito, John L., "Religion and Global Affairs: Political Challenges" *SAIS Review* Summer-Fall, 1998, 19-24.

———, The *Islamic Threat: Myth or Reality?* 2nd ed., Oxford: Oxford University Press, 1995.

Esposito, John L. and John O. Voll, "Islam and the West: Muslim Voices of Dialogue" *Millennium* 29 (3), 2000, 613-639.

Falconer, Alan D., "The Role of Religion in Situations of Armed Conflict: The Case of Northern Ireland" *Bulletin of Peace Proposals* 21 (3), 1990, 273-280.

Fawcett, Liz, *Religion, Ethnicity, and Social Change*, New York: St. Martins, 2000.

Fein, Helen "Genocide: A Sociological Perspective" *Current Sociology* 38 (1), Spring 1990, 1-126.

Fenn, Richard, "The Sociology of Religion: A Critical Survey" in Tom Bottimore, Stefan Nowak, and Magdalena Sokolowska eds., *Sociology: The State of the Art*, London: Sage, 1982, 101-128.

Fenn, Richard K., "Malaise in the Sociology of Religion: A Prescription" *Sociological Analysis* 46 (4), 1985, 401-414.

Fenton, Steve, *Ethnicity: Racism, Class, and Culture*, London: McMillan, 1999.

Fields, Echo E., "Understanding Activist Fundamentalism" *Sociological Analysis* 52 (2), 1991, 175-190.

Feierabend, Ivo and Rosiland Feierabend, "Systemic Conditions of Political Aggression: An Application of Frustration=Aggression Theory" in Ivo Feierabend, et al., eds., *Anger, Violence and Politics*, New York: Prentice-Hall, 1973.

Foster-Carter, A., "The Sociology of Development" in M. Haralambos ed., *Sociology: New Directions*, Ormskirk, Lancashire: Causeway, 1985.

Fox, Jonathan, "The Salience of Religious Issues in Ethnic Conflicts: A Large-N Study" *Nationalism and Ethnic Politics* 3 (3), Aut 1997, 1-19.

————, "Do Religious Institutions Support Violence or the Status Quo?" *Studies in Conflict and Terrorism* 22 (2), 1999a, 119-139.

————, "The Influence of Religious Legitimacy on Grievance Formation by Ethnoreligious Minorities" *Journal of Peace Research* 36 (3), 1999b, 289-307.

————, "Is Islam More Conflict Prone than Other Religions? A Cross-Sectional Study of Ethnoreligious Conflict" *Nationalism and Ethnic Politics* 6 (2), 2000a, 1-23.

————, "Religious Causes of Ethnic Discrimination" *International Studies Quarterly* 44 (3), September 2000b, 423-450.

————, "The Effects of Religious Discrimination on Ethnic Protest and Rebellion" *Journal of Conflict Studies* 20 (2), Fall, 2000c, 16-43.

————, "Islam and the West: The Influence of Two Civilizations on Ethnic Conflict" *Journal of Peace Research* 38 (4), July, 2001, 459-472.

Frank, Andre G., *Capitalism and Underdevelopment in Latin America: Historical Studies of Chile and Brazil*, Harmonsworth: Penguin, 1971.

Friedman, Jonathan, "Religion, the Subject and the State" in Mart Bax, Peter Kloos and Adrianus Koster eds., *Faith and Polity: Essays in Religion and Politics*, Amsterdam: VU University Press, 1992, 1-26.

Friedrichs, Robert W., "The Uniquely Religious: Grounding the Social Scientific Study of Religion Anew" *Sociological Analysis* 1985, 46 (4), 361-366.

Frykenberg, Robert Eric, "Accounting for Fundamentalisms in South Asia: Ideologies and Institutions in Historical Perspective" in Martin E. Marty and R. Scott Appleby eds., *Accounting for Fundamentalisms: The Dynamic Character of Movements*, Chicago: University of Chicago Press, 1994, 591-618.

Fuller, Graham E. and Ian O. Lesser, *A Sense of Siege: The Geopolitics of Islam and the West*, Boulder Colo: Westview, 1995.

Fulton, John, "Religion and Politics in Gramsci: An Introduction" *Sociological*

Analysis 1987, 48 (3), 197-216.

Garvey, John H., "Introduction: Fundamentalism and Politics" in Martin E. Marty and R. Scott Appleby eds., *Fundamentalisms and the State: Remaking Politics, Economies, and Militance*, Chicago: University of Chicago Press, 1991, 13-27.

Geertz, Clifford, "Centers, Kings and Charisma: Reflections on the Symbolics of Power" in J. Ben-David and C. Nichols Clark eds., *Culture and its Creators*, Chicago: Chicago University Press, 1977.

————, *The Interpretation of Culture*, New York: Basic Books, 1973.

————, "Religion as a Cultural System" in Michael Banton ed., *Anthropological Approaches to the Study of Religion*, London: Tavistock Publications, 1966, 1-46.

Gellner, Ernest, *Postmodernism, Reason and Religion*, London: Routledge, 1992.

Gill, Anthony, *Rendering Unto Caesar: The Catholic Church and the State in Latin America*, Chicago: University of Chicago Press, 1998.

Gill, Anthony and Arang Keshavarzian, "State Building and Religious Resources: An Institutional Theory of Church-State Relations in Iran and Mexico" *Politics and Society* 27 (3), 1999, 431-465.

Ginsburg, Faye, "Saving America's Souls: Operation Rescue's Crusade against Abortion" Martin E. Marty, and R. Scott Appleby eds., *Fundamentalisms and the State: Remaking Politics, Economies, and Militance*, Chicago: University of Chicago Press, 1991, 557-588.

Girard, Rene, *Violence and the Sacred*, trans. Patrick Gregory, Baltimore Md.: Johns Hopkins University Press, 1977.

Glasner, Peter E., *The Sociology of Secularization: A Critique of a Concept*, London: Routledge, 1977.

Goldstone, Jack A., *Revolution and Rebellion in the Early Modern World*, Berkeley: University of California, 1991.

Goldstone, Jack A., Ted Robert Gurr, and Farrokh Moshiri, eds., *Revolutions of the Late Twentieth Century*, Boulder, Colo.: Westview, 1991.

Gopin, Marc, *Between Eden and Armageddon: The Future of World Religions, Violence, and Peacemaking*, Oxford: Oxford University Press, 2000.

Greely, Andrew M., *Religion: A Secular Theory*, New York: Free Press, 1982.

Greenawalt, Kent, *Religious Convictions and Political Choice*, Oxford: Oxford University Press, 1988.

Greenfeld, Liah, *Nationalism: Five Roads to Modernity*, Cambridge, Mass.: Harvard University Press, 1992.

Gregg, Donald P., "A Case for Continued U.S. Engagement" *Orbis* 41 (3) 1997, 375-384.

Gungwu, Wang, "A Machiavelli for Our Times" *The National Interest* (46) 1997a, 69-73.

————, "Learn from the Past" *Far Eastern Economic Review* 160 (18), May 1 1997b, 37-38.

Gurr, Ted R., *Peoples Versus States: Minorities at Risk in the New Century*, Washington, D.C.: United States Institute of Peace Press, 2000.

Quarterly 13 (1), Spring 1997, 11-23.

———, "Minorities, Nationalists, and Ethnopolitical Conflict" in Chester A. Crocker and Fen O. Hampson eds., *Managing Global Chaos: Sources of and Responses to International Conflict*, Washington, D.C.: United States Institute of Peace Press, 1996, 53-77.

———, "Peoples Against the State: Ethnopolitical Conflict and the Changing World System" *International Studies Quarterly*, 38 (3), 1994, 347-377.

———, *Minorities At Risk: A Global View of Ethnopolitical Conflict*, Washington, D.C.: United States Institute of Peace, 1993a.

———, "Why Minorities Rebel" *International Political Science Review* 14 (2), 1993b, 161-201.

———, "War Revolution, and the Growth of the Coercive State" *Comparative Political Studies* 21 (1), April 1988, 45-65.

———, *Why Men Rebel*, Princeton: Princeton University 1970.

Gurr, Ted R. and Barbara Harff, *Ethnic Conflict in World Politics*, Boulder, Colo.: Westview, 1994a.

———, "Conceptual, Research and Policy Issues in Early Warning Research: An Overview" *Journal of Ethno-Development* 4 (1), 1994b, 3-14.

Gurr, Ted R. and Will H. Moore, "Ethnopolitical Rebellion: A Cross-Sectional Analysis of the 1980s with Risk Assessments for the 1990s" *American Journal of Political Science* 41 (4), 1997, 1079-1103.

Hadden, Jeffrey E., "Religious Broadcasting and the Mobilization of the New Christian Right" *Journal for the Scientific Study of Religion* 26 (1), 1987, 1-24.

Halliday, Fred, *Nation and Religion in the Middle East*, Boulder, Colo.: Lynne Rienner, 2000.

———, "A New World Myth" *New Statesman* 10 (447), 1997, 42-43.

Halpern, "Toward Further Modernization of the Study of New Nations" *World Politics* October 1964, 17, 157-181.

Hannigan, John A., "Social Movement Theory and the Sociology of Religion: Toward a New Synthesis" *Sociological Analysis* 52 (4), 1991, 311-331.

Hannum, Hurst, *Autonomy, Sovereignty, and Self-Determination: The Accommodation of Conflicting Rights*, Philadelphia: University of Philidelphia Press, 1990.

Hardacre, Helen, "The Impact of Fundamentalisms on Women, the Family, and Interpersonal Relations" in Martin E. Marty and R. Scott Appleby eds., *Fundamentalisms and Society: Reclaiming the Sciences, the Family, and Education*, Chicago: University of Chicago Press, 1993, 129-150.

Hardjono, Ratih, "The Clash of Civilizations and the Remaking of World Order" *Nieman Reports* 51 (1), 1997, 87-88.

Harff, Barbara and Ted R. Gurr, "Systematic Early Warning of Humanitarian Emergencies" *Journal of Peace Research* 35 (5), 1998, 551-579.

Harris, Robin "War of the World Views" *National Review* 48 (20), 1996, 69.

Hassner, Pierre, "Morally Objectionable, Politically Dangerous" *The National Interest* (46), Winter 1997a, 63-69.

———, "Clashing On" *The National Interest* (48), Summer 1997b, 105-111.

————, "Clashing On" *The National Interest* (48), Summer 1997b, 105-111.

Hayes, Bernadette C., "The Impact of Religious identification on Political Attitudes: An International Comparison" *Sociology of Religion* 56 (2), 1995, 177-194.

Haynes, Jeff, *Religion in Third World Politics*, Boulder, Colo.: Lynne Rienner, 1994.

Heilbrunn, Jacob, "The Clash of Samuel Huntingtons" *The American Prospect* (39), 1998. 22-28.

Heisler, Martin O., "The Uses and Limitations of Perspective" in Peter Suedfeld ed., *Light from the Ashes: Early Disruption by the Holocaust and the Later Life of Social Scientists*, Ann Arbor: University of Michigan Press, 2000.

Henderson, Errol A., "The Democratic Peace through the Lens of Culture, 1820-1989" *International Studies Quarterly* 42 (3), September 1998, 461-484.

————, "Culture or Contiguity: Ethnic Conflict, the Similarity States, and the Onset of War,1820-1989" *Journal of Conflict Resolution* 41 (5), October 1997, 649-668.

Henderson, Errol A. and J. David Singer, "Civil War in the Post-Colonial World, 1946-1992" *Journal of Peace Research* 37 (3), 2000, 275-299.

Hickey, John, *Religion and the Northern Ireland Problem*, Totowa, N.J.: Barnes and Noble, 1984.

Hobsbawm, E.J., *Nations and Nationalism since 1789: Programme, Myth, Reality*, Cambridge: Cambridge University Press, 1990.

Hoffman, Bruce, "'Holy Terror': The Implications of Terrorism Motivated by a Religious Imperative" *Studies in Conflict and Terrorism* 18, 1995, 271-284.

Horowitz, Donald L., *Ethnic Groups in Conflict*, Berkeley: University of California Press, 1985.

Hunter, Shirleen T., *The Future of Islam and the West: Clash of Civilizations or Peaceful Coexistence?*, Westport, Conn.: Praeger, with the Center for Strategic and International Studies, Washington, D.C., 1998.

Huntington, Samuel P., *The Clash of Civilizations and the Remaking of the World Order*, New York: Simon & Schuster, 1996a

————, "The West: Unique, Not Universal" *Foreign Affairs* 75 (6), 1996b, 28-46.

————, "The Clash of Civilizations?" *Foreign Affairs* 72 (3), 1993, 22-49.

————, *Political Order in Changing Societies*, New Haven, Conn.: Yale University Press, 1968.

Iannaccone, Laurence R., "Voodoo Economics? Reviewing the Rational Choice Approach to Religion" *Journal for the Scientific Study of Religion* 34 (1), 1995a, 76-89.

————, "Second Thoughts: A Response to Chaves, Demerath, and Ellison" *Journal for the Scientific Study of Religion* 34 (1), 1995b, 113-120.

Ikenberry, John G., "Just Like the Rest" *Foreign Affairs* 76 (2), 1997, 162-163.

Isaacs, Harold A., *Idols of the Tribe: Group Identity and Political Change*, New York: Harper and Row, 1975.

Polity III Data" *Journal of Peace Research* 3, (4), 1995, 469-482.

Janosik, Robert J., "Religion and Political Involvement: A Study of Black African Sects" *Journal for the Scientific Study of Religion* 13, 1974, 161-175.

Johnston, Douglass "The Churches and Apartheid in South Africa" in Douglas Johnston and Cynthia Sampson eds., *Religion, the Missing Dimension of Statecraft,* Oxford: Oxford University Press, 1994, 177-207.

Johnston, Hank and Jozef Figa, "The Church and Political Opposition: Comparative Perspectives on Mobilization Against Authoritarian Regimes" *Journal for the Scientific Study of Religion* 27 (1), 1988, 32-47.

Juergensmeyer, Mark, "Terror Mandated by God" *Terrorism and Political Violence* 9 (2), Summer 1997, 16-23.

————, *The New Cold War?* Berkeley: University of California, 1993.

————, "Sacrifice and Cosmic War" *Terrorism and Political Violence* 3 (3), 1991, 101-117.

Kabalkova, Vendulka, "Towards and International Political Theology" *Millennium* 29 (3), 2000, 675-704.

Kader, Zerougui A., "The Clash of Civilizations and the Remaking of World Order" *Arab Studies Quarterly* 20 (1),1998, 89-92.

Kalberg, Stephen, "The Rationalization of Action in Max Weber's Sociology of Religion" *Sociological Theory* 8 (1), Spring 1990, 58-84.

Kamrava, Mehran, *Understanding Comparative Politics: A Framework For Analysis,* London: Routledge, 1996.

Kasfir, Nelson, "Explaining Political Participation" *World Politics* 31, 1979, 365-388.

Kautsky, J., *The Political Consequences of Modernization,* New York: John Wiley, 1972.

Keddie, Nikki R., "Shi'ism and Revolution" in Bruce Lincoln ed., *Religion, Rebellion and Revolution,* London: Macmillin, 1985

Kennedy, Robert, "Is One Person's Terrorist Another's Freedom Fighter? Western and Islamic Approaches to 'Just War' Compared" *Terrorism and Political Violence* 11 (1), 1999, 1-21.

Kent, Stephan, A., "Relative Deprivation and Resource Mobilization: A Study of Early Quakerism" *British Journal of Sociology* 33 (4), 1982, 529-544.

Kirkpatrick, Jeane J. et. al., "The Modernizing Imperative" *Foreign Affairs* 72 (4), 1993, 22-26.

Kolas, Ashild, "Tibetan Nationalism: The Politics of Religion" *Journal of Peace Research* 33 (1), 1996, 51-66.

Kokosalakis, Nikos, "Legitimation, Power and Religion in Modern Society" *Sociological Analysis* 46 (4), 1985, 367-376.

Kowalewski, David and Arthur L. Greil, "Religion as Opiate: Religion as Opiate in Comparative Perspective" *Journal of Church and State* 1990, 511-526.

Kramer, Martin ed., *Shi'ism, Resistance and Revolution,* Boulder: Westview, 1987

Kriesberg, Louis, "Preventing and Resolving Destructive Communal Conflicts" in David Carment and Patrick James eds, *Wars in the Midst of Peace,* Pittsburgh:

David Carment and Patrick James eds, *Wars in the Midst of Peace*, Pittsburgh: University of Pittsburgh Press, 1997, 232-251.

Kumar, Radha, "The Troubled History of Partition" *Foreign Affairs* 76 (1), 1997, 22-34.

Kuran, Timur, "Fundamentalism and the Economy" in Martin E. Marty and R. Scott Appleby eds., *Fundamentalisms and the State: Remaking Politics, Economies, and Militance*, Chicago: University of Chicago Press, 1991, 289-301.

Lambert, Yves, "Religion in Modernity as a New Axial Age: Secularization or New Religious Forms" *Sociology of Religion* 60 (3), 303-333.

Lang, Graeme, "Correlations Versus Case Studies: The Case of the Zulu in Swanson's *The Birth of the Gods*" *Journal for the Scientific Study of Religion* 28 (3), 1989, 273-282.

Latin, David, "Religion, Political Culture, and the Weberian Tradition" *World Politics* 30 (4), 1978, 563-593.

Latkin, Carl, "From Device to Vice: Social Control and Intergroup Conflict at Rajneeshpuram", *Sociological Analysis* 52 (4), 1991, 262-278.

Lawrence, Bruce B., *Defenders of God: The Fundamentalist Revolt against the Modern Age*, San Francisco: Harper and Row, 1989.

Laustsen, Carsten B. and Ole Waever, "In Defense of Religion: Sacred referent Objects for Securitization" *Millennium* 29 (3), 2000, 705-739.

Layachi, Azzedine and Abdel-Kader Halreche, "National Development and Political Protest: Islamists in the Maghreb Countries" *Arab Studies Quarterly* 14 (2 and 3), 1992, 69-92.

Layton-Henry, Zig, *The Political Rights of Migrant Workers in Western Europe*, London: Sage, 1990.

Leak, Gary K. and Brandy A. Randall, "Clarification of the Link Between Right-Wing Authoritarianism and Religiousness: The Role of Religious Maturity" *Journal for the Scientific Study of Religion* 34 (2), 1995, 245-252.

Lechner, Frank A., "The Case Against Secularization: A Rebuttal" *Social Forces* 69 (4), June 1991, 1103-1119.

Levine, Daniel H., *Religion and Political Conflict in Latin America*, Chapel Hill: University of North Carolina, 1986a.

Levine, Daniel H., "Religion and Politics in Comparative and Historical Perspective" *Comparative Politics* 19 (1), 1986b, 95-122.

Lewis, Bernard, *Islam and the West*, Oxford: Oxford University Press, 1993.

Lewy, Gunther, *Religion and Revolution*, New York: Oxford University Press, 1974.

Lichbach, Mark I., "An Evaluation of 'Does Economic Inequality Breed Political Conflict?': Studies" *World Politics* 1989, 431-470.

Lincoln, Bruce ed., *Religion, Rebellion and Revolution*, London: Macmillin, 1985.

Little, David, "Belief, Ethnicity, and Nationalism" *Nationalism and Ethnic Politics* 1 (2) 1995.

———, *Sri Lanka: The Inversion of Enmity*, Washington, D.C.: United States Institute of Peace Press, 1994.

————, *Ukraine: The Legacy of Intolerance*, Washington, D.C.: United States Institute of Peace Press, 1991.

Luckman, Thomas, *The Invisible Religion*, New York: Macmillan, 1967.

Luttwak, Edward, "The Missing Dimension" in Douglas Johnston and Cynthia Sampson eds., *Religion, the Missing Dimension of Statecraft*, Oxford: Oxford University Press, 1994, 8-19.

Mahbubani, Kishore "The Dangers of Decadence" *Foreign Affairs* 72 (4), 1993, 10-14.

Manor, James, "Organizational Weakness and the Rise of Sinhalese Buddhist Extremism" in Martin E. Marty and R. Scott Appleby eds., *Accounting for Fundamentalisms: The Dynamic Character of Movements*, Chicago: University of Chicago Press, 1994, 770-784.

Marshall, Paul, "Religion and Global Affairs: Disregarding Religion" *SAIS Review* Summer-Fall 1998, 13-18.

Marshall, Gordon, "Which Way for the Sociology of Religion? A Review Article" *Comparative Studies in Society and History* 29, 1987, 375-80.

Martin, David A., *A General Theory of Secularization*, Oxford: Blackwell, 1978.

Martin, Richard C., "The Study of Religion and Violence" in David C. Rapoport, and Yonah Alexander, eds., *The Morality of Terrorism: Religious and Secular Justifications*, 2nd ed. New York: Columbia University Press, 1989, 349-373.

Marty, Martin E. and R. Scott Appleby, eds., *Accounting for Fundamentalisms: The Dynamic Character of Movements*, Chicago: University of Chicago Press, 1994.

————, eds, *Fundamentalisms and Society: Reclaiming the Sciences, the Family, and Education*, Chicago: University of Chicago Press, 1993.

————, eds, *Fundamentalisms and the State: Remaking Politics, Economies and Militance*, Chicago: University of Chicago Press, 1991.

Marx, Gary T., *Protest and Prejudice*, New York: Harper and Row, 1967a.

————, "Religion: Opiate or Inspiration of Civil Rights Militancy among Negroes" *American Sociological Review* 1967b, 64-72.

McAdam, Doug, *Political Process and the Development of Black Insurgency 1930-1970*, Chicago: University of Chicago Press,1982.

McArthy, John D. and Mayer N. Zald, "Resource Mobilization and Social Movements: A Partial Theory" *American Journal of Sociology* 82 (6), 1976, 1212-1241.

McLoughlin, William G., "The Role of Religion in the Revolution" in Steven G. Kurtz and James H. Hutson eds., *Essays on the American Revolution*, Chapel Hill: University of North Carolina, 1973.

McNeil, William H., "Epilogue: Fundamentalism and the World of the 1990s" in Martin E. Marty and R. Scott Appleby eds., *Fundamentalisms and Society: Reclaiming the Sciences, the Family, and Education*, Chicago: University of Chicago Press, 1993, 558-573.

Mearsheimer, John J., "Why We Will Soon Miss the Cold War" *The Atlantic* 266 (2), 1990, 35-50.

Mendelsohn, Everett, "Religious Fundamentalism and the Sciences" in Martin E. Marty and R. Scott Appleby eds., *Fundamentalisms and Society: Reclaiming the Sciences, the Family, and Education*, Chicago: University of Chicago Press, 1993, 23-41.

Meny, Yves, *Government and Politics in Western Europe*. Oxford: Oxford University Press, 1993.

Merkl, Peter H. and Ninian Smart eds., *Religion and Politics in the Modern World*, New York: New York University Press, 1983.

Midlarsky, Manus I., "Democracy and Islam: Implications for Civilizational Conflict and the Democratic Peace" *International Studies Quarterly* 42 (3), 1998, 458-511.

Miller, Alan S., "The Influence of Religious Affiliation on the Clustering of Social Attitudes" *Review of Religious Research* 37 (3), March 1996, 123-136.

Miller, Mark, J., *Foreign Workers in Western Europe: An Emerging Political Force*, New York: Praeger, 1981.

Misztal, Bronislaw and Anson Shupe eds., *Religion and Politics in Comparative Perspective: Revival of Religious Fundamentalism in East and West*, Westport, Conn.: Praeger, 1992.

Moaddel, Mansoor, *Class, Politics, and Ideology in the Iranian Revolution*, New York: Columbia, 1993.

Moen, Matthew C., and Lowell S. Gustafson, eds., *The Religious Challenge to the State*, Philadelphia: Temple University Press, 1992.

Monshipouri, Mahmood, "The West's Modern Encounter with Islam: From Discourse to Reality" *Journal of Church and State* 40 (1), 1998, 25-56.

Montville, Joseph, ed., *Conflict and Peacemaking in Multiethnic Societies*, Lanham, Md.: Lexington Books, 1990.

Mortimer, Robert, "Islam and Multiparty Politics in Algeria" *Middle East Journal* 1991, 25 (4), 575-593.

Moshiri, Farrokh, "Iran: Islamic Revolution Against Westernization" in Jack A. Goldstone, Ted Robert Gurr, and Farrokh Moshiri eds., *Revolutions of the Late Twentieth Century*, Boulder: Westview, 1991, 116-135.

Mortimer, Edward, *Faith and Power: The Politics of Islam*, New York: Vintage, 1982.

Moyser, George ed., *Politics and Religion in the Modern World*, New York: Routledge, 1991.

Murphey, Dwight C., "The Clash of Civilizations" *The Journal of Social, Political, and Economic Studies* 23 (2), 1998, 215-216.

Naff, William E., "The Clash of Civilizations and the Remaking of World Order" *Annals of the American Academy of Political and Social Science* 556, 1998, 198-199.

Nasr, Vali, "Religion and Global Affairs: Secular States and Religious Oppositions" *SAIS Review* Summer-Fall 1998, 32-37.

Neckermann, Peter, "The Promise of Globalization or the Clash of Civilizations" *The World and I* 13 (12), 1998.

The World and I 13 (12), 1998.

Nielson, Michael E. and Jim Fultz, "Further Examination of the Relationships of Religious Orientation to Religious Conflict" *Review of Religious Research* 36 (4), June 1995.

Nodjomi, Mohssen, "From Popular Revolution to Theocratic Absolutism: Iran 1979-1981" *Socialism and Democracy* 1988, 31-55.

Oberschall, Anthony, *Social Movements: Ideologies, Interests, and Identities*, New Brunswick, U.S.A.: Transaction Publishers, 1993.

————, *Social Conflicts and Social Movements*, Englewood Cliffs, N.J.: Prentice-Hall, 1973.

Olson, Mancur, Jr., *The Logic of Collective Action*, Cambridge, Mass.: Harvard University Press, 1971.

————. "Rapid Growth as a Destabalizing Force" *Journal of Economic History* 23, 1963.

Olson, Daniel V.A. and Jackson W. Carroll, "Religiously Based Politics: Religious Elites and the Public" *Social Forces* 70 (3), 1992, 765-786.

Olzak, Susan, "Ethnic Protest in Core and Periphery States" *Ethnic and Racial Studies*, 21 (2), 1998, 187-217.

————, *The Dynamics of Ethnic Competition and Conflict*, Stanford: Stanford University Press, 1992.

Olzak, Susan and Joane Nagel, eds., *Competitive Ethnic Relations*, New York: Academic Press, 1986.

Oommen, T.K., "Religious Nationalism and Democratic Polity: The Indian Case" *Sociology of Religion* 55 (4), 1994, 455-472.

Osiander, Andreas, "Religion and Politics in Western Civilization: The Ancient World as Matrix and Mirror of the Modern" *Millennium* 29 (3), 2000, 761-790.

Pelletiere, Stephen C., *A Theory of Fundamentalism: An Inquiry into the Origin and Development of the Movement*, The U.S. Army War College, 1995.

Pfaff, William, "The Reality of Human Affairs" *World Policy Journal* 14 (2), 1997, 89-96.

Philpott, Daniel, "The Religious Roots of Modern International Relations" *World Politics* 52, 2000, 206-245.

Piererd, Richard V., "Religion and the East German Revolution" *Journal of Church and State* 1990, 501-509.

Pickering, W. S. F., *Durkheim's Sociology of Religion: Themes and Theories*, London: Routledge, 1984.

————, *Durkheim on Religion: A selection of Readings with Bibliographies*, London: Routledge, 1975

Piekalkiewiez Jaroslaw, "Poland: Nonviolent Revolution in a Socialist State" in Jack A. Goldstone, Ted Robert Gurr, and Farrokh Moshiri eds., *Revolutions of the Late Twentieth Century*, Boulder, Colo.: Westview, 1991, 136-161.

Piscatori, James, "Accounting for Islamic Fundamentalisms" in Martin E. Marty and R. Scott Appleby eds., *Accounting for Fundamentalisms: The Dynamic*

373.

Poe, Steven C., C. Neal Tate, and Linda Camp Keith, "Repression of the Human Right to Personal Integrity Revisited: A Global Cross-National Study Covering the Years 1976-1993" *International Studies Quarterly* 43 (2), 1999, 291-313.

Popkin, Samuel L., *The Rational Peasant*, Berkeley: University of California, 1979.

Pottenger, John R., "Liberation Theology: Its Methodological Foundation for Violence" in David C. Rapoport, and Yonah Alexander, eds. *The Morality of Terrorism: Religious and Secular Justifications*, 2nd ed. New York: Columbia University Press, 1989, 99-123.

Pye, Lucien W., *Aspects of Political Development*, Boston: Little, Brown, 1966.

Randall, V. and R. Theobald, *Political Change and Underdevelopment: A Critical Introduction to Third World Politics*, London: Macmillan, 1985.

Ranstorp, Magnus, "Terrorism in the Name of Religion" *Journal of International Affairs* 50 (1), 1996, 41-60.

Rapoport, David C., "Some General Observations on Religion and Violence" *Journal of Terrorism and Political Violence* 3 (3), 1991a, 118-139.

————, "Comparing Fundamentalist Movements and Groups" in Martin E. Marty, and R. Scott Appleby eds., *Fundamentalisms and the State: Remaking Politics, Economies, and Militance*, Chicago: University of Chicago Press, 1991b, 489-461.

————, "Sacred Terror: A Contemporary Example from Islam" in Walter Reich ed. *Origins of Terrorism: Psychologies, Ideologies, Theologies, States of Mind*, Cambridge, Mass.: Cambridge University Press, 1990, 103-130.

————, "Messianic Sanctions for Terror" *Comparative Politics* 20 (2), January 1988, 195-213.

————, "Fear and Trembling: Terrorism in Three Religious Traditions" *American Political Science Review* 78, 1984, 658-677.

Rawking, P., "Terror from the Heart of Zion: The Political Challenge of the Jewish Underground in the West Bank" *Middle East Focus* 7 (5), January 1985.

Regan, Patrick M., "Choosing to Intervene: Outside Interventions in Internal Conflicts" *The Journal of Politics* 60 (3), 1998, 754-779.

Reudy, John, *Modern Algeria: The Origins and Development of a Nation*, Bloomington: Indiana University Press, 1992.

Richards, Alan and John Waterbury, *A Political Economy of the Middle East*, Boulder, Colo.: Westview, 1990.

Riis, Ole, "The Role of Religion in Legitimating the Modern Structarian Society" *Acta Sociologica* 32 (2), 1989, 137-153.

Robbins, Thomas, "The Transformative Impact of the Study of New Religions on the Sociology of Religion" *Journal for the Scientific Study of Religion* 27 (1), 1988, 12-31.

————, "Nuts, Sluts and Converts: Studying Religious Groups as Social Problems: A Comment" *Sociological Analysis* 46 (2), 1985, 171-178.

Robbins, Thomas, "The Beach is Washing Away: Controversial Religion and the Sociology of Religion" *Sociological Analysis* 44 (3), 1983, 207-214.

Roberts, Hugh, "Radical Islam and the Dilemma of Algerian Nationalism: The Embattled Africans if Algiers" *Third World Quarterly* 1988, 556-589.

Robertson, Roland, "Beyond the Sociology of Religion?" *Sociological Analysis* 46 (4), 1985, 355-360.

Roelofs, H. Mark, "Liberation Theology: The Recovery of Biblical Radicalism" *American Political Science Review* 88 (2), 1988, 549-566.

Rosecrance, Richard, "The Clash of Civilizations and the Remaking of World Order" *American Political Science Review* 92 (4), 1998, 978-980.

Rosser, J. Barkley Jr., "Belief: Its Role in Thought and Action" *American Journal of Economics and Sociology* 52 (3), July 1993, 355-368.

Rostow, W., *The Stages of Economic Growth: A Non-Communist Manifesto*, Cambridge: Cambridge University Press, 1959.

Rubenstein, Richard L., *Spirit Matters: The Worldwide Impact of Religion on Contemporary Politics*, New York: Paragon, 1987.

Rubin, Barry, "Religion and International Affairs" in Douglas Johnston and Cynthia Sampson eds., *Religion, the Missing Dimension of Statecraft*, Oxford: Oxford University Press, 1994, 20-34.

Rude, George, *Ideology and Popular Protest*, New York: Pantheon, 1980.

Rule, James B., *Theories of Civil Violence*, Berkeley: University of California Press, 1988.

Rummel, Rudolph J., "Is Collective Violence Correlated with Social Pluralism?" *Journal of Peace Research* 34 (2), 1997, 163-175.

Russett, Bruce, John R. Oneal, and Michalene Cox, "Clash of Civilizations, or Realism and Liberalism Deja Vu? Some Evidence" *Journal of Peace Research* 37 (5), 2000.

Salehi, M. M., *Insurgency Through Culture and Religion*, New York: Praeger, 1988.

Sahliyeh, Emile, ed., *Religious Resurgence and Politics in the Contemporary World*, New York: State University of New York Press, 1990.

Sandler, Shmuel, "Religious Zionism and the State: Political Accommodation and Radicalism in Israel" *Terrorism and Political Violence* 8 (2), 1996, 135-154.

Schbley, Ayla Hammond, "Torn Between God, Family, and Money: The Changing Profile of Lebanon's Religious Terrorists" *Studies in Conflict and Terrorism* 23, 175-196, 2000.

Scheepers, Peer and Frans Van Der Silk, "Religion and Attitudes on Moral Issues: Effects of Individual, Spouse and Parental Characteristics" *Journal for the Scientific Study of Religion* 37 (4), 1998, 678-691.

Schoenfeld, Eugen, "Militant and Submissive Religions: Class, Religion and Ideology" *British Journal of Sociology* 43 (1), March 1992, 111-140.

Seamon, Richard, "The Clash of Civilizations: And the Remaking of World Order" *United States Naval Institute. Proceedings* 124 (3), 1998, 116-118.

Segal, Haggai, *Dear Brothers: The West Bank and the Jewish Underground*, Jerusalem: Keter, 1987.

Senghass, Dieter, "A Clash of Civilizations–An Idea Fixe?" *Journal of Peace*

Senghass, Dieter, "A Clash of Civilizations–An Idea Fixe?" *Journal of Peace Research* 35 (1), 1998, 127-132.

Serpa, Eduardo, "The Fundamentalist Reaction and the Future of Algeria" *Africa Insight* 21 (3), 1991, 194-203.

Seul, Jefferey R., "'Ours is the Way of God': Religion, Identity and Intergroup Conflict" *Journal of Peace Research* 36 (3), 1999, 553-569.

Shragai, Nadav, *The Temple Mount Conflict*, Jerusalem: Keter, 1995.

Shupe, Anson, "The Stubborn Persistence of Religion in the Global Arena" in Emile Sahliyeh ed., *Religious Resurgence and Politics in the Contemporary World*, New York: State University of New York Press, 1990.

Silk, Mark, *Spiritual Politics*, New York: Simon and Schuster, 1988.

Sivan, Emmanuel, *Radical Islam: Medieval Theology and Modern Politics*, New Haven, Conn.: Yale University Press, 1985.

Skocpol, Theda, "Rentier State and Shi'a Islam in the Iranian Revolution" *Theory and Society* 11, 1982, 265-304.

————, *States and Social Revolutions*, Cambridge: Cambridge University 1979

Smart, Ninian, "Religion, Myth, and Nationalism" in Peter H. Merkl and Ninian Smart eds., *Religion and Politics in the Modern World*, New York: New York University Press, 1983.

————, *Beyond Ideology: Religion and the Future of Western Civilization*, San Francisco, Calif. Harper and Row, 1981.

Smith, Anthony D., "The Sacred Dimension of Nationalism" *Millennium* 29 (3), 2000, 791-814.

————, "Ethnic Election and National Destiny: Some Religious Origins of Nationalist Ideals" *Nations and Nationalism* 5 (3), 1999, 331-355.

————, *The Ethnic Revival in the Modern World*, London: Cambridge University Press, 1981.

Smith, Bardwell L., ed., *Religion and Social Conflict in South Asia*, The Netherlands: Leiden, 1976

Smith, Donald E., "The Limits of Religious Resurgence" in Emile Sahliyeh ed., *Religious Resurgence and Politics in the Contemporary World*, New York: State University of New York Press, 1990, 33-44.

————, ed., *Religion and Political Modernization*, New Haven, Conn.: Yale University Press, 1974

————, *Religion, Politics, and Social Change in the Third World*, New York: Free Press, 1971.

————, *Religion and Political Development*, Boston: Little, Brown, 1970.

Smith, Tony, "Dangerous Conjecture" *Foreign Affairs* 76 (2), 1997, 163-164.

Smock, David R., *Religious Perspectives on War*, Washington, D.C.: United States Institute of Peace Press, 1992.

Snow, David A., E. Burke Rochford Jr., Steven K. Worden, and Robert D. Benford, "Frame Alignment Processes, Micrmobilization and Movement Participation" *American Sociological Review* 51, 1986, 464-481.

Soloveitchik, Haym, "Rupture and Reconstruction: The Transformation of Contem-

Spencer, Claire, "Algeria in Crisis" *Survival* 36 (2), 1994, 149-163.

Spiro, Melford E., "Religion: Problems of Definition and Explanation" in Michael Banton, ed., *Anthropological Approaches to the Study of Religion*, London: Tavistock Publications, 1966, 85-126.

Sprinzak, Ehud, "Models of Religious Violence: The Case of Jewish Fundamentalism in Israel" in Martin E. Marty, and R. Scott Appleby eds., *Fundamentalisms and the State: Remaking Politics, Economies, and Militance*, Chicago: University of Chicago Press, 1991, 462-490.

Stack, John F. Jr., "The Ethnic Challenge to International Relations Theory" in David Carment and Patrick James eds, *Wars in the Midst of Peace*, Pittsburgh: University of Pittsburgh Press, 1997, 11-25.

Stark, Rodney, "Secularization, R.I.P." *Sociology of Religion* 60 (3), 249-273.

Stark, Rodney and William Bainbridge, *The Future of Religion: Secularization, Revival and Cult Formation*, Berkeley: University of California Press, 1985.

Sutton, Frank, "Social Theory and Comparative Politics" in Harry Eckstein and David Apter eds., *International Encyclopedia of the Social Sciences*, New York: Macmillan, 1968.

Swanson, Guy E., *The Birth of the Gods: The Origin of Primitive Beliefs*, Ann Arbor: University of Michigan Press, 1960.

Swatos, William H. Jr. and Kevin J. Christiano, "Secularization Theory: The Course of a Concept" *Sociology of Religion* 60 (3), 1999, 209-228.

————, *A Future for Religion? New Paradigms for Social Analysis*, Newbury Park, Calif.: Sahe, 1993.

Tarrow, Sidney, *Democracy and Disorder: Protest and Politics in Italy 1965-1975*, Oxford: Clarendon, 1989.

Taylor, Bron, "Religion, Violence, and Radical Environmentalism: From Earth First! To the Unabomber to the Earth Liberation Front" *Terrorism and Political Violence* 10 (4), 1998, 1-42.

Taylor, Maxwell, *The Fanatics*, London: Brassey's, 1991.

Tehranian, Majid, "Fundamentalist Impact on Education and the Media: An Overview" in Martin E. Marty and R. Scott Appleby eds., *Fundamentalisms and Society: Reclaiming the Sciences, the Family, and Education*, Chicago: University of Chicago Press, 1993, 313-340.

Thomas, Scott M., "Taking Religious and Cultural Pluralism Seriously: The Global Resurgence of Religion and the Transformation of International Society" *Millennium* 29 (3), 2000, 815-841.

Tibi, Bassam, "Post-Bipolar Disorder in Crisis: The Challenge of Politicized Islam" *Millennium* 29 (4), 2000, 843-859.

Tilly, Charles, "National Self-Determination as a Problem for All of Us" *Deadalus* 122, 1993, 29-36.

————, *From Mobilization to Revolution*, Reading, Mass.: Addison-Wesley, 1978.

Tipson, Frederick S., "Culture Clash-ification: A Verse to Huntington's Curse" *Foreign Affairs* 76 (2), 1997, 166-169.

Foreign Affairs 76 (2), 1997, 166-169.

Turner, Brian S., *Religion and Social Theory*, 2nd ed. London: Sage, 1991.

Underhill, Ralph "Economic and political Antecedents of Monotheism: A Cross-Cultural Study" *American Journal of Sociology* 80, 1975.

Van der Vyver, Johan D, "Religious Fundamentalism and Human Rights" *Journal of International Affairs* 50 (1), 1996, 21-40.

Vatin, Jean-Claude, "Revival in the Maghreb: Islam as an Alternative Political Language" in Ali E. Hillal ed., *Islamic Resurgence in the Arab World*, New York: Praeger, 1982.

Verweij, Johan, Peter Ester, and Rein Nauta, "Secularization as an Economic Cultural Phenomenon: A Cross-National Analysis, *Journal for the Scientific Study of Religion* 36 (2), 1997, 309-324.

Viorst, Milton "The Coming Instability" *The Washington Quarterly* 20 (4) 1997, 153-167.

Voye, Liliane, "Secularization in a Context of Advanced Modernity" *Sociology of Religion* 60 (3), 1999, 275-288.

Walid, Abdurrahman, "Future Shock" *Far Eastern Economic Review* 160 (18), May 1 1997, 38-39.

Wallerstein, Immanuel, *The Modern World System*, New York: Academic, 1974a.

————, "The Rise and Future Demise of the World Capitalist System" *Comparative Studies in Society and History* 16, 1974b, 387-415.

————, "Crisis: The World Economy, the Movements, and the Ideologies" in Albert Bergson ed., *Crisis in the World System*, Newbury Park, Calif.: Sage, 1983.

Walt, Stephen N., "Building Up New Bogeymen" *Foreign Policy* 106, 1997, 177-189.

Walzer, Michael, *Just and Unjust Wars*, New York: HarperCollins, 1977.

Warner, R. Stephen, "Work in Progress toward a New Paradigm for the Sociological Study of Religion in the United States" *American Journal of Sociology* 98 (5), March 1993, 1044-1093.

Wayland, Sarah V., "Religious Expression in Public Schools: Kirpans in Canada, Hijab in France" *Ethnic and Racial Studies* 20 (3), 1997, 545-561.

Webb, Keith et al., "Etiology and Outcomes of Protests" *American Behavioral Scientist* 26 (3), January/February 1983, 311-331.

Weber, Max, *Sociology of Religion*, Boston: Beacon Press, 1963.

Weigel, George, "Religion and Peace: An Argument Complexified" in Sheryl J. Brown and Kimber M. Schraub eds., *Resolving Third World Conflict: Challenges for a New Era*, Washington, D.C.: United States Institute for Peace Press, 1992, 172-192.

Wentz, Richard, *Why People Do Bad Things in the Name of Religion*, Macon, Ga.: Mercer, 1987

Westhus, Kenneth, "The Church in Opposition" *Sociological Analysis* 37 (4), 1976, 299-314.

Williams, Rhys H., "Movement Dynamics and Social Change: Transforming

Fundamentalist Ideologies and Organizations" in Martin E. Marty and R. Scott Appleby eds., *Accounting for Fundamentalisms: The Dynamic Character of Movements*, Chicago: University of Chicago Press, 1994, 785-833.

Williamson, Roger, "Why is Religion Still a Factor in Armed Conflict?" *Bulletin of Peace Proposals* 21 (3), 1990, 243-53.

Wilson, Bryan R,. *Religion in Sociological Perspective*, Oxford: Oxford University Press, 1982.

————, "Aspects of Secularization in the West" *Japanese Journal of Religious Studies* 3 (4), 1976, 259-276.

————, *Religion in Secular Society*, Baltimore, Md.: Penguin, 1966.

Worden, Steven and E. Burke Rochford Jr., "Frame Alignment Processes, Micromobilization and Movement Participation" *American Sociological Review* 51, 1986, 464-481.

Wright, Robin, "Islam's New Political Face" *Current History* 1991, 25-28.

Wuthrow, Robert ed., *The Religious Dimension: New Directions in Quantitative Research*, New York: Academic Press, 1979.

Yamane, David, "Secularization on Trial: In Defense of a Neosecularization Paradigm" *Journal for the Scientific Study of Religion* 36 (1), 1997, 109-122.

Yaron, Zvi, *The Philosophy of Rabbi Kook*, Jerusalem: World Zionist Organization, 1974.

Yinger, John Milton, *The Scientific Study of Religion*, New York: Macmillan, 1970.

Zartman, W. I. and W. M. Habeeb, *Polity and Society in North Africa*, Boulder, Colo.: Westview, 1993.

Index

249

About the Author

Jonathan Fox is a lecturer in the Political Studies department of Bar-Ilan University in Ramat Gan, Israel. He received his Ph.D. in Government and Politics from the University of Maryland in College Park in May 1997. He has been the recipient of the Israel Science Foundation grant and has written numerous articles on the influence of religion on ethnic conflict and on Samuel Huntington's civilizations theory, including articles in the *British Journal of Political Science, International Political Science Review, International Studies Quarterly, International Studies Review*, and *Journal of Peace Research*. This is his first book.